THANK YO

In the 2014 Astrologica

- All twleve signs
  personalized look at *each month* in the year to come
- The days that will be most memorable for you
- Answers to many questions
- And much more!

"Astrology told me about my life even before I wrote it as an autobiography." — Bette Davis

"Whether or not I would have succeeded without astrology, I don't know." — Sylvester Stallone

SYDNEY OMARR'S®

ASTROLOGICAL
GUIDE
FOR YOU IN

2014

by Trish MacGregor
with Rob MacGregor

A SIGNET BOOK

SIGNET
Published by the Penguin Group
Penguin Group (USA) Inc., 375 Hudson Street,
New York, New York 10014, USA

USA | Canada | UK | Ireland | Australia | New Zealand | India | South Africa | China

Penguin Books Ltd., Registered Offices: 80 Strand, London WC2R 0RL, England
For more information about the Penguin Group visit penguin.com.

First published by Signet, an imprint of New American Library,
a division of Penguin Group (USA) Inc.

First Printing, July 2013

 REGISTERED TRADEMARK — MARCA REGISTRADA

ISBN 978-0-451-41379-6

Printed in the United States of America
10 9 8 7 6 5 4 3 2 1

PUBLISHER'S NOTE
While the author has made every effort to provide accurate telephone numbers and Internet addresses at the time of publication, neither the publisher nor the author assumes any responsibility for errors, or for changes that occur after publication. Further, publisher does not have any control over and does not assume any responsibility for author or third-party Web sites or their content.

CONTENTS

1

The Basics

When our daughter was born, we made sure we were watching a clock so that we would know her exact time of birth. Her first breath, her first cry, came at 8:10 P.M. Three days later we went over to a New Age bookstore with her birth information and had her chart drawn up. This was in the days before astrology software was so readily available, and we were delighted to have her actual birth chart.

From an astrological point of view your exact time of birth is one of the most valuable pieces of information you can have. From this blueprint all kinds of information can be extracted. And any kind of predictive astrology begins with your birth chart. But if you don't have your time of birth time, don't panic. There are ways around it.

How much do you know about the day you were born? What was the weather like that day? If you were born at night, had the moon already risen? Was it full or the shape of a Cheshire cat's grin? Was the delivery ward quiet or bustling with activity? Unless your mom or dad has a very good memory, you'll probably never know the full details. But there's one thing you can know for sure: on the day you were born, the sun was located in a particular zone of the zodiac, an imaginary 360-degree belt that circles the earth. The belt is divided into twelve 30-degree portions called signs.

If you were born between March 21 and April 19, then the sun was passing through the sign of Aries, so we say that your sun sign is Aries. Each of the twelve signs has distinct attributes and characteristics. Aries individuals, for example, are independent pioneers, fearless and passionate. Virgos, born between August 23 and September 22, are perfectionists with discriminating intellects and a genius for details. Geminis, born between May 21 and June 20, are networkers and communicators.

The twelve signs are categorized according to element and quality or modality. The first category reads like a basic science lesson—fire, earth, air, and water—and describes the general physical characteristics of the signs.

Fire signs—Aries, Leo, Sagittarius—are warm, dynamic individuals who are always passionate about what they do.

Earth signs—Taurus, Virgo, Capricorn—are the builders of the zodiac, practical and efficient, grounded in everything they do.

Air signs—Gemini, Libra, Aquarius—are people who live mostly in the world of ideas. They are terrific communicators.

Water signs—Cancer, Scorpio, Pisces—live through their emotions, imaginations, and intuitions.

The second category describes how each sign operates in the physical world, how adaptable it is to circumstances.

Cardinal signs—Aries, Cancer, Libra, Capricorn—are initiators. These people are active, impatient, restless. They're great at starting things, but unless a project or a relationship holds their attention, they lose interest and may not finish what they start.

Fixed signs—Taurus, Leo, Scorpio, Aquarius—are deliberate, controlled. These individuals tend to move more slowly than cardinal signs, are often stubborn, and resist change. They seek roots, stability.

Mutable signs—Gemini, Virgo, Sagittarius, Pisces—are adaptable. These people are flexible, changeable, communicative. They don't get locked into rigid patterns or belief systems.

Sun Signs

Sign	Date	Element	Quality
Aries ♈	March 21–April 19	Fire	Cardinal
Taurus ♉	April 20–May 20	Earth	Fixed
Gemini ♊	May 21–June 21	Air	Mutable
Cancer ♋	June 22–July 22	Water	Cardinal
Leo ♌	July 23–August 22	Fire	Fixed
Virgo ♍	August 23–September 22	Earth	Mutable
Libra ♎	September 23–October 22	Air	Cardinal
Scorpio ♏	October 23–November 21	Water	Fixed
Sagittarius ♐	November 22–December 21	Fire	Mutable
Capricorn ♑	December 22–January 19	Earth	Cardinal
Aquarius ♒	January 20–February 18	Air	Fixed
Pisces ♓	February 19–March 20	Water	Mutable

The Planets

The planets in astrology are the players who make things happen. They're the characters in the story of your life. This story always begin with the sun, the giver of life.

Your sun sign describes your self-expression and primal energy, the essence of who you are. It's the archetypal pattern of your Self. When you know another person's sun sign, you already have a great deal of information about that person. Let's say you're a Taurus who has just started dating a Gemini. How compatible are you? On the surface it wouldn't seem that you have much in common. Taurus is a fixed earth sign; Gemini is a mutable air sign. Taurus is persistent, stubborn, practical, a cultivator as opposed to an initiator. Gemini is a chameleon, a communicator, social, with a mind as quick as lightning. Taurus is ruled by Venus, which governs the arts, money, beauty, love, and romance, and Gemini is ruled by Mercury, which governs communication and travel. There doesn't seem to be much common ground. But before we write off this combination, let's look a little deeper.

Suppose the Taurus has Mercury in Gemini and suppose the Gemini has Venus in Taurus? This would mean that the Taurus and Gemini each have their rulers in the other person's sign. They probably communicate well and probably enjoy travel and books (Mercury) and would see eye to eye on romance, art, and music (Venus). They might get along so well, in fact, that they collaborate on creative projects.

Each of us is also influenced by the other eight planets (the sun and moon are treated like planets in astrology) and the signs they were transiting when you were born. Suppose our Taurus and Gemini have the same moon sign? The moon rules our inner needs, emotions and intuition, and all that makes us feel secure within ourselves. Quite often, compatible moon signs can overcome even the most glaring difference in sun signs because the two people share similar emotions.

In the sections on monthly predictions your sun sign always takes center stage, and every prediction is based on the movement of the transiting planets in relation to your sun sign. Let's say you're a Sagittarius. Between November 16 and December 10 this year Venus will be transiting your sign. Venus rules romance, so you can expect your love life to pick up significantly during these weeks. Other people will find you attractive and be more open to your ideas, and you'll radiate a certain charisma. Your creative endeavors will move full steam ahead.

The following table provides an overview of the planets and the signs that they rule. Keep in mind that the moon is the swiftest-moving planet, changing signs about every two and a half days, and Pluto is the snail of the zodiac, taking as long as thirty years to transit a single sign. Although the faster-moving planets—the moon, Mercury, Venus, and Mars—have an impact on our lives, it's the slow pokes—Uranus, Neptune, and Pluto—that bring about the most profound influence and change. Jupiter and Saturn fall between the others in terms of speed.

In the section on predictions the most frequent references are to the transits of Mercury, Venus, and Mars. In the daily predictions for each sign the predictions are based primarily on the transiting moon.

Now glance through the table. When a sign is in parentheses, it means the planet corules that sign. This assignation dates back to when we thought there were only seven planets in the solar system. But since there were still twelve signs, some of the planets had to do double duty!

The Planets

Planet	Rules	Attributes of Planet
Sun ☉	Leo	Self-expression, primal energy, creative ability, ego, individuality
Moon ☽	Cancer	Emotions, intuition, mother or wife, security
Mercury ☿	Gemini, Virgo	Intellect, mental acuity, communication, logic, reasoning, travel, contracts
Venus ♀	Taurus, Libra	Love, romance, beauty, artistic instincts, the arts, music, material and financial resources
Mars ♂	Aries (Scorpio)	Physical and sexual energy, aggression, drive
Jupiter ♃	Sagittarius (Pisces)	Luck, expansion, success, prosperity, growth, creativity, spiritual interests, higher education, law
Saturn ♄	Capricorn (Aquarius)	Laws of physical universe, discipline, responsibility, structure, karma, authority
Uranus ♅	Aquarius	Individuality, genius, eccentricity, originality, science, revolution
Neptune ♆	Pisces	Visionary self, illusions, what's hidden, psychic ability, dissolution of ego boundaries, spiritual insights, dreams
Pluto ♇	Scorpio	The darker side, death, sex, regeneration, rebirth, profound and permanent change, transformation

Houses and Rising Signs

In the instant you drew your first breath one of the signs of the zodiac was just passing over the eastern horizon. Astrologers refer to this as the rising sign or ascendant. It's what makes your horoscope unique. Think of your ascendant as the front door of your horoscope, the place where you enter into this life and begin your journey.

Your ascendant is based on the exact moment of your birth, and the other signs follow counterclockwise. If you have Taurus rising, for example, that is the cusp of your first house. The cusp of the second would be Gemini, of the third Cancer, and so on around the horoscope circle in a counterclockwise direction. Each house governs a particular area of life, which is outlined below.

The best way to find out your rising sign is to have your horoscope drawn up by an astrologer. For those of you with access to the internet, though, there are sites that provide free birth horoscopes, such as www.astro .com.

In a horoscope the ascendant (cusp of the first house), IC (cusp of the fourth house), descendant (cusp of the seventh house), and MC (cusp of the tenth house) are considered to be the most critical angles. Any planets that fall close to these angles are extremely important in the overall astrological picture of who you are. By the same token, planets that fall in the first, fourth, seventh, and tenth houses are also considered to be important.

Now here's a rundown on what the houses mean.

ASCENDANT OR RISING: THE FIRST OF FOUR IMPORTANT CRITICAL ANGLES IN A HOROSCOPE

- How other people see you
- How you present yourself to the world
- Your physical appearance

FIRST HOUSE, PERSONALITY

- Early childhood
- Your ego
- Your body type and how you feel about your body
- General physical health
- Defense mechanisms
- Your creative thrust

SECOND HOUSE, PERSONAL VALUES

- How you earn and spend your money
- Your personal values
- Your material resources and assets
- Your attitudes toward money
- Your possessions and your attitude toward those possessions
- Your self-worth
- Your attitudes toward creativity

THIRD HOUSE, COMMUNICATION AND LEARNING

- Personal expression
- Intellect and mental attitudes and perceptions
- Siblings, neighbors, and relatives
- How you learn
- School until college

- Reading, writing, teaching
- Short trips (the grocery store versus Europe in seven days)
- Earth-bound transportation
- Creativity as a communication device

IC OR FOURTH HOUSE CUSP: THE SECOND CRITICAL ANGLE IN A HOROSCOPE
- Sign on IC describes the qualities and traits of your home during early childhood
- Describes roots of your creative abilities and talents

FOURTH HOUSE, YOUR ROOTS
- Personal environment
- Your home
- Your attitudes toward family
- Early childhood conditioning
- Real estate
- Your nurturing parent

Some astrologers say this house belongs to Mom or her equivalent in your life, others say it belongs to Dad or his equivalent. It makes sense to me that it's Mom because the fourth house is ruled by the moon, which rules mothers. But in this day and age, when parental roles are in flux, the only hard and fast rule is that the fourth house belongs to the parent who nurtures you most of the time.

- The conditions at the end of your life
- Early childhood support of your creativity

FIFTH HOUSE, CHILDREN AND CREATIVITY
- Kids, your first-born in particular
- Love affairs
- What you enjoy
- Gambling and speculation
- Pets

Traditionally, pets belong in the sixth house. But that definition stems from the days when pets were chattel. These days we don't even refer to them as pets. They are animal companions who bring us pleasure.

- Creative ability

SIXTH HOUSE, WORK AND RESPONSIBILITY
- Day-to-day working conditions and environment
- Competence and skills
- Your experience of employees and employers
- Duty to work, to employees
- Health
- Daily work approach to creativity

DESCENDANT/SEVENTH HOUSE CUSP: THE THIRD CRITICAL ANGLE IN A HOROSCOPE
- The sign on the house cusp describes the qualities sought in intimate or business relationships
- Describes qualities of creative partnerships

SEVENTH HOUSE, PARTNERSHIPS AND MARRIAGE
- Marriage
- Marriage partner
- Significant others

- Business partnerships
- Close friends
- Open enemies
- Contracts

EIGHTH HOUSE, TRANSFORMATION
- Sexuality as transformation
- Secrets
- Death, taxes, inheritances
- Resources shared with others
- Your partner's finances
- The occult (read: astrology, reincarnation, UFOs, everything weird and strange)
- Your hidden talents
- Psychology
- Life-threatening illnesses
- Your creative depths

NINTH HOUSE, WORLDVIEW
- Philosophy and religion
- The law, courts, judicial system
- Publishing
- Foreign travels and cultures
- College, graduate school
- Spiritual beliefs

MC OR CUSP OF TENTH HOUSE: THE FOURTH CRITICAL ANGLE IN A HOROSCOPE
- Sign on cusp of MC describes qualities you seek in a profession
- Your public image
- Your creative and professional achievements

TENTH HOUSE, PROFESSION AND CAREER
- Public image as opposed to a job that merely pays the bills (sixth house)
- Your status and position in the world
- The authoritarian parent and authority in general
- People who hold power over you
- Your public life
- Your career/profession

ELEVENTH HOUSE, IDEALS AND DREAMS
- Peer groups
- Social circles (your writers' group, your mother's bridge club)
- Your dreams and aspirations
- How you can realize your creative dreams

TWELFTH HOUSE, PERSONAL UNCONSCIOUS
- Power you have disowned that must be claimed again
- Institutions—hospitals, prisons, nursing homes— what is hidden
- What you must confront this time around, your karma, issues brought in from other lives
- Psychic gifts and abilities
- Healing talents
- What you give unconditionally

In the section on predictions you'll find references to transiting planets moving into certain houses. These houses are actually solar houses that are created by putting your sun sign on the ascendant. This technique is how most predictions are made for the general public rather than for specific individuals.

Lunations

Every year there are twelve new moons and twelve full moons, with some years having thirteen full moons. The extra full moon is called the Blue Moon. New moons are typically when we should begin new projects, set new goals, seek new opportunities. They're times for beginnings.

Two weeks after each new moon there's a full moon. This is the time of harvest, fruition, when we reap what we've sown.

Whenever a new moon falls in your sign take time to brainstorm what you would like to achieve during weeks and months until the full moon falls in your sign. These goals can be in any area of your life. Or you can simply take the time on each new moon to set up goals and strategies for what you would like to achieve or manifest during the next two weeks—until the full moon—or until the next new moon.

Here's a list of all the new moons and full moons during 2014. The asterisk beside any new moon entry indicates a solar eclipse; the asterisk next to a full moon entry indicates a lunar eclipse.

New Moons
January 1—Capricorn
January 30—Aquarius
March 1—Pisces
March 30—Aries
April 29—Taurus*
May 28—Gemini

Full Moons
January 15—Cancer
February 14—Leo
March 16—Virgo
April 15—Libra *
May 14—Scorpio*
June 13—Sagittarius

June 27—Cancer
July 26—Leo
August 25—Virgo
September 24—Libra
October 23—Scorpio*
December 6—Gemini

July 12—Capricorn
August 10—Aquarius
September 8—Pisces
October 8—Aries*
November 22—Sagittarius
December 21—Capricorn

Every year there are two lunar and two solar eclipses, separated from each other by about two weeks. Lunar eclipses tend to deal with emotional issues and our internal world and often bring an emotional issue to the surface related to the sign and house in which the eclipse falls. Solar eclipses deal with events and often enable us to see something that has eluded us. They also symbolize beginnings and endings.

Look to the entries for each month for more information. I also recommend Celeste Teal's excellent book, *Eclipses.*

Mercury Retrograde

Every year Mercury—the planet that symbolizes communication and travel—turns retrograde three times. During these periods our travel plans often go awry, communication breaks down, computers go berserk, cars or appliances develop problems. You get the idea. Things in our daily lives don't work as smoothly as we would like.

In the overview for each sign check out the dates for this year's Mercury retrogrades and how these retrogrades are likely to impact you.

Using This Book

This book can be used alone, to get a sense of the patterns that may be coming up for you in a particular month, or it can be used along with the book for your sun sign that contains daily predictions. Whether you use one or both, the information is intended to inform you ahead of time about possible issues, challenges, situations, and relationships that may be surfacing in your life. To be informed is to be empowered.

2

Aries

The Big Picture in 2014

Welcome to 2014, Aries! And what a lucky year this should be for you. It's an 8 year, and 8s suggest money, power, playing with power, an interest in metaphysical areas, an awakening to your own intuitive and psychic abilities, fame, and recognition. In other words it's a year for professional achievements. Now that you've survived the tumult of 2012 and the realignment of 2013, you're ready for everything the universe brings your way.

So let's look at how specific areas of your life may be impacted and which dates will be of vital importance to you.

ROMANCE/CREATIVITY

The best news all year for your love life and creativity occurs between July 16, 2014, and August 11, 2015, when expansive Jupiter transits fellow fire sign Leo, your solar fifth house. Jupiter expands everything it touches, so during this period your romantic options burgeon. If you're in a committed relationship already—or are married—

you and your partner may rediscover all the camaraderie that brought you together in the first place.

Jupiter is also about excess, and while it's in Leo you may have a tendency to be boastful or to see yourself and your romantic relationships in an unrealistic light. Your expectations could be overblown. But once you're aware of this tendency, you can draw on Jupiter's positive energy to bring about significant change in your own life.

Creatively Jupiter's transit through Leo should bring ample opportunities to strut your abilities and talents. Doors open, helpful people arrive, you're on a roll.

Jupiter turns retrograde on December 8 and doesn't turn direct again until April 8, 2015. During this period the planet is essentially in a dormant state. But before the retro starts, you have a prolonged period when it's functioning at optimal levels, working to make things happen.

Other excellent dates:

August 12 to September 5, when Venus joins Jupiter in Leo. This period infuses your love life with excitement and harmony and brings your muse up close and personal.

July 26 features a new moon in Leo that could usher in new romantic and creative opportunities. Jupiter is closely conjunct this moon, so any opportunities that surface are likely to be big.

CAREER

Jupiter's transit through Leo, of course, will help every facet of your life, even your career. The caveat with career matters, though, is that if you're doing something you love, you benefit tremendously. If you're working in a field that doesn't excite you, that has become rather humdrum and routine, then Jupiter, Venus, and your ruler, Mars, could help you to break away and find something that is more aligned with your passions.

Let's take a closer look at the beneficial career times:

January 1 to March 5: Venus transits Capricorn, your solar tenth house and career area. During this period peers and bosses are impressed with your work, skills, and organizational talents. A promotion or raise could be forthcoming. Venus is moving retrograde between January 1 and 31, so things don't start to move along until after the 31.

October 26 to December 4: This period will be very high energy. Your ruler, Mars, transits Capricorn. This is the time to implement new projects, brainstorm with colleagues, launch new projects, start a business, or even move your office location. Fortunately Mercury turns direct on October 25, so Mars won't be weakened.

The new moon in your career area occurs on New Year's Day, a wonderful way to start 2014. In addition to the new moon Pluto, Mercury, and Venus are all in Capricorn too. So make the first your brainstorming day, and be ready to dive into career stuff as soon as you return to work. Your physical energy and focus should be quite good.

FINANCES

Let's look at Venus transits first for beneficial dates for finances. Your solar second house, which rules money, is Taurus. The period to watch for, then, falls between May 28 and June 23. During this three-week period you could get a raise, bonus, unexpected insurance, or royalty check, or someone could repay money they owe you. You may feel an urge to spend on a luxury item—jewelry, for instance, or art.

During this period Jupiter is moving through Cancer, a water sign compatible with Taurus. This could boost your earnings in a way that also expands some other area of your life. Maybe you launch a home-based business, Aries. With Uranus still in your sign, whatever occurs is likely to be sudden and unexpected.

April 29 features a new moon in Taurus. It's also a solar eclipse. Mercury forms a close conjunction with the eclipse degree. New opportunities surface in finances, but you may have to give up something else before you reap the benefits.

MERCURY RETROGRADES

Every year Mercury—the planet of communication and travel—turns retrograde three times. During these periods it's wise not to sign contracts (unless you don't mind renegotiating when Mercury is moving direct), to check and recheck travel plans, and to communicate as succinctly as possible. Refrain from buying any large-ticket items or electronics during this time too. Often computers and appliances go on the fritz, cars act up, data is lost . . . you get the idea. Be sure to back up all files before the dates below:

February 6–28: Mercury retrograde in Pisces, your solar twelfth house. This one impacts your personal unconscious. Old issues surface. Mercury slips back into Aquarius before it turns direct, so your friendships are also impacted.

June 7–July 1: Mercury retrograde in Cancer, your solar fourth house. Appliances at home may go on the fritz, and there could be communication mishaps with parents or other family members.

October 4–25: Mercury retrograde in Scorpio, your solar eighth house. It won't be a favorable period for applying for a mortgage or loan. Your partner or spouse may experience some sort of snafus with his or her paycheck, royalties, or a loan.

ECLIPSES

Solar eclipses tend to trigger external events that bring about change according to the sign and house in which they fall. Lunar eclipses trigger inner, emotional events according to the sign and house in which they fall. Any eclipse marks both beginnings and endings. The solar and lunar eclipse in a pair falls in opposite signs. If you're interested in detailed information on eclipses, take a look at Celeste Teal's excellent and definitive book, *Eclipses: Predicting World Events & Personal Transformation.*

If you were born under or around the time of an eclipse, it's to your advantage to take a look at your birth chart to find out exactly where the eclipses will impact you.

Most years feature four eclipses—two solar, two lunar—with the set separated by about two weeks. Let's take a closer look.

April 15: Lunar eclipse in Libra, your opposite sign and your seventh house. This may bring up emotional issues with a partner—business or romantic. But the emotions you experience look to be positive, and the day is energized.

April 29: Solar eclipse in Taurus, your solar second house. New financial opportunities are headed your way, Aries. With Mercury forming a close conjunction to the eclipse degree and Jupiter forming a beneficial angle to it, be on your toes and ready to seize the opportunity as soon as it occurs.

October 8: Lunar eclipse in your sign, Aries! Uranus is closely conjunct the moon, so you can expect sudden and unexpected emotional reactions to stuff in your personal life. The thing to remember is this: before snapping someone's head off, mull over what you want to say, take deep breaths, and maintain your cool.

October 23: Solar eclipse in Scorpio. New financial opportunities for both you and your partner. This eclipse is at 0 degrees Scorpio and so is Venus, so it's apt to be quite positive for you.

LUCKIEST DAYS OF THE YEAR
Every year there are one or two days when Jupiter and the sun meet up, and luck, serendipity, and expansion are the hallmarks. This year those days fall on July 25–26. Circle the dates. Do whatever you enjoy!

January—Aries

Between January 11 and 31 your social life should pick up big time. Mercury in Aquarius is moving through your solar eleventh house. Accept any invitation you receive, Aries, because you never know which event may lead you to new romantic or creative possibilities. In fact your ruler, Mars, is moving direct in Libra, your partnership area, between January 1 and March 1, so your soul mate and future partner may be within a group of friends or acquaintances.

Lovely Venus begins the year retrograde in Capricorn, the career area of your chart. It's not all that serious, but it means that Venus isn't functioning at optimum levels, and there could be some bumps and bruises at work. Romantic relationships can be a bit more challenging now too. But on the 31, Venus turns direct again, setting you up for a beautiful February!

Jupiter starts the year retrograde in Cancer, your solar fourth house. This retro, like that of Venus, isn't such a big deal. Certainly not like a Mercury retrograde. It simply means that things aren't expanding as quickly as you would like. If you've been planning renovations to your home, plans may be delayed until after March 6, when Jupiter turns direct again. Once Jupiter turns direct, though, get ready for a wild ride in your domestic environment. Someone may move in—a parent or other relative, or perhaps an adult child who recently graduated from college. If you and your partner have been considering starting a family, a pregnancy could occur when Jupiter is direct.

Saturn begins the year in Scorpio, your solar eighth house. This placement may make it more difficult for you to obtain mortgages and loans or could bring some restrictions to your partner's income. It could also simply mean that you'll have to be more responsible and diligent about your money! It's moving direct until March 6, so if you are applying for a loan or mortgage, do it before then!

Uranus begins the year in your sign, where it has been since 2010. It slipped back into Pisces for a while that year, then in mid-March 2011 it went into Aries, where it will be for the next seven years. You should be accustomed to this energy by now. Uranus' job is to shake up the status quo, so you can expect plenty of excitement and unpredictability in many areas of your life. While some events may seem initially jarring, remember that Uranus helps you to make room for the new.

Neptune begins the year in Pisces, where it has been off and on since 2011. In February 2012 it returned to Pisces and will be there until 2026. This lengthy transit helps to deepen your spirituality and brings higher inspiration in all that you do.

Then there's Pluto, in Capricorn since 2008, the career of your chart. This transit transforms your professional life in a profound way. You may quit your job or find a new career with better pay that satisfies you emotionally.

IMPORTANT DATES
January 1: New moon in Capricorn, your career area. This one could bring new professional opportunities. Three other planets are also in Capricorn at this time, so your career will have plenty of astrological support.

January 11: Mercury enters Aquarius, your friendship and social area.

January 15: Full moon in Cancer, your solar fourth house. This full moon joins Jupiter in the home area of your chart and lights up your domestic life. If things are a bit nuts around this time, just try to go with the flow.

January 31: Mercury enters Pisces, your solar twelfth house, and Venus turns direct in Capricorn, your career area. The Mercury transit lasts until April 7 and should facilitate dream recall. Your personal unconscious is more accessible to you. Between February 6 and 28 Mercury will be retrograde.

Also on January 31 there's a new moon in Aquarius, which should be very nice for you, Aries. New opportunities surface with friends and groups, and Uranus in your sign forms a beneficial angle to this moon, so it's accompanied by excitement and an unpredictability.

February—Aries

For the first five days of February Mercury is moving direct in Pisces. Then on February 6 it turns retrograde until February 28. This period could feel unsettling for you. Old issues surface, or old friends, former lovers, or spouses may suddenly reappear in your life. Memories from other lives could surface in dreams, while you're meditating, even while you're simply relaxing.

If you're going to be traveling, try to do it on either side of the retrograde dates. Be sure to back up your computer before the retro begins, and don't buy any large-ticket items during the retrograde period. On February 12 Mercury slides back into Aquarius, where it will be when it turns direct again. There could be some misunderstandings with friends.

With Venus now in direct motion again, your professional life should be humming along at a perfect pitch. You're clear about your daily goals and also the long-range things you would like to accomplish. Bosses and peers are supportive of your ideas and projects. A raise or promotion could be in the offing. Venus is traveling close to Pluto in Capricorn at this time, which suggests powerful forces at work in your career and love life.

As February begins you're still enjoying the effects of the new moon in compatible air sign Aquarius. On February 14 right in time for Valentine's Day there's a full moon in fellow fire sign Leo, your solar fifth house. This one highlights your love life, creativity, and children and should be quite enjoyable for you in spite of Mercury retrograde.

IMPORTANT DATES
February 6: Mercury turns retrograde in Pisces.

February 12: Retrograde Mercury slides back into Aquarius.

February 14: Full moon in Leo, the romance area of your chart.

February 28: Mercury turns direct in Aquarius. Time to celebrate, pack your bags, hit the road!

March—Aries

March is an exceptionally busy month, with a number of planets changing signs or turning retrograde and three lunations. Let's take a closer look.

Mars in Libra, your opposite sign, turns retrograde on March 1 and remains that way until May 19. This retrograde can throw a wrench into your partnerships—both business and professional. In your personal life you and your partner may not be seeing eye to eye on things. Something may feel *off.* Your sex life may falter. Things generally don't move as quickly as you would like. Your ambition may not be as strong as it usually is. It's a good time to take things at an easier, more leisurely pace.

Saturn turns retro in Scorpio, your solar eighth house, on March 2 and doesn't turn direct again until July 20. During this period you may be scrutinizing your joint finances and trying to establish a realistic budget and should probably not apply for a mortgage or a loan. This retro period encourages you to go within for answers to difficult questions and situations.

Venus enters Aquarius on March 5, a perfect spot for you, Aries. This transit, which ends on April 5, heats up your social life. You may join a group whose interests and purposes suit yours, and someone you meet through friends or who is already a friend may become something more.

Jupiter turns direct in water sign Cancer on March 6, a major plus for your home life. Proceed with your home expansion and refurbishment plans, redecorate your house, bring in plants and fresh flowers, get a cat or dog, have a party, set up your home office.

On March 17 Mercury—moving direct again—enters Pisces, your solar twelfth house. Now you'll experience some of the same things you did in February, when Mercury was moving direct in Pisces. In fact you can work more actively now to recall your dreams, visualize, and uncover your core beliefs. This transit makes your conscious mind much more intuitive.

On March 1 the new moon in Pisces joins Neptune in your solar twelfth house. What an imaginative combination! With Jupiter forming a beneficial angle to this new moon, expansion is the name of the game. New opportunities surface to use your imagination in a creative endeavor, delve into your own unconscious, and work behind the scenes in some capacity.

The full moon in Virgo two weeks later on March 16 falls in your solar sixth house. Your daily work routine or the way you maintain your health is illuminated in some way. Saturn forms a close, beneficial angle to this full moon, suggesting that something you've been working on now reaches fruition. It has the right structure, a solid foundation.

The new moon in your sign on March 30 rocks! It comes around just once a year and sets the tone for the next twelve months. What would you like to experience and achieve in the next year? What do you wish for and dream about? Make a list. Uranus is closely conjunct, so any new opportunities that surface will do so quickly and unexpectedly. Do something special for yourself today.

IMPORTANT DATES

March 1: Mars turns retrograde in Libra, new moon in Pisces.

March 2: Saturn turns retro in Scorpio.

March 5: Venus enters Aquarius.

March 6: Jupiter turns direct in Cancer.

March 16: Full moon in Virgo.

March 17: Mercury enters Pisces.

March 30: New moon in Aries.

With the dates lined up like this, you can see why March is not only a busy month, but a bit crazy too.

April—Aries

This month is going to sweep you along into a kind of wonderful madness. Mercury occupies three signs in April, so your conscious mind will be up and down and sideways, all over the place.

Between April 1 and 7 Mercury is in water sign Pisces, your solar twelfth house, a continuation of energy since March 17. This transit enables you to access your own unconscious more easily. Dreams are easier to recall and are a source of insight and information. You're much more intuitive. It's a great time to tie up loose ends, complete projects, and clear the deck for Mercury's transit through your sign between April 7 and 23.

Once Mercury enters your sign, Aries, you're on a roll. You're filled with ideas, and your mind is restless, inventive, and entrepreneurial. You're an intellectual trailblazer. Take risks, and expect them to pay off.

Between April 23 and May 7 Mercury transits earth

sign Taurus, your financial area. Your attention turns to your money—how to earn more, save more, whether you're sticking to your budget. You may be applying for jobs or deciding to return to school to attain new skills.

Lovely Venus transits Pisces between April 5 and May 2, so for a couple of days early on it will be traveling with Mercury through your solar twelfth house, a pleasant, romantic, and creative time.

For all of April Mars retrograde continues its transit through Libra, your partnership area. Ouch. The retrograde may create some tensions with partners—business or personal. Just remember: this too shall pass. The retro ends on May 19.

There are two eclipses in April, which adds to the general chaos and madness! April 15 features a lunar eclipse in Libra, and even though Mars retrograde is also in Libra, the eclipse should highlight something positive for you in the partnership area. The solar eclipse on April 29 falls in Taurus, your financial area, and Mercury forms a close conjunction to the eclipse degree. Prediction? New financial opportunities surface and may be tied to communication, travel, or education.

IMPORTANT DATES

April 15: Lunar eclipse in Libra. Lunar eclipses can bring news and insight. Balance is key. Even if the world around you seems a tad crazy, maintain your grounded center.

April 29: Solar eclipse in Taurus. New money opprtunities. Start visualizing!

May—Aries

Mercury is something of a trickster at times. And this month the planet of communication may seem to be more mischievous than usual. It begins the month in Taurus, your financial area, so there's a carryover from late April, with your focus on finances. You may be more stubborn and fixed in your opinions until Mercury enters Gemini on May 7.

Mercury rules Gemini, so it's happy here, and this air sign is compatible with your fire-sign sun. With this transit, which lasts until May 29, you've got the gift of gab and may be socializing more than usual. Travel may be front and center of your thoughts, and whether you go somewhere or not could all boil down to money—can you afford a trip now? Maybe a car trip would satisfy the itch to travel.

From May 29 to June 7 Mercury moves through Cancer, your solar fourth house, bringing your conscious focus to home, family, your domestic situation. Cancer is an intuitive sign, so your psychic antennae are twitching frequently. You may decide to beautify your home in some way, even if it's just a coat of fresh paint in a room.

Between May 2 and 28 Venus transits your sign. This is one of the most romantic and creative periods for you all year. Other people look to you to lead the way and are receptive to you and your ideas. In terms of love and romance, Aries, it doesn't get much better than this. If you're involved already, then you and your partner should get along well during this transit. You are courted and dined, Aries! If you're not involved, then it's possible that you meet someone special before this transit ends.

Mars finally turns direct on May 19 in Libra, your solar seventh house. From now until September 13 a lot of your energy is poured into partnerships—business and personal—and things begin to happen. You may be networking more, and some of these connections prove professionally valuable.

The full moon in Scorpio on May 14 falls in your solar eighth house. Something about your partner's finances is highlighted. Saturn is closely conjunct this full moon, so there's either a somberness about it, or you are urged to take more responsibility for resources you share with others.

The new moon in Gemini on May 28 should delight you no end, Aries. New opportunities surface in communication and travel. Uranus forms a wide, beneficial angle to this new moon, suggesting an element of excitement and unpredictability.

IMPORTANT DATES

May 2: Venus enters your sign. This transit is something to anticipate!

May 19: Circle it. Since Mars rules your sign, its transits affect you more than other signs. When it turns direct on this date, things in your life will begin to move forward again and at a pace that suits you.

May 28: Venus enters Taurus, your financial area. That could attract more income. You may also be spending more.

June—Aries

The second Mercury retrograde of 2014 starts on June 7 and ends on July 1. It's in Cancer, your solar fourth house. This one may bring chaos to your domestic life. Suddenly it seems that no one is listening to anyone else. Miscommunication abounds. Mercury retrogrades back into Gemini, so that's where it is when it turns direct. For you the retro in Gemini could impact your travel plans in a big way.

The other notable transit this month occurs on June 23, when Venus enters Gemini, your solar third house. Love and romance may be as close as your neighborhood. It could happen with someone you already know—a friend, perhaps—and suddenly the chemistry is just right. Your communication skills are highlighted with this transit. If you've been hoping to move, you may find exactly the right neighborhood for you and your family. Just don't sign any contracts—for selling your home or buying another—until after Mercury turns direct on July 1!

The full moon in fellow fire sign Sagittarius on June 13 should be very much to your liking. You may feel a sudden urge to travel far and wide, return to college, or go to graduate school. You may explore a new aspect of your spirituality. Uranus forms a wide and beneficial angle to this full moon, so buckle up, Aries. It's going to be a wild, unpredictable ride.

June 27 features a new moon in Cancer, your solar fourth house. This lunation should bring new opportunities in your domestic situation: a pregnancy, the birth of a child, someone moves in (like your significant other), you have a chance to refurbish your home or build an addition. However the opportunities unfold, all you have to do is recognize and then seize them.

IMPORTANT DATE
In addition to the dates mentioned above, take note of June 17, when retrograde Mercury moves back into Gemini.

July—Aries

July is a super-busy month astrologically, with several planets changing signs or turning direct or retrograde. Let's take a closer look.

On July 1 Mercury turns direct in Gemini. Time to celebrate. Pack your bags and hit the road, send out résumés or manuscripts, touch base with clients, play catchup with friends. Then on July 12 Mercury enters Cancer again, so anything you didn't get right last month can be tried again. In fact any time between July 12 and 31 would be a good time to put your home on the market or buy a new place.

Until July 18 Venus continues its transit of Gemini and lights up your communication skills. Between July 18 and August 12, Venus transits Cancer. You and your partner may decide to move in together or get married, and your love life enjoys a quiet hum of intuitive guidance and insights.

Expansive Jupiter enters fellow fire sign Leo, your solar fifth house, on July 16 and remains there until August 11, 2015. This beautiful transit is sure to expand your love life, creativity, and everything you do for fun and pleasure. Having Jupiter in your court is always a good thing, and with this transit it will be easier for you to manifest your desires. If you don't have a meditation practice yet, Aries, get moving.

Read more about this transit in the overview for your sign for 2014.

On the 20 Saturn turns direct gain in Scorpio, your solar eighth house. This movement helps you strengthen any financial resources you share with others. Since the eighth house is also about ghosts, life after death, and communication with the dead, you may be looking into those areas in a more serious way.

Uranus has been in your sign since 2011, and it turns retrograde once a year. This year it turns retro on July 21 and remains that way until December 21. It means that Uranus' energy is turned inward, so you may feel edgy, more restless than usual.

IMPORTANT DATES
July 12: Full moon in Capricorn, your career area. This one should bring a professional matter to light or news related to your career. Saturn forms a close, beneficial angle to it, suggesting support and structure.

July 25: Mars enters Scorpio, a sign it corules, your solar eighth house. This transit lasts until September 13 and brings plenty of activity concerning joint resources. It would be an excellent time to procure a mortgage or loan.

On July 26 the new moon falls in fellow fire sign Leo and joins Jupiter in your solar fifth house. Wow. New opportunities in love and romance, creativity, with children, and in everything you do for pleasure. With Jupiter's proximity, these new opportunities expand your life in a significant way.

August—Aries

Mercury occupies just two signs this month—Leo, which it went into on July 31, and Virgo, which it enters on August 15. The first transit is very much to your liking since it falls in your romance and creativity area. It means your thoughts are going to be on those areas in which your muse is tagging you like a faithful puppy.

Once Mercury enters Virgo, your solar sixth house, you become quite focused on your daily work. You may be prompted to change your diet in some way, begin a regular exercise routine, or expand an existing routine. Virgo is detail oriented, so you may find yourself reading fine print quite closely. It's a good time to schedule appointments with doctors, dentists, and other health-care professionals.

August 12 marks the beginning of a romantic and creative period for you, one of two this year that should be extraordinary. Venus enters fellow fire sign Leo and transits that sign until September 5. During this period you actively pursue enjoyment and romance and should plunge into your creative endeavors. Other people will be receptive to you, your ideas, and your presence. This transit should be so pleasant that you'll wonder why life can't always be so good!

There's an added bonus to Venus' transit: it will be

traveling with Jupiter, which expands whatever it touches. So if you've got creative endeavors that you shelved, retrieve them, dust them off, and let Venus and Jupiter do the rest!

The full moon on August 10 falls in Aquarius, an air sign compatible with your sun. For four days on either side of this full moon life could get a bit nuts. Uranus forms a close, beneficial angle to this moon, lending an unexpected suddenness to events and any news you hear. This full moon should ramp up your social life, though, and you may join a group whose interests are in line with your own.

The new moon in Virgo on August 25 falls in your solar sixth house of daily work. This moon should usher in new opportunities related to your employment. If you're unemployed and have been looking for work, this moon may attract the opportunity you need. It could also attract opportunities to bolster your health.

IMPORTANT DATE
August 10: That full moon in Aquarius is one to antici-pate.

September—Aries

Mercury is a busy bee again this month. On September 2 it enters Libra, your partnership area, and your conscious attention turns to your personal and business partners. Libra is a social sign, so you may be spending more time than usual with friends and could be networking too with social media.

On September 27 Mercury enters Scorpio, your solar eighth house. Your conscious attention turns to the mundane—insurance, taxes, mortgages, finances you share with others and to the esoteric—ghosts, communication with the dead, things that go bump in the night. Until October 4 Mercury is moving direct in Scorpio. But between October 4 and 25 Mercury is retro. More on that in next month's roundup.

Venus is busy this month too. It starts off September in fellow fire sign Leo, that area of your chart that governs romance and creativity. It's traveling with expansive Jupiter, so go back and read the section in last month's roundup about the energy this duo generates.

Between September 5 and 29 Venus moves through Virgo, your solar sixth house. This transit helps smooth over any issues or challenges in your daily work. You're paying close attention to details, to how the minutiae connect. There could also be a flirtation with a coworker that quickly turns into something else.

Venus moves through Libra, your partnership area, between September 29 and October 23, so you and your partner may take your relationship to a deeper level of commitment. On the business front this transit helps with professional partnerships too. The right person comes along at the right time with the money and energy to help you launch your business. Or you find a manager, agent, or other professional whose skills are exactly what you need.

Your ruler, Mars, enters fellow fire sign Sagittarius on September 13 and remains there until October 26, sure to be a highly charged period for you. You may succumb to the lure of exotic places, decide to go to graduate school, or to take courses in something that interests you. Your physical and sexual energy is remarkable! Whenever Mars makes a favorable angle to your sun, as it does during this transit, it's much easier to make things happen.

September 8 brings a full moon in Pisces, your solar twelfth house. Saturn forms a beneficial angle to it, suggesting that whatever is illuminated, whatever news you hear, enables you to create a solid foundation and structure in some area of your life.

The new moon in Libra on September 24 is something to anticipate! You and your partner may get engaged or even married. New opportunities emerge with business partnerships. Mars forms a beneficial angle to this new moon, indicating action, forward thrust, pizazz!

IMPORTANT DATE
September 22: Pluto turns direct in Capricorn, your career area. This movement should enable professional matters to move forward again.

October—Aries

Okay, the Mercury news first. The last Mercury retro of the year begins October 4 in Scorpio and ends on October 25 in Libra. You probably know the drill by now, but let's review it. Since this retro occurs in your solar eighth house, it's wise not to apply for mortgages or loans, and some financial stuff you thought was resolved may be revisited. Make travel plans on either side of this time frame, and be sure to back up all your computer files before the retro begins.

For the first twenty-three days of the month Venus continues its transit of Libra, your partnership area. Re-read last month's section about this position for Venus. Between October 23 and November 8 it transits Scorpio, your solar eighth house. Despite Mercury's retro, this Venus transit favors your partner's income—a raise? a bonus? It also favors things like mortgages and loans as well as insurance settlements and tax breaks. If you're in the midst of a divorce and property settlement, it looks like things fall in your court, Aries. Be patient!

Your ruler, Mars, remains in Sagittarius, your solar ninth house, until October 23, then it enters your career area until December 14. With Mars in your professional court, things get done. It's much easier to move your professional agenda forward, and people look to you as the leader, the one with the knowhow and organization to do whatever needs to be done.

The two eclipses this month promise a lot of activity, insights, and excitement. On October 8 the lunar eclipse in your sign stirs emotions related to your personal life. Uranus is closely conjunct the eclipse degree, so whatever surfaces does so suddenly and unexpectedly. Mars forms a beneficial angle to the lunar eclipse, suggesting a lot of forward thrust and activity.

The solar eclipse on October 23 falls in Scorpio, your solar eighth house. This eclipse should usher in new opportunities to investigate and research the hidden, mysterious undercurrents of life. You may encounter opportunities related to taxes, insurance, or mortgages, and/or your partner could see a spike in his or her income. Venus is conjunct the eclipse degree, so in romance and creativity things are intense and passionate.

IMPORTANT DATE

October 8: The lunar eclipse in your sign is something to plan for. Be sure you've got yourself lined up internally before it begins. Expect insights and answers to come to you from unexpected sources. Synchronicities are likely to flourish.

November—Aries

As you enter the last two months of the year, you may feel pressed for time or wonder where the year went or both. So much still to achieve—right, Aries? Let's take a closer look at how you can maximize your time for the month of November.

During the first week of November Mercury is steaming ahead through Libra, the sign in which it turned direct on October 25. This is the time to straighten out anything that went wrong with a partner when Mercury was retro. You regain your balance and feel as if you're on solid ground again.

Between November 8 and 27 Mercury transits Scorpio, your solar eighth house. It travels with Venus for about a week, between November 8 and 16, which should prove to be highly charged emotionally. You're digging for information, insights into a relationship or a creative endeavor. Your mind and heart are in synch.

On November 25 Mercury enters fellow fire sign Sagittarius, a much more comfortable fit for you. Your head is filled with ideas, you feel restless for travel and change, and routine is anathema to you now. You're preparing for the Thanksgiving holidays, perhaps getting ready to leave town for a few days. That would suit Mercury! This transit ends on December 16.

The full moon of November 6 falls in earth sign Taurus, your financial area. Some facet of your financial picture becomes much clearer, or there's news about money. With Pluto forming a close, beneficial angle to this full moon, you're in the power seat, Aries, just where you like to be.

The new moon on November 22 is one to plan for! It's in fellow fire sign Sagittarius, and Venus is widely conjunct. New opportunities surface in romance and creative endeavors, with publishing, education, and long-distance travel. You may be meeting people from other countries and cultures either here at home or, of course, while traveling abroad.

IMPORTANT DATES

November 15: Neptune turns direct in Pisces, your solar twelfth house. Dream recall, synchronicity, and psychic experiences proliferate once again.

The new moon in Sagittarius on November 22 is excellent for the upcoming Thanksgiving holidays.

December—Aries

A busy month! Mercury occupies three signs this month, Venus occupies two signs, Mars changes signs, Jupiter turns retrograde, Saturn enters a new sign. Whew! So let's get started.

December begins with Mercury's continued transit through Sagittarius. Reread that section in last month's roundup to refresh your memory about what you may experience. Between December 16 and January 5, 2015, Mercury transits Capricorn, your career area. Your communication skills turn toward your career. You pitch ideas and explain your current projects and what you would like to tackle next. Your strategy is sound, your goals are clear, and you gather the support of coworkers and bosses.

For the first ten days of December Venus continues its transit of Sagittarius, a glorious time for you, Aries. Love and romance find you in unlikely places—while you're traveling abroad, taking a workshop or seminar, sitting in a graduate school class, or researching your novel. Between December 10 and January 4, 2015, Venus transits Capricorn, your solar tenth house. During most of this transit Venus is traveling with Mercury through the same area of your chart, and this duo helps you gain the professional support you might need. A raise or bonus could be in the offing; a romantic flirtation or fling is possible with a coworker or boss.

On December 4 Mars enters Aquarius, an air sign compatible with your fire-sign sun. It remains there until January 12, 2015, and should heat up your social life just in time for the holidays. You may be inundated with opportunities for all kinds of social activities and should accept as many of them as you possibly can. Think of it as networking. Be sure to have business cards with all your contact data.

December 6 features a full moon in air sign Gemini, which is compatible with your sun sign. Uranus forms a close and favorable angle to it, so whatever is headed toward you occurs suddenly and unexpectedly. Excitement, Aries. Jupiter forms a wide, beneficial angle to this full moon, and that indicates expansion of whatever you're feeling.

December 21 features a new moon in Capricorn, your career area. So between now and the first full moon in 2015, new professional opportunities surface. Mercury is widely conjunct, suggesting the opportunities could be connected to communication and travel.

IMPORTANT DATES
December 8: Jupiter turns direct in Leo.

December 21: Uranus turns direct in your sign.

December 23: Saturn enters fellow fire sign Sagittarius, where it will be for the next two and a half years. During this period it forms a beneficial angle to your sun, Aries, so all the seeds you've been planting will begin to sprout and flourish. Saturn will help you to solidify the existing structures in your life.

HAPPY NEW YEAR!

3

Taurus

The Big Picture in 2014

Welcome to 2014, Taurus! It's a 9 year for you, with many beginnings and endings. It's your year to tie up loose ends; an old cycle is ending and a new cycle is about to begin. You're making room in your life for new relationships, a new job, perhaps even a new career path. Now that you've the tumult of 2012 and the realignment of 2013 behind you, you're ready for everything the universe brings your way.

So let's look at how specific areas of your life may be impacted and which dates will be of vital importance to you.

ROMANCE/CREATIVITY

One of the most romantic and creative times for you all year occurs between May 28 and June 23, when Venus transits your sign. During this period your muse is at your beck and call, and you feel so creative that everything you touch illustrates how your muse is working for you. You feel more self-confident. Others pick up on that vibe and are attracted to you and your ideas, persona, and creative projects. So if you have these ready, start submitting and exhibiting them, doing whatever you need to do in order to advertise your products.

If a relationship begins during this period, it's likely to be sensuous and deeply satisfying for you. The romantic interests you attract are a reflection of who you are within the deepest parts of your soul. If you're already involved in a relationship, this transit helps to define it. You and your partner may deepen your commitment to each other

The other terrific period for romance and creativity occurs between September 5 and 29, when Venus transits fellow earth sign Virgo, your solar fifth house. This transit stimulates you to do whatever it is you most enjoy. If it's travel, you go traveling. If your passion is politics, you dive into the political arena in some way. It's a perfect time for romance, the kind of romance that entails candlelit dinners, midnight walks on a beach, kayaking through some mysterious shaded part of a river . . . you get the idea.

Between January 1 and July 16 Jupiter is completing its transit of Cancer that began last year. Cancer is a water sign compatible with your earth-sign sun, Taurus, so this transit should be expanding all your communication venues. Your communication skills are heightened during this period, and this makes it easier for you to talk about what you feel in any relationship.

Jupiter's transit through Cancer forms a strong angle to your sun and heightens your intuition, nurturing qualities, and love of home and family (that's the Cancer part of it!). If you're in a committed relationship already, you and your partner may decide to move in together or get married.

On July 15 Jupiter enters Leo, where it will be until August 11, 2015. If you have a lot of fire-sign planets in your natal chart, this transit will benefit you tremendously. If not, it could create excesses in some area of your life, but you still benefit. Jupiter turns retrograde on December 8 and doesn't turn direct again until April 8, 2015.

Other excellent dates:

January 15, when a full moon in Cancer shines brightly with Jupiter.

July 18 to August 12, when Venus joins Jupiter in Cancer. This period infuses your love life with harmony and brings your muse up close and personal.

CAREER

Jupiter's transit through Cancer, of course, will help every facet of your life, even your career. The caveat with career matters, though, is that if you're dong something you love, you benefit tremendously. If you're working in a field that doesn't excite you, that has become rather humdrum and routine, then Jupiter, Mars, and your ruler, Venus, could help you to break away and find something that is more aligned with your passions.

Let's take a closer look at the beneficial career times:

January 11 to 31: Mercury transits your career area, making this period an excellent one for communication with bosses and peers. Pitch your ideas; gather your support among coworkers. Think as far outside the box as your dare, then allow your practical Taurus sun to translate these abstract concepts and ground them. During this period peers and bosses are impressed with your work, skills, and organizational talents. A promotion or raise could be forthcoming.

March 5 to April 5: During this period while Venus transits career area your professional life hums along at a perfect pitch. This is the time to implement new projects, especially those that have captured your passions.

The new moon in your career area occurs on January 30 and should usher in new professional opportunities. Uranus forms a tight, beneficial angle to this new moon, suggesting that opportunities seem to come out of the blue. Just be ready to seize them.

Between December 4, 2014, and January 13, 2015, Mars transits Aquarius, your solar tenth house. This period will be highly energetic and active, and you'll feel you can do it all. Guard against spreading yourself too thinly. It's a great time to brainstorm with coworkers.

FINANCES
Let's look at Venus transits first for beneficial dates for finances. Your solar second house, which rules money, is Gemini. The period to watch for, then, falls between June 23 and July 18. During this three-week period you could get a raise, bonus, or unexpected insurance or royalty check, or someone could repay money they owe you. You may feel an urge to spend on a luxury item—jewelry, for instance, or art.

Once Jupiter enters Leo on July 16, you could see some spikes in expenses related to your home. Jupiter's transit through Leo lasts until late June 2015. It could result in an expansion in your home—you move, add a room, buy property, all if which would cost money. But not to worry, Taurus. You have the money to spend.

May 28 features a new moon in Gemini, your financial area. New opportunities surface in finances, and with Uranus forming a wide, harmonious angle, these may surface unexpectedly.

MERCURY RETROGRADES

Every year Mercury—the planet of communication and travel—turns retrograde three times. During these periods it's wise not to sign contracts (unless you don't mind renegotiating when Mercury is moving direct), to check and recheck travel plans, and to communicate as succinctly as possible. Refrain from buying any large-ticket items or electronics during this time too. Often computers and appliances go on the fritz, cars act up, data is lost . . . you get the idea. Be sure to back up all files before the dates below:

February 6–28: Mercury retrograde in Pisces, your solar eleventh house. This one impacts your friendships and social circles. Mercury slips back into Aquarius before it turns direct, so it impacts your career too.

June 7–July 1: Mercury retrograde in Cancer, your solar third house. This retrograde affects communication and travel. Be sure to make travel plans on either side of the retrograde period. If you have to travel while Mercury is retrograde, regard it as an adventure!

October 4–25: Mercury retrograde in Scorpio, your solar seventh house. This one impacts your business and romantic partnerships. You and a partner may rehash old issues. There are likely to be communication mixups and general confusion about priorities.

ECLIPSES

Solar eclipses tend to trigger external events that bring about change according to the sign and house in which they fall. Lunar eclipses trigger inner, emotional events according to the sign and house in which they fall. Any eclipse marks both beginnings and endings. The solar and lunar eclipse in a pair falls in opposite signs. If you're interested in detailed information on eclipses, take a look at Celeste Teal's excellent and definitive book, *Eclipses: Predicting World Events & Personal Transformation.*

If you were born under or around the time of an eclipse, it's to your advantage to take a look at your birth chart to find out exactly where the eclipses will impact you.

Most years feature four eclipses—two solar, two lunar—with the set separated by about two weeks. Let's take a closer look.

April 15: Lunar eclipse in Libra, your solar sixth house. This may bring up emotional issues related to your daily work routine or health. It should be a positive eclipse, though, so go with the flow and enjoy!

April 29: Solar eclipse in your sign. This eclipse should bring plenty of new opportunities that are personally satisfying. You may have to give up something before you can take advantage of these opportunities, but it won't be a difficult choice to make! With Mercury forming a close conjunction to the eclipse degree and Jupiter forming a beneficial angle to it, be on your toes and ready to seize the opportunity as soon as it occurs.

October 8: Lunar eclipse in Aries, your solar twelfth house. Uranus is closely conjunct the moon, so you can expect sudden and unexpected emotional reactions to something that surfaces from your own unconscious. It could be a past-life memory or something from early childhood, and its appearance catches you off guard.

October 23: Solar eclipse in Scorpio, your solar seventh house. New partnership opportunities. If you're already in a committed relationship, this eclipse could deepen your commitment—you get engaged or married. You also could find exactly the right partner for your business. This eclipse is at 0 degrees Scorpio, and so is Venus, so it's apt to be quite positive for you.

LUCKIEST DAYS OF THE YEAR

Every year there are one or two days when Jupiter and the sun meet up, and luck, serendipity, and expansion are the hallmarks. This year those days fall on July 25–26. Circle the dates. Do whatever you enjoy!

January—Taurus

The year begins with Mercury in fellow earth sign Capricorn, your solar ninth house. This transit brings greater clarity to your goals and professional ambition. Your conscious mind is constantly busy with plans and strategies, and you can envision how to bring everything together with a particular project.

Between January 11 and 31 Mercury transits Aquarius, your career area. The seeds you planted and whatever you planned during Mercury's transit through Capricorn can now be implemented. Think as far outside the box as you can. Bosses and coworkers will be impressed with your ideas. You get help from people who are experts in their field.

Mercury enters Pisces on January 31 and will be there for quite a while because of a retrograde. We'll discuss that in the February roundup.

Your ruler, Venus, begins the year retrograde in Capricorn and remains that way until January 31. Mainly this retro can cause misunderstandings in your most intimate relationships—with a partner or the women in your life. It's wise not to purchase any large-ticket items until Venus is direct again. Keep track of what's going on with your bank accounts and investments too.

Once Venus turns direct on January 31, your love life is in much better shape, your creative drive and inspiration function more smoothly, and if you're traveling abroad, everything should unfold the way it should. Venus travels direct in Capricorn until March 5.

Mars begins 2014 moving direct in Libra, your solar sixth house. This transit galvanizes your daily work. You're able to accomplish more than usual and are motivated and energetic. Since the planet is in Libra, you may be networking and socializing a lot with coworkers.

Jupiter, the planet of luck and expansion, begins the year retrograde in Cancer, your solar third house, and turns direct again on March 6. During this period your inner awareness is heightened, particularly in regard to the content of your conscious thoughts. You're more aware of negative thinking and are able to pivot those thoughts into something more positive.

Saturn, the planet of discipline, responsibility, structure, begins the year direct in Scorpio, your opposite sign. You and a business or romantic partner may be committing to each other more deeply, perhaps by moving in together, getting engaged or married. In business you find the right partner at the right time, whose abilities and skills balance yours.

Uranus starts 2014 in Aries, your solar twelfth house, where it has been since 2011. You should be accustomed to this erratic energy by now. It's helping you to deal with issues and beliefs that you may have buried over the years and rid yourself of beliefs and relationships that no longer serve your best interest.

Neptune has been in Pisces since February 2012 and continues its journey in that sign. It's moving in direct motion until June 9, so during this period your ideals and idealism are played out among friends and among any groups to which you belong. This transit also deepens your spirituality.

Then we come to Pluto, still moving at a snail's pace through Capricorn, your solar ninth house. It forms a strong, beneficial angle to your sun, so you're in the power seat, Taurus, and deal successfully with important issues.

IMPORTANT DATES

January 1: The new moon in Capricorn, your solar ninth house, is a terrific way to start the new year. Expect opportunities to surface in spirituality, higher education, publishing, foreign travel, and your career. Pluto is closely conjunct this new moon, indicating that opportunities which surface may be deeply transformative.

January 15: Full moon in Cancer, your solar third house. Communication is highlighted. There could be news related to a writing or communication project or something in your domestic situation. A sibling or a parent plays an important role.

January 30: New moon in Aquarius, your career area. New professional opportunities are likely. Thanks to a beneficial angle from Uranus, the opportunities could surface suddenly and unexpectedly. Just be ready to seize them!

February—Taurus

All right, bad news first. On February 6 Mercury turns retrograde for the first time this year, in Pisces, your solar eleventh house. Since the retrograde begins when Mercury is in the early degrees of Pisces, it retrogrades back into Aquarius, your career area, where it turns direct on February 28. During the retro period you may experience communication snafus with friends. Be sure to check and double-check appointments, back up your computers before the retrograde begins, and take nothing for granted!

Venus turned direct in Capricorn on January 31 and now zips along toward its appointment with Aquarius on March 5. During its transit through Capricorn you may take a workshop or seminar in something that interests you or perhaps to enhance your professional skills. If you travel overseas during this transit, romance could come knocking at your door when you least expect it. However, try not to travel during Mercury's retrograde, unless you don't mind sudden, unexpected changes in your itinerary.

Until March 1 Mars continues to move direct in Libra,

your solar sixth house. Take advantage of this transit while Mars is behaving. Set up appointments and pitches, network with employees and coworkers, and burn your candle at both ends. Your physical energy this month is good, and if you don't have a regular exercise routine already, start one!

On February 14 the full moon in Leo occurs in your solar fourth house and illuminates something in your domestic environment. Mars forms an exact and beneficial angle to this full moon, suggesting increased social activities, drama, warmth, and love. Quite a mix!

IMPORTANT DATES
February 6–28: Mercury's retrograde in Pisces and Aquarius.

March—Taurus

Some major activity is happening this month, and it all gets off to a running start on March 1, when Mars turns retrograde in Libra. Suddenly everything at work seems to slow down, become sluggish. Your physical energy isn't quite what it was during February, so indulge your need to sleep in on weekends and take a day off from work. The retrograde period lasts until May 19.

On March 2 Saturn turns retrograde in Scorpio, your opposite sign, and remains that way until July 20. During this period partnerships—both personal and professional—don't move along as smoothly as you would like. Just remind yourself that it's all temporary.

Your ruler, Venus, enters Aquarius and your career

area on March 5 and stays there until April 5. During this month professional matters flow your way. Bosses and peers tap you for answers and insights. People are receptive to you and your ideas. A flirtation or romance could start up with someone in your work environment. If you've been applying for jobs, this transit of Venus could help you land a job you love.

March 6 is a day to circle. Jupiter in Cancer turns direct after being retrograde for months. This movement proves beneficial for your writing and other communication projects, and your mind is now less sluggish. Foreign travel is a distinct possibility, and if that opportunity unfolds, the trip goes well.

Mercury transits Pisces from March 17 to April 4. You may be spending more time with friends or participating in groups than you usually do. You and your friends may get together to form a band, brainstorm ideas, or even take a road trip somewhere. Your conscious mind is particularly intuitive during this transit.

IMPORTANT DATES

This month, as January, there are three lunations, so jot these dates on your calendar:

March 1: New moon in Pisces. New opportunities surface in friendships and with groups. You may have an opportunity to use your imagination and/or intuition in new ways. With Neptune closely conjunct to this new moon, you could have an opportunity to write a novel or screenplay.

March 16: The full moon in fellow earth sign Virgo should be terrific for you. A romantic relationship or creative project is highlighted. If you've applied for jobs or submitted creative endeavors (like a manuscript or portfolio), there will be positive news. Insights you gain into a romantic relationship will be positive.

March 30: The new moon in Aries brings an opportunity to work behind the scenes in some capacity. Thanks to a close conjunction of Uranus, opportunities surface suddenly and unexpectedly. Be ready to seize them!

April—Taurus

Here comes another busy month, so buckle up, Taurus, things could get wild! Between April 5 and May 2 Venus transits Pisces, your solar eleventh house. This one could bring about a romance with someone you already know as a friend or with someone you meet through friends. Your social life should be quite active and busy during this transit—everyone seeks your company!

Between April 7 and 23 Mercury moves through Aries, your solar twelfth house. This transit is perfect for working behind the scenes, in solitude or near solitude, writing or preparing for something in order to meet a deadline. You may be doing research that requires you to be focused.

Once Mercury moves into your sign on April 23, you feel much more comfortable. It remains in Taurus until May 7, and during this period your conscious mind is grounded, you're able to take abstract ideas and make them comprehensible to others, and your communication skills shine.

The other noteworthy events this month are the two eclipses—a lunar eclipse in Libra on April 15 and a solar eclipse in your sign on April 29. The first one stirs up emotions connected to your work. The emotions, however, look positive. Mars forms a wide conjunction to the eclipse degree, however, which suggests a lot of energy and activity.

The solar eclipse in your sign is like a double new moon—double the opportunities. With Mercury forming a close conjunction to the eclipse degree, it looks as if at least one of the opportunities involves writing/communication and travel. With Jupiter in compatible water sign Cancer forming a wide, beneficial angle to the eclipse degree, these opportunities somehow expand your venue creatively, spiritually, personally.

IMPORTANT DATES
In addition to all the dates already mentioned, add this one: April 14. Pluto in Capricorn turns retrograde and will be like that until September 22. This could be a period during which you're on some sort of spiritual quest or are defining your career options.

May—Taurus

It's another one of those months when numerous transits bring heightened activity and energy into your life. Mercury, for instance, occupies three signs in May. From May 1 to 7, it's in your sign, Taurus, so you're in your element. Your communication skills are excellent, and you may be more stubborn than usual.

Between May 7 and 29 Mercury transits air sign Gemini, your second house. This brings your conscious focus to finances—what you earn and spend and your beliefs about money. As a Taurus, you're careful about money but do enjoy occasional extravagances. Just be sure to pay in cash!

Between May 29 and July 13 Mercury transits Cancer (although it slips back into Gemini for a time), your solar third house. However, the planet will be retrograde between June 7 and July 1. More on that in next month's roundup.

Your ruler, Venus, moves through Aries, your solar twelfth house, between May 2 and 28. During this period there's a lot going on behind the scenes. You and a romantic interest may be spending a lot of time alone together, or you could be working on a creative endeavor, perhaps in order to meet a deadline. A period to anticipate occurs between May 28 and June 23, when Venus moves through your sign. More on that in next month's roundup!

After a retrograde of about ten weeks, Mars finally turns direct again on May 19 in Libra. This will enable you to move ahead with plans in your daily work routine. Projects that were stalled will once again be on the front burner. You may be socializing more with employees and coworkers.

After last month's eclipses, which may have been a bit too frenetic for your tastes, you'll enjoy the full moon in Scorpio on May 14 and the new moon in Gemini on May 28. Saturn is closely conjunct to this full moon, suggesting that any news you receive will be solid, genuine. Also, Jupiter forms a beautiful angle to this moon, indicating expansion. If you've been applying for jobs, you may land one of them around this time.

The new moon in Gemini on the 28 brings new financial opportunities. Thanks to a challenging angle from Neptune, there could be something confusing about one of these opportunities. Uranus forms a wide, beneficial angle to this moon, suggesting an air of excitement and unpredictability.

IMPORTANT DATES
May 29: Mercury enters Cancer and is going to turn retrograde in that sign on June 7 until July 1. This transit affects your solar third house—communication, travel, the conscious mind.

By now you know how to prepare for these retro periods. But to refresh your memory, reread the appropriate section under The Big Picture for 2014.

June—Taurus

All right, bad news first. Mercury is retrograde between June 7 and July 1 in Cancer. This retro not only impacts the areas mentioned earlier, but because it's in Cancer it will affect your domestic environment too. This period favors the three Rs—rethinking, revising, reviewing. It's not a good time to start anything new. Wait until after July 1 for that.

Since Mercury is in the early degrees of Cancer when it retrogrades, it will slide back into Gemini, your financial area, and turn direct in that sign on July 1. Be sure to check and recheck bank statements.

On May 28 Venus entered your sign, marking one of the most romantic and creative periods for you all year. Other people find you attractive and are receptive to your ideas and presence. They are generally helpful. Your muse is at your beck and call during this transit, Taurus, so put him/her to work by dusting off those creative projects you stashed away in a drawer somewhere. This transits lasts until June 23.

Between June 23 and July 18 Venus moves through Gemini, your solar second house. This transit should bolster your income in some way—a raise, a loan repaid, royalty check, even income from a second job. You may be tempted to buy large-ticket items. If you do, make sure you pay in cash.

With Mars now moving direct in Libra, your social life should be ramping up once more, and your daily work is moving at a swift clip. You may be working longer hours, but as long as it's work on something you love and believe in, you don't mind.

The full moon in Sagittarius on June 13 brings to light something concerning a mortgage, loan, your partner's income—i.e., other people's money. Uranus forms a wide, beneficial angle to this full moon, so any news you hear is apt to be sudden and unexpected.

The new moon in Cancer on June 27 brings new opportunities for you in communication and travel and with neighbors and siblings. Saturn retrograde forms an exact, beneficial angle to this new moon, an indication that the opportunities warrant your serious consideration. Think them through, then decide.

IMPORTANT DATES
June 7: Mercury turns retrograde in Cancer.

June 9: Neptune turns retrograde in Pisces, your solar eleventh house, and will remain that way until November 15. During this period you're reflecting on what you desire in friendships. Do you and your friends share common ideals and spiritual beliefs?

July—Taurus

This month's pace is going to feel a bit too accelerated for you, unless you're the kind of Taurus who relishes change. Let's take a closer look.

July 1 features great news: Mercury turns direct again in Gemini, your financial area. Breathe deeply, and let the exhalation be a contented sigh! On June 17 Mercury enters Cancer again and moves toward its appointment with Leo on July 31. While it's in Cancer, your communication skills are enhanced, you may be checking out neighborhoods that would be more suitable for you and/or your family, and you could put your home on the market.

On July 18 Venus enters Cancer, and your solar third house, where it will be until August 12. This transit could bring about a flirtation or romance with a neighbor or with someone you meet through a sibling. It also favors an ease in communication that could result in unexpected bonuses—a speaking engagement, for instance, or a book deal.

Jupiter begins its transit of fire sign Leo, your solar fourth house, on July 15. This transit lasts about a year and may result in an expansion in your family—a birth, a parent or relative moves in, an adult child returns home. Or you may refurbish your home, add a room, or even buy a large piece of property. One way or another, Jupiter expands everything it touches.

On July 20 Saturn emerges from its lengthy retrograde, in Scorpio, your opposite sign. This could signal that a partnership—romantic or professional—takes a more serious and committed turn.

Saturn turns direct, and a day later Uranus in Aries turns retrograde, which will last until December 21. While Uranus is retro, you may tend to look inward more frequently for answers and insights. You may also be revisiting issues you thought were resolved.

Mars also enters another sign this month—Scorpio, on July 25. This one brings a lot of activity and energy into the partnership area. Your sexuality is definitely heightened.

IMPORTANT DATES
July 12 features a full moon in fellow earth sign Capricorn, your solar ninth house. It illuminates an issue connected with your worldview, spiritual beliefs, higher education, publishing, or foreign travel, or there's news in one or several of these areas. Pluto is widely conjunct, suggesting the news or insight gained is potentially transformative.

On July 26 a new moon in Leo brings new opportunities in your domestic environment. With expansive Jupiter closely conjunct, the possibilities are practically infinite. Maybe you find your dream home. Or if you're female, you discover that you're pregnant. Or perhaps you and your partner move in together.

On July 31 Mercury enters Leo, your domestic area. We'll talk more about that in the August roundup.

August—Taurus

Let's start with Mercury. As of July 31, it's now in Leo, your solar fourth house—your domestic environment. This transit may bring an element of drama into your home life, particularly if you have children. That said, it also triggers a lot of discussion and conversation. Perhaps you or someone at home is writing a book or has a speaking engagement of some kind. Some conversations revolve around that.

On August 15 Mercury enters fellow earth sign Virgo, the romance/creativity section of your chart. One thing is for sure with this transit. Any romantic interest you meet during this period will have to seduce your intellect first! On the creative front, this transit ramps up your communication skills. It's an excellent transit for writing, so perhaps it's time to dust off those old manuscripts, Taurus, and get to work.

Your ruler, Venus, spends the first twelve days of the month in compatible water sign Cancer, your solar third house. Lucky you! This transit has a distinctive intuitive element. Your conscious mind absorbs information easily, your intuition is particularly powerful, and you're quite comfortable in your own skin.

Between August 12 and September 5 Venus moves through fire sign Leo, your domestic area. You may be refurbishing rooms in your home, adding color, freshly cut flowers, potted plants, redoing things from the inside out. The transit is especially good for your love life, Taurus, just like Venus' transit through Cancer, but has a different flavor and texture to it. What's particularly nice about this Venus transit is that the planet is traveling with Jupiter. When these two planets travel together, life feels pleasing.

Mars continues its transit through Scorpio this month, a sign it corules, and you and your partner continue to enjoy a heightened sexuality. You may not agree on everything, but as long as you don't try to pick a fight, the storm passes quickly.

IMPORTANT DATES
August 10: The full moon in Aquarius should illuminate a career matter. If you've been job-hunting, then this full moon could bring sudden, unexpected, and positive news from a prospective employer. Uranus forms a close, beneficial angle to this full moon, so there could be a lot going on in your career. It's exciting, but perhaps exhausting.

August 25: The new moon in fellow earth sign Virgo is a beauty. This one should usher in new opportunities in romance and creativity. Make a list of what you're looking for in romance, Taurus, and what you hope to achieve creatively. Visualize, back these visualizations with emotion, then let the universe do its work!

September—Taurus

It's another busy month astrologically, Taurus, and you may get caught up in the whirl. On September 2 Mercury enters Libra, your solar sixth house. This transit, which lasts until September 27, should bring your conscious attention to your daily work. But because it's in Libra, there may be a big social aspect to this period. You could be spending more social time with employees and co-workers.

Between September 27 and October 4 Mercury transits Scorpio, your solar seventh house, then turns retro on October 4, slides back into Libra, and turns direct in that sign on October 25. More on that part of the transit in next month's roundup. While Mercury is moving direct in Scorpio, there's a bottom-line intensity to your intellect. Easy answers won't suit you. This transit favors research and investigation.

Venus occupies three signs this month. Until September 5 it continues its journey through Leo. Then it enters Virgo, where it remains until September 29, when it begins its transit of Libra. Let's talk about the second transit, through Virgo.

This period of twenty-four days should be one of the most romantic and creative and joyful times for you all year. In romance and love, things go your way. Your current romantic interest just can't get enough of you. If you aren't involved when the transit begins, you could be before it ends, and if not, it doesn't matter. You're having too much fun. Creatively your muse shadows you 24/7, so you've got plenty of support in all your creative endeavors.

We'll talk about Venus' transit through Libra in next month's roundup.

Between September 13 and October 26 Mars transits fire sign Sagittarius, your solar eighth house. This period favors obtaining a mortgage or loan, except when Mercury is retrograde. There's also activity concerning your partner's income and resources you share with others in terms of energy and time. Your hunger for travel may increase—that's the Sagittarius part of the equation. Be sure to schedule your travel plans on either side of the Mercury retrograde. There could also be activity with publishing, higher education, the courts, attorneys.

September 22 marks the day that Pluto finally turns direct again, in fellow earth sign Capricorn. Projects and endeavors that felt sluggish or even stalled now pick up and move forward again.

IMPORTANT DATES
September 8: The full moon in Pisces should be a good one for you, Taurus. There could be news about a friendship or some dream or wish that you have. Pluto forms a beneficial angle to this full moon, suggesting the news could be transformative. Your social life picks up, and you may be meeting people whose ideals align with your own.

September 24: A new moon in Libra, your solar sixth house should usher in new work opportunities. A promotion, perhaps? Greater responsibility? With the moon in Libra, opportunities could surface in public relations, music, or the arts in general.

September 27: Mercury enters Scorpio. We'll talk about this in October's roundup.

October—Taurus

For the first four days of the month, Mercury is moving in direct motion through Scorpio, your opposite sign. You and your business and romantic partners share excellent communication and may be dealing with the absolute bottom lines in your discussions. Between October 4 and 25 Mercury move retrograde through Scorpio, slips back into Libra, your solar sixth house, then turns direct in Libra and enters Scorpio again on November 8. This is the last Mercury retro of the year, so by now you know the ins and outs, right? Just to refresh your memory, though, reread the section on Mercury retrograde in the overview section for your sign.

While Mercury is retrograde in Scorpio, you and your partners may experience miscommunications, so be sure that in discussions, in email exchanges, you communicate clearly. Take nothing for granted.

Two days before Mercury turns direct in Libra, Venus enters Scorpio, where it will be until November 16. You and your partner may commit to each other more deeply—you get engaged, move in together, get married.

Mars continues its transit of Sagittarius until October 26, when it enters fellow earth sign Capricorn. During this transit, which lasts until December 4, you're focused about your professional goals and move full speed ahead on projects that are important to you. There could be some overseas travel too, Taurus. Or you could be debating about going to graduate school.

IMPORTANT DATES
October 8: A lunar eclipse in Aries, your solar twelfth house, stirs emotions concerning something long buried that comes to light. Given the close proximity of Uranus to the eclipse degree, the discovery is sudden and unexpected. Mars forms a beneficial angle to both Uranus

and the eclipse degree, suggesting that you are spurred into action.

October 23: A solar eclipse in Scorpio, your solar seventh house. Venus is exactly conjunct this eclipse degree. This one ushers in new partnership opportunities in both business and romance. If you're involved already, then you and your significant other may deepen your commitment to each other by getting married. If it's in business partnerships, then you find exactly the right agent, manager, accountant, or financial backer.

October 25: Mercury turns direct in Libra.

November—Taurus

Now that Mercury is moving in direct motion again, life unfolds with greater smoothness and less confusion. Mercury now heads toward its appointment with Scorpio (again) on November 8. You and a business or romantic partner may have a heart-to-heart about your individual expectations in the relationship. A romantic relationship may be taken to the next level—you get engaged, married, buy a home together, decide to start a family. This transit lasts until November 27.

For the first sixteen days of the month Venus continues its transit of Scorpio, your solar seventh house. Whatever is going on between you and a partner is intense sexually and emotionally. Is it love, Taurus? Or is it hormones? On November 16 Venus enters Sagittarius, your solar eighth house. This transit, which lasts until December 10, favors obtaining mortgages, loans, and help from others. Your partner's income may be high-lighted in some way—a raise, perhaps?

Mars entered Capricorn, your solar ninth house, on October 26 and will remain there until December 4. This transit acts as a professional booster rocket, prompting you to lay down a career strategy and figure out how you will achieve what you want. You're grounded during this transit and quite focused. Your physical energy and stamina are powerful.

On November 15 Neptune turns direct again in Pisces, your solar eleventh house. You're more conscious now of how your social connections reflect your spiritual values and ideals.

IMPORTANT DATES
November 6: The full moon in your sign should bring news of a personal nature. Thanks to a strong, beneficial angle from Pluto, the news puts you in the driver's seat, Taurus. Not a bad place to be, right?

November 22: The new moon in Sagittarius should be enormously satisfying for you. It ushers in new opportu-nities in any of these areas: travel, publishing, metaphys-ics, and higher education. Venus is widely conjunct this new moon, so there could be a new romance or creative endeavor underway too.

December—Taurus

Now that we're in the last month of 2014, you might want to take some time to reflect on the year behind you—and the year ahead. Have you achieved what you set out to do this year? Focus on the positive highlights and bring that energy into the new year with you!

Until December 16 Mercury continues its journey through Sagittarius, your solar eighth house. In addition to the areas mentioned in last month's roundup about this transit, you may be delving into the weird and the strange—UFOs, ghosts, communication with the dead, and things that go bump in the night.

Between December 16 and January 5, 2015, Mercury transits fellow earth sign Capricorn, your solar ninth house. This transit favors professional discussions, strategy sessions, and also foreign travel. Perhaps you're going to spend your holidays in the Greek isles and will usher in 2015 from the oracle at Delphi! But even if you spend the holidays at home, this transit is a good one for you for welcoming the new year.

Venus also changes signs this month. Between December 10 and January 4 it transits Capricorn, so it will be traveling with Mercury right into the new year. You and your partner may be discussing spending the holidays abroad and take steps to make the dream a reality. If you're not involved right now, then you may meet a romantic interest while traveling. Your muse is up close and personal during this transit, so take advantage of it by diving into your creative endeavors.

On December 4 Mars enters Aquarius, your career area, where it will be until January 12, 2015. This transit galvanizes you into action concerning your career, and it could be that you take on more than you can realistically handle. So perhaps you need to step back and take a broader view. Set your goals for 2015!

Circle December 23. Saturn enters Sagittarius, your solar eighth house, that day, for a stay of two and a half years. This transit brings structure to resources you share with others. You are urged to meet your responsibilities concerning mortgages and loans. Sources of income that were available to you before may be restricted in some way.

IMPORTANT DATES

December 6: The full moon in Gemini illuminates something in your financial area and with communication and travel. Uranus forms a close, beneficial angle to this moon, suggesting that news you hear or insights you gain are sudden and unexpected. Jupiter forms a wide, beneficial angle to the moon, so whatever you hear or learn expands your life and opportunities in a significant way.

December 21: The new moon in fellow earth sign Capricorn should be exciting for you. It brings in new opportunities related to your professional life, publishing, foreign travel, and higher education. Mercury forms a wide conjunction to this moon, so new opportunities with communication are also possible.

HAPPY NEW YEAR!

4

Gemini

The Big Picture in 2014

Welcome to 2014, Gemini! It's a 1 year for you, which puts you in the power seat and favors new beginnings in all areas of your life. Think of this year as a new chapter that's laying the foundation for subsequent years. Now that you've the tumult of 2012 and the realignment of 2013 behind you, you're ready for everything the universe brings your way.

So let's look at how specific areas of your life may be impacted and which dates will be of vital importance to you.

ROMANCE/CREATIVITY

One of the most romantic and creative times for you all year occurs between June 23 and July 18, when Venus transits your sign. During this period your muse is at your beck and call, and you feel so creative that everything you touch illustrates how your muse is working for you. You feel more self-confident, and others pick up on that vibe and are attracted to you, your ideas, persona, and creative projects. So if you have these ready, start submitting and exhibiting them, doing whatever you need to do in order to advertise your products.

If a relationship begins during this period, it's likely to be intellectually lively. You and your partner will have similar interests and a solid base for communication. The romantic interests you attract are a reflection of who you are within the deepest parts of your soul. If you're already involved in a relationship, this transit helps to define it. You and your partner may deepen your commitment to each other.

The other terrific period for romance and creativity occurs between September 29 and October 23, when Venus transits fellow air sign Libra, your solar fifth house. This transit stimulates you to do whatever it is you most enjoy. If it's travel, you go traveling. If your passion is politics, you dive into the political arena in some way. It's a perfect time for romance, the romantic kind of romance that entails long talks, candlelit dinners, concerts, exchanging ideas, browsing bookstore aisles together, doing the sorts of things so many Geminis enjoy.

Between July 16 and August 11, 2015, Jupiter transits compatible fire sign Leo and forms a strong, beneficial angle to your sun. This transit through your third house expands your communication venues and your romantic and creative possibilities.

Jupiter turns retrograde on December 8 and doesn't turn direct again until April 8, 2015. During this period the planet is essentially in a dormant state. But before the retro starts, you have a prolonged period where it's functioning at optimal levels, working to make things happen.

Other excellent dates:

April 15, when a lunar eclipse in Libra, your solar fifth house, stirs up emotions in a positive way about a romance, creative project, child, or something you're doing for enjoyment.

August 12 to September 5, when Venus joins Jupiter in Leo. This period infuses your love life with harmony and brings your muse up close and personal.

CAREER

Jupiter's transit through Leo will help every facet of your life, even your career. The caveat with career matters, though, is that if you're dong something you love, you benefit tremendously. If you're working in a field that doesn't excite you, that has become rather humdrum and routine, then Jupiter, Mars, Venus, and your ruler, Mercury, could help you to break away and find something that is more aligned with your passions.

Let's take a closer look at the beneficial career times:

February 12 to 28 and March 17 to April 7: Mercury is moving direct in Pisces, through your career area. This period favors communication with bosses and peers. Pitch your ideas, gather your support among coworkers. Think as far outside the box as your dare, then allow your lively intellect to play around with them, redefining them. During this period peers and bosses are impressed with your work, skills, and organizational talents. A promotion or raise could be forthcoming. Your conscious mind is particularly intuitive.

Between those two sets of dates Mercury is retrograde. Read more about that under the Mercury retrograde section.

April 5 to May 2: During this period, while Venus transits career area, your professional life hums along at a perfect pitch. This is the time to implement new projects, especially those that have captured your passions. During part of this transit Mercury will be in compatible fire sign Aries, urging you to be innovative and daring.

The new moon in Pisces, your career area, on March 1 should usher in new professional opportunities. Neptune forms a beneficial conjunction with this new moon, suggesting a spiritual element to any new opportunities that surface. Perhaps you'll be able to integrate your spiritual beliefs or your idealism more readily into your professional life.

Between July 25 and September 13 Mars transits Scorpio and forms a beneficial angle to your career area. This transit should provide you with excellent research and investigative skills and confers a kind of determined resoluteness to your professional endeavors.

FINANCES

Let's look at Venus transits first for beneficial dates for finances. Your solar second house, which rules money, is Cancer. The period to watch for, then, falls between July 18 and August 12. During this three-week period you could get a raise, bonus, or unexpected insurance or royalty check, or someone could repay money they owe you. You may feel an urge to spend on a luxury item—jewelry, for instance, or art.

Between January 1 and July 16 Jupiter transits Cancer, your financial area. You've been experiencing this transit since last year, but this period should be especially favorable. You could see a significant rise in your income. You could get a raise or royalty check, your partner could land a raise, money could come through an insurance settlement. Regardless of the source, this transit benefits your finances.

June 27 features a new moon in Cancer. New opportunities surface in finances. With Neptune forming a close, beneficial angle to the new moon, it looks as if creativity that is deeply inspired may be part of the equation.

MERCURY RETROGRADES

Every year Mercury—the planet of communication and travel—turns retrograde three times. During these periods it's wise not to sign contracts (unless you don't mind renegotiating when Mercury is moving direct), to check and recheck travel plans, and to communicate as succinctly as possible. Refrain from buying any large-ticket items or electronics during this time too. Often computers and appliances go on the fritz, cars act up, data is lost . . . you get the idea. Be sure to back up all files before the dates below:

February 6–28: Mercury retrograde in Pisces, your solar tenth house. This one impacts your career. Mercury slips back into Aquarius before it turns direct, so it also impacts your involvement with higher education, publishing, and foreign travel.

June 7–July 1: Mercury retrograde in Cancer, your solar second house. Ouch. This one impacts your finances. Check and double-check financial statements, don't buy large-ticket items during this period—unless you don't mind returning them later!—and try to pay cash for everything.

October 4–25: Mercury retrograde in Scorpio, your solar sixth house. This one impacts your daily work routine. Be sure to communicate succinctly and clearly with everyone in your work environment—employees, coworkers, bosses. If you receive a worrisome health report, get rechecked after Mercury turns direct again.

ECLIPSES

Solar eclipses tend to trigger external events that bring about change according to the sign and house in which they fall. Lunar eclipses trigger inner, emotional events according to the sign and house in which they fall. Any eclipse marks both beginnings and endings. The solar and lunar eclipse in a pair falls in opposite signs. If you're interested in detailed information on eclipses, take a look at Celeste Teal's excellent and definitive book, *Eclipses: Predicting World Events & Personal Transformation.*

If you were born under or around the time of an eclipse, it's to your advantage to take a look at your birth chart to find out exactly where the eclipses will impact you.

Most years feature four eclipses—two solar, two lunar—with the set separated by about two weeks. Let's take a closer look.

April 15: Lunar eclipse in Libra, your solar fifth house. This may bring up emotional issues related to a romantic relationship or creativity project. The emotions are positive, though!

April 29: Solar eclipse in Taurus, your solar twelfth house. New opportunities for working behind the scenes in some capacity. If you're so inclined, now is the time to start therapy, work with your dreams, or start a meditation program. This eclipse also favors a past-life regression or the spontaneous surfacing of a past-life memory. With Mercury forming a close conjunction to the eclipse degree and Jupiter forming a beneficial angle to it, the opportunities will be expansive.

October 8: Lunar eclipse in Aries, your solar eleventh house. Uranus is closely conjunct the moon, so you can expect sudden and unexpected emotional reactions to a friendship or some sort of group endeavor.

October 23: Solar eclipse in Scorpio, your solar sixth house. New work opportunities. This eclipse is at 0 degrees Scorpio, and so is Venus, so it's apt to be quite positive for you.

LUCKIEST DAYS OF THE YEAR

Every year there are one or two days when Jupiter and the sun meet up, and luck, serendipity, and expansion are the hallmarks. This year those days fall on July 25–26. Circle the dates. Do whatever you enjoy!

January—Gemini

Aren't you the lucky one, Gemini! Between January 11 and 31 Mercury, your ruler, transits fellow air sign Aquarius. Your communication skills are powerful, you think outside the box, you're versatile, and can sell anything to anyone just through your gift of gab. It's moving through your solar ninth house, which rules higher education, publishing, and overseas travel. You're in your element. Enjoy it.

A word about the first eleven days of the month, when Mercury moves through earth sign Capricorn, your solar eighth house. During this transit your conscious focus is on resources you share with others. Your partner's income may be the subject of discussion. Your career goals are clear, and you're able to strategize well.

Venus starts the year retrograde in Capricorn and turns direct on the 31. While retrograde, you may be revisiting issues with joint resources that you thought were solved. Don't buy any large-ticket items, and be sure to double-check bank statements. Your love life could be a bit bumpy too. But by January 31, everything is smoothed over and you're a happy camper again.

Mars begins the year in Libra, a fellow air sign, and certainly revs up your love life, your creativity, and everything you do for fun and enjoyment. You may be spending more time with friends and groups during this transit, that's the Libra component. You may go to museums, concerts, and /or buy art or musical instruments.

Jupiter begins the year retrograde in Cancer, your financial area. During the retro period, which lasts until March 6, money owed to you may be delayed in arriving. You may be rethinking your financial priorities and strategies during this period.

Saturn begins the year in Scorpio, moving in direct motion in your daily work area. This transit helps to stabilize your routine and may indicate that you will have more responsibility. Just do the work, Gemini, and watch it pay off down the line.

Uranus continues its journey through compatible fire sign Aries, your solar eleventh house. This transit started in 2011 and won't finish until early March 2019. You probably are accustomed to the energy by now, but keep in mind that Uranus shakes up the status quo and does so by triggering sudden, unexpected events.

Neptune begins the year in direct motion in Pisces, your career area. This transit began in 2012 and continues for fourteen years. During this period you seek to integrate your ideals and idealism more readily into your professional life. If you don't have a meditation practice, you may start one. Your metaphysical experiences are likely to be numerous, so it would behoove you to develop your intuition.

Then there's Pluto, continuing its journey through earth sign Capricorn, your solar eighth house. This very long transit (until 2024) is altering your shared resources from the bottom up.

IMPORTANT DATES

There are three lunations in January—two new moon and a full moon. Let's take a look:

January 1: The new moon in earth sign Capricorn should usher in new opportunities in terms of income—yours and your partner's, your joint resources. Pluto forms a close conjunction with this new moon, indicating that you're in the power seat. It is now easier for you to obtain a loan or mortgage and get breaks on insurance and taxes.

January 15: Full moon in Cancer, your solar second house. This moon highlights something in your finances or brings news about finances. Jupiter forms a wide conjunction, so any news you hear is likely to be positive and may expand your financial base in some way.

January 30: New moon in fellow air sign Aquarius,

your solar ninth house. New opportunities surface in the areas of foreign travel, higher education, publishing, and your spiritual beliefs.

February—Gemini

The first Mercury retrograde of the year begins on February 6 and ends on February 28. It begins in Pisces, moves back to Aquarius, and goes direct in that sign. While it's retrograde in your career area, things may not go as planned. Don't start new projects; back up computers and plan your travel on either side of the retro, if possible. If you hear career news during this period that seems negative, don't worry about it. Once Mercury turns direct again you will probably discover that the news was wrong!

Last month on January 31 Venus turned direct in Capricorn, and now you enjoy its benefits! There should be professional bonuses with this transit—perhaps a raise, a promotion, or maybe you're tagged for a team project that you really want to work on. There could also be unexpected benefits with insurance, an inheritance, a mortgage, or loan. With Venus traveling with Pluto for part of its transit, you're in the driver's seat when it comes to romance and creativity.

Mars continues its journey through Libra, your solar fifth house. You pour a lot of energy into romance, creative endeavors, and everything you do for fun and pleasure. Mars symbolizes your physical energy and your sexuality, so both will be ramped up. You're in the mood not just for love, Gemini, but for sex.

IMPORTANT DATES

February 14: It's somehow appropriate that the only lunation in February falls on Valentine's Day. The moon is in dramatic, warm-hearted Leo, your solar third house. Mars forms an exact and beneficial angle to this full moon, and Mercury opposes it. Be patient with the one you love during this full moon—there could be some communication snafus—and go out of your way to express what you feel, when you feel it.

February 28: Mercury, your ruler, turns direct in Aquarius.

March—Gemini

Compared to February, March is a Boeing 777 racing from one end of the world to the other in the blink of an eye. Lots going on, Gemini.

Circle March 1: Mars turns retrograde in Libra, in that area of your chart that governs romance, creativity, and what you do for fun and pleasure. This movement, which lasts until May 19, slows things down and may impact your romantic relationship. You and your partner may be at odds now and then during this period. Your creative endeavors may not move forward as quickly as you would like, and your sex life could be somewhat erratic. It's a good time to keep up your regular exercise routine.

Between March 5 and April 5 Venus transits fellow air sign Aquarius, your solar ninth house. This transit should be a good one for you, Gemini. You may have an opportunity to travel abroad, could sign up for a workshop or seminar in something that interests you, may decide to go to college or graduate school. Your world-view and spiritual beliefs are highlighted.

In romance things go your way. Other people find you appealing and seek out your company. Your creative endeavors go well. Your muse is ready and willing to help out, and ideas come to you rapidly, unexpectedly. Be sure to jot them down.

Mercury turned direct on February 28 in Aquarius and continues its transit through that sign until March 17, when it enters Pisces, your career area. During this transit, which lasts until April 7, Mercury facilitates your professional communications. Your conscious mind is extremely intuitive, so rely on your hunches!

Jupiter, the planet of expansion and luck, turns direct in Cancer on March 6, a welcome development, particularly for your finances! Now financial matters that have been slow to develop or which seem to have been delayed should move along briskly.

IMPORTANT DATES
March features three lunations. The first is on March 1, a new moon in water sign Pisces, your career area. New professional opportunities should come your way with this moon. With Neptune forming a close conjunction, it's possible that at least one of the opportunities could enable you to integrate your ideals and spiritual beliefs more readily into your career.

March 16: The full moon in Virgo falls in your domestic area. Expect something to be highlighted in that environment. Saturn forms a close, beneficial angle to this full moon, suggesting that any news you hear around the time of this lunation brings a more solid foundation to your home life.

March 30: New moon in compatible fire sign Aries, your solar eleventh house. Expect new friendships to surface and new opportunities to achieve your wishes and dreams.

On March 2 Saturn turns retrograde in Scorpio, your solar sixth house. This movement lasts until July 20 and slows down your daily work routine in some way.

April—Gemini

Mercury's transits impact you and Virgo most strongly because it rules both signs. This month it's in three signs. Let's take a closer look.

From April 1 to April 7, Mercury continues its transit through Pisces, your career area, so you've got the week to make your pitches, submit manuscripts, ideas, and to brainstorm with coworkers and bosses. From April 7 to 23 Mercury moves through Aries, a transit that should heat up your social life and allow you to network with people who share your interests.

Between April 23 and May 7 Mercury transits earth sign Taurus, your solar twelfth house. This transit favors work that requires patience and persistence. You may be in a hibernation period, perhaps to meet a looming deadline. Pay close attention to your dreams during this period; they may hold insights and information.

Venus transits water sign Pisces, your career area, between April 5 and May 2, a super period for you professionally. Bosses and coworkers are receptive to you and your ideas, and your popularity in the office increases. If you're self-employed, clients seek you out. In terms of romance, this transit could bring about an intuitive connection that blossoms into something beautiful.

IMPORTANT DATES
The lunar eclipse in Libra on April 15 should be quite positive for you. It occurs in your solar fifth house. You may hear good news related to romance, creativity, or your children and are thrilled. Mars forms a wide conjunction with the moon, suggesting a lot of activity that is perhaps connected to the news you hear.

April 29 features a solar eclipse in Taurus. This one could bring new opportunities in writing and other forms of communication. You may have an opportunity to work behind the scenes in some way on a project that interests you.

Pluto turns retrograde in Capricorn on April 14, your solar eighth house. This retro lasts until September 22. During this period you may be rethinking resources you share with others and could be reading about and studying metaphysics.

May—Gemini

Okay, it's another busy month in the zodiac! It all begins with your ruler, Mercury. Between May 1 and May 7 Mercury finishes up its transit of Taurus, which we covered under last month's roundup. From May 7 to May 29 Mercury transits your sign, Gemini, and you are in rare form! Your communication skills are powerful, and you catch up with friends and acquaintances—in person or through email, blogging, Facebook. Your mind is quicker than usual, and you tackle a variety of projects and endeavors.

On May 29 Mercury conjuncts Cancer, your financial area. This transit is long, thanks to a retrograde between June 7 and July 1, when Mercury turns direct again in Gemini. The planet then speeds toward its appointment with Leo on July 31. More on this transit in the June roundup.

Between May 2 and May 28 Venus transits compatible fire sign Aries, your solar eleventh house. This transit should heat up your social life and bring a kind of daringness to projects you take on, relationships in which you get involved, and the ways in which you attempt to achieve your dreams. If you're not involved, you may meet someone through friends or through a group to which you belong.

Between May 28 and June 23 Venus moves through earth sign Taurus, your solar twelfth house. We'll talk more about this transit in the June roundup.

Mars turns direct in Libra on May 19, a welcome change for sure. Creative endeavors, romantic relationships, your sexuality, whatever you do for enjoyment, now straighten out and move at a pace with which you're comfortable. You're more motivated, and your physical energy is stronger.

IMPORTANT DATES
May 14: The full moon in Scorpio occurs in your solar sixth house. This moon illuminates something or brings news about your daily work routine and the daily main-

tenance of your health. Saturn forms a close conjunction with this moon, suggesting that the news you hear may concern responsibility, and it's serious stuff.

May 28: This is a new moon to anticipate and plan for—it's in your sign, Gemini. This moon comes along just once a year and sets the tone for the next twelve months. So make a list of what you hope to experience and achieve, and then release it so the universe can deliver!

June—Gemini

Ok, here comes the second Mercury retrograde of 2014. It's in Cancer, your financial area, and it extends from June 7 to July 1, when it turns direct in Gemini. While retro in Cancer, be sure to check and recheck bank statements, mail payments early, and follow your online banking closely. Read over the section on Mercury retrograde under The Big Picture section for 2014 and follow the recommendations.

For the first twenty-three days of the month Venus is in Taurus, your solar twelfth house. This transit favors work done in solitude, dream recall, and greater access to your unconscious. It would be a good time for therapy, if you're so inclined, and is favorable for starting a meditation practice, if you don't have one already. You and a romantic interest may be spending more time alone together.

Between June 23 and July 18 Venus moves through your sign. This period is one of the most romantic and creative for you all year. Other people find you and your ideas appealing. If you're in sales, you can anticipate an extraordinarily productive period. Your muse shadows you like a faithful puppy during this transit, so make the most of it. If you're not involved right now, chances are you will meet someone special before the transit ends.

On June 9 Neptune in Pisces turns retrograde, and it will be that way until November 15. This retro occurs in your career area. During this period you may be mulling over how to integrate your idealism and spiritual beliefs more readily into your professional life. There can be some confusion about career matters.

IMPORTANT DATES

June 13: The full moon in Sagittarius sheds light on a romantic or business partnership. Uranus forms a wide, beneficial angle to this moon, suggesting a suddenness to any news that you hear—news that comes out of the blue. And it looks positive!

June 27: The new moon in Cancer occurs in your financial area. New financial opportunities should surface that enable you to incorporate your ideals and spirituality. Thank Neptune for that. It forms a close, beneficial angle to this new moon. Your hunches about money are right on target.

July—Gemini

The best news this month happens on July 1: Mercury turns direct in your sign and now rushes along toward its appointment with Cancer on July 12. While it's in your sign, your communication skills are heightened, you can sell anything to anyone, and you feel quite in synch with life generally.

When Mercury transits your financial area between July 12 and 31, money is uppermost in your conscious mind. You're eager to make and save more and to spend less. You may have to establish a realistic budget and forget paying with credit cards. It's possible that you make additional income through writing or public speaking.

Venus continues its journey through your sign until July 18, then enters Cancer, where it will be until August 12. During this period you may earn more money, receive an unexpected check or the repayment of a loan, and could meet a romantic interest whose beliefs are similar to yours. Your intuition should be quite powerful during this period, so listen to that inner voice and act on its guidance.

Mars turned direct on May 19 in Libra and continues in that sign until July 25, when it enters Scorpio, your solar sixth house. It will be there until September 13. During this period your daily schedule ramps up. You may be up against deadlines; your workload may increase. Your sexuality is heightened too, so a work flirtation could turn into something much more.

From July 20 to December 23 Saturn is moving direct in Scorpio, so it will be traveling with Mars for a while. Saturn helps to ground you and makes sure you meet your responsibilities and obligations.

IMPORTANT DATES
July 12: The full moon in Capricorn falls in your solar eighth house and brings news about or highlights other

people's money: your partner's income, a mortgage or loan, an insurance claim or inheritance. Since the moon is in Capricorn, your professional ambitions are highlighted in some way. With Pluto forming a wide conjunction to the moon, you're in the driver's seat.

July 26: The new moon in Leo should be very much to your liking. It brings new opportunities in communication, with siblings, in your neighborhood or community. In some way, you have a chance to strut your stuff, Gemini, to exhibit your talents.

July 31: Mercury enters Leo. We'll discuss this transit in next month's roundup.

August—Gemini

As Mercury transits Leo from July 31 to August 15, your gift of gab is powerful, and you're eager to show off your communication skills. You and your siblings may be spending more time together than you usually do. You also could be checking out new neighborhoods in anticipation of a move.

Between August 15 and September 2 Mercury moves through Virgo, a sign that it rules. This transit occurs in your domestic area, so you can anticipate lively discussions with your family, travel, and plenty of activity at home in general. If you have kids, then your home is the place where everyone congregates.

From August 12 to September 5 Venus moves through compatible fire sign Leo, your solar third house. This transit can certainly facilitate your search for a new neighborhood, and smooths rough edges in a relationship with a sibling or with neighbors. Romance is possible with someone you meet through friends or with someone who lives in your neighborhood. If you're involved already, then you and your partner may opt for a romantic getaway.

Venus travels with Jupiter during its transit of Leo, a major plus for you. Jupiter's influence helps to expand all your romantic and pleasurable feelings.

Throughout August Mars continues its transit through Scorpio, a sign it corules, your solar sixth house. The primary thing to watch out for during this transit is doing too much and burning out.

IMPORTANT DATES

August 10: The full moon in Aquarius, a fellow air sign, illuminates your solar ninth house and brings news about a trip abroad, higher education, publishing, or your spiritual beliefs/worldview. Since Uranus forms a close and beneficial angle to this full moon, news arrives out of the blue, suddenly and unexpectedly.

August 25: A new moon in Virgo, your solar fourth house, brings new opportunities in your domestic environment. You may move or put your home on the market, someone may move in or out, or you could refurbish your home.

September—Gemini

It's a busy month astrologically, Gemini, so be prepared for a wild, exciting ride! It all gets off to a running start on September 2, when your ruler, Mercury, enters fellow air sign Libra, your solar fifth house. This transit, which lasts until September 27, stimulates conversation between you and a romantic interest, you and your muse, you and your children. Travel for fun and pleasure is certainly possible during this transit. Your creative drive is powerful, so indulge your creative endeavors at this time, and don't hesitate to try new ideas.

On September 27 Mercury enters Scorpio, but we'll talk about that transit in next month's roundup since it leads to the last Mercury retrograde of the year.

Venus enters Virgo, your solar fourth house, on September 5 and remains there until September 29. During this period things at home unfold with greater smoothness. You and your partner are more compatible, you may team up for a creative endeavor, or you may decide to redecorate your house or refurbish it. Your attention to details during this transit is important.

On September 29 Venus enters fellow air sign Libra, your romance area. We'll discuss this important transit in next month's roundup!

Mars enters Sagittarius, your opposite sign, on September 13 and remains there until October 26. During this transit partnerships, both business and personal, take center stage. A lot of your energy goes into these relationships as you work with the bigger picture of whatever is transpiring.

IMPORTANT DATES

September 8: The full moon in Pisces illuminates or brings news about professional matters. Saturn forms a close, beneficial angle to this full moon, suggesting that the news deserves your serious consideration. Could a promotion be in the offing, Gemini?

September 24: A new moon in Libra ushers in new opportunities in romance, creativity, and whatever you do for fun and enjoyment. If you're female and have been trying to get pregnant, this new moon may bring a wonderful surprise!

September 22: Pluto turns direct in Capricorn, your solar eighth house.

October—Gemini

Okay, let's talk about the last Mercury retro of 2014. On September 27 Mercury entered Scorpio, your solar sixth house, and your conscious attention turned to your daily work routine and how you maintain your daily health. On October 4 Mercury turns retro in Scorpio, slides back into Libra on the 10, and turns direct in that sign on the 25. By now you know what to expect during these retro periods, but to refresh your memory, reread the appropriate section under The Big Picture for your sign. While Mercury is retro in Scorpio, research and investigation may encounter snafus, your daily work routine gets confusing, messages and emails may get lost. Clear communication is paramount. Once Mercury slides back into Libra, your love life may suffer from miscommunication.

On September 29 Venus entered Libra, your solar fifth house, where it will be until October 23. This period marks once of the most romantic and creative for you all year. If you're not involved when the transit begins, you probably will be by the time it ends. If you are involved, things between you and your partner go extremely well. You're on the same page. Your muse tags you faithfully during this period, whispering ideas, urging you to get moving with your various endeavors and stretch your creativity in new, exciting ways. Of course, the best meaning of this transit is that you're encouraged to do what you love and have ample opportunities to do that.

Between October 23 and November 16 Venus transits Scorpio. This period is apt to be intense emotionally, sexually, and spiritually. In your work you're after the bottom line in everything you tackle. The one risk here is that you take on too much!

Until the 26 Mars continues its transit of Sagittarius, your solar seventh house, creating a lot of activity in partnerships. Between October 26 and December 4 Mars transits Capricorn, your solar eighth house. This transit stirs up a lot of activity in the areas of mortgages, loans, taxes, insurance. However, the Capricorn part of the equation suggests activity connected to your professional life/career.

IMPORTANT DATES

October 8: A lunar eclipse in Aries, your solar eleventh house, may trigger emotions related to a friendship or a group to which you belong. If there's news, it comes out of the blue, totally unexpected. Mars forms a close and beneficial angle to the eclipse degree, so there's a lot of activity swirling around you at this time.

October 23: A solar eclipse in Scorpio ushers in new work opportunities. If you're unemployed—or underemployed—this eclipse could change all that in a heartbeat. Venus is exactly conjunct the eclipse degree, so there's plenty of good stuff on its way into your life. Some possibilities? A new romantic interest, creative endeavor, or even a raise.

October 25: Mercury turns direct in Libra!

November—Gemini

On November 8 Mercury enters Scorpio again and you experience some of the same energy that you did back in late September and early October. This transit lasts until November 27 and snaps your attention to your daily work and the way you maintain your health. You might, for instance, take up meditation during this transit; the Scorpio part of the equation would welcome that. Your conscious mind is exceptionally intuitive now, so take advantage of it.

On November 27 Mercury enters Sagittarius, a transit that lasts until December 16. We'll discuss that more in the December roundup.

Venus is active this month too. For the first sixteen days of the month it continues it journey through Scorpio, your daily work area. Between November 16 and December 10 it transits through Sagittarius, your opposite sign. This period should be pleasant for you and your partner. You may get away for a romantic weekend, take off from some exotic port of call, or perhaps become partners in some creative endeavor. If you've been in a relationship for a while, this transit could help to deepen your commitment to each other.

Throughout November Mars continues its movement toward Capricorn, your solar eighth house. This transit helps to ground your ideas. It's easier to set your sights on a goal and take steps to achieve it.

The full moon of November 6 falls in Taurus, your solar twelfth house. This moon illuminates something that is hidden—an issue from the past, power you've disowned over the years, or perhaps a belief that is holding you back. Your dreams hold insights and information that may help you in some way.

The new moon in Sagittarius on November 22 should be very much to your liking. It ushers in new partnerships—personal and professional. In an existing relationship you and your partner may decide to deepen your commitment to each other. Be ready to seize whatever comes your way, Gemini.

IMPORTANT DATE
November 15: Neptune turns direct in Pisces. There won't be as much confusion now related to professional matters and relationships.

December—Gemini

Mercury spends the first sixteen days in Sagittarius, continuing a transit that began last month. This transit brings your conscious awareness to partners—your spouse, business partner, lover. Lots of conversation and discussion with this one!

Between December 16 and January 5, 2015, Mercury transits earth sign Capricorn, your solar eighth house. You're able to strategize, plan, and communicate your ideas in a realistic manner. Even with the holidays approaching, your focus is excellent.

Venus enters Capricorn on December 10 and stays there until January 4, 2015, so for a time Venus and Mercury travel together. The combination suggests that romance may find you through a career-related event, in a seminar or workshop on an esoteric subject, or through some type of writing or public speaking in which you're involved.

On December 4 Mars changes signs and enters fellow air sign Aquarius, where it will be until January 2, 2015. This transit should be quite good for you. It stimulates your worldview, spirituality, foreign travel, and also publishing and higher education. You may be hanging out with really unusual people who are idiosyncratic, geniuses in their professions, or visionaries.

The full moon of December 6 falls in your sign! You'll enjoy this one, even if things are a bit hectic. Jupiter forms a wide, beneficial angle to it, and Uranus forms a closer, beneficial angle, so the stage is set for expansion of whatever you're feeling and a sudden, unexpected quality to your insights and whatever news you hear.

The new moon on December 21 falls at 0 degrees 6 minutes of Capricorn, with Mercury widely conjunct and Neptune forming a close, beneficial angle to it. What kinds of new opportunities can you expect? That depends on where you place your focus, but some possibilities: professional opportunities, new opportunities for your partner to increase his or her income, a break in taxes, insurance, mortgages, or loans. Since the new moon occurs in your eighth house, there could also be some experiences with things that go bump in the night.

IMPORTANT DATES
December 8: This is a date to mark. Jupiter turns direct in Leo, your solar third house. Now you benefit from this planet's expansion in a way that is tangible, visible. You move, find a better neighborhood for yourself and your family, or perhaps you welcome a sibling into the world. Tine to showcase your talents, Gemini. Get busy.

December 21: Uranus turns direct in Aries, the area of friendships, groups, your wishes and dreams.

December 23: Saturn enters Sagittarius for a transit that will last about two and a half years. Read about this one in The Big Picture section for your sign.

With all the planets now moving in direct motion, you're ready to greet 2015!

HAPPY NEW YEAR!

5

Cancer

The Big Picture in 2014

Welcome to 2014, Cancer! It's a 2 year for you, which emphasizes partnerships, cooperation, team work. It's a year when it's easier for two people joined together to achieve something than it is for two separate individuals to accomplish the same thing. Now that the tumult of 2012 and the realignment of 2013 are behind you, you're ready to embark on yet another journey.

So let's look at how specific areas of your life may be impacted and which dates will be of vital importance to you.

ROMANCE/CREATIVITY

One of the most romantic and creative times for you all year occurs between July 18 and August 12, when Venus transits your sign. During this period your muse is at your beck and call, and you feel so creative that everything you touch illustrates how your muse is working for you. You feel more self-confident. Others pick up on that vibe and are attracted to you, your ideas, persona, and creative projects. So if you have these ready, start submitting and exhibiting them, doing whatever you need to do in order to advertise your products.

If a relationship begins during this period, it's likely to be deeply intuitive. You and your partner will have similar interests and a solid base for communication. The romantic interests you attract are a reflection of who you are within the most profound depths of your soul. If you're already involved in a relationship, this transit helps to define it. You and your partner may deepen your commitment to each other.

The other terrific period for romance and creativity occurs between October 23 and November 16, when Venus transits fellow water sign Scorpio, your solar fifth house. This transit stimulates you to do whatever it is you most enjoy. Many Scorpios enjoy exploring metaphysics, so you may undertake a spiritual quest of some kind. Or you may be doing extensive research into something. It's a perfect time for romance, the romantic kind of romance that entails long talks, candlelit dinners, concerts, exchanging ideas, browsing bookstore aisles together, doing the sorts of things so many Cancers enjoy.

Between January 1 and July 16 Jupiter moves through your sign, a continuation of a transit that began last year. Jupiter expands whatever it touches, so this entire transit should be magnificent for you in all areas. Between July 16 and August 11, 2015, Jupiter moves through Leo, your financial area, so this period should improve your monetary situation! When you feel secure financially, other areas of your life tend to flow more easily.

Other excellent dates:

April 5 to May 2, when Venus in fellow water sign Pisces forms a beautiful angle to your sun and Jupiter. Heightened intuition in all areas of your life. Romance may find you while you're traveling or involved in creative work.

October 23, a new moon in Scorpio, your solar fifth house. This one should bring new romantic possibilities and a chance to do something new creatively. You may also uncover new enjoyments and pleasures.

CAREER

Jupiter's transit through Leo will help every facet of your life, even your career. The caveat with career matters, though, is that if you're doing something you love, you benefit tremendously. If you're working in a field that doesn't excite you, that has become rather humdrum and routine, then Jupiter, Mars, Venus, Mercury, and your ruler, the moon, could help you to break away and find something that is more aligned with your passions.

Let's take a closer look at the beneficial career times:

April 7 to 23: Mercury is moving direct in Aries, your career area. This period favors communication with bosses and peers. This is the time to pitch your ideas and move professional matters forward. Start a blog, put up a Web site, advertise your products/services or those of your company. Your conscious mind is quite free spirited and independent.

May 2 to 28: During this period, while Venus transits career area, your professional life is exciting, perhaps even somewhat feverish. This time frame is perfect for pushing your own ideas and beliefs forward in your work.

Coworkers and bosses are impressed with your ideas and the way you implement them.

March 30: The new moon in Aries, your career area, should usher in new professional opportunities. Uranus forms a close conjunction with this new moon, suggesting an unexpected quality to any opportunities that surface.

Between September 13 and October 26 Mars in Sagittarius forms a beneficial angle to your career area. This transit may bring foreign travel connected to professional matters. Your desire for independence is strong. Maybe this is the time to launch your own business?

FINANCES

Let's look at Venus transits first for beneficial dates for finances. Your solar second house, which rules money, is Leo, so the entire thirteen months that Jupiter is in Leo should be terrific for your monetary situation. Those dates: July 16, 2014, to August 11, 2015. You could see a significant rise in your income. You could get a raise or royalty check, your partner could land a raise, money could come through an insurance settlement. Regardless of the source, this transit benefits your finances.

Other good dates? August 12 to September 5, when Venus is in Leo.

July 26 features a new moon in Leo, which could attract new financial opportunities and sources of income.

MERCURY RETROGRADES

Every year Mercury—the planet of communication and travel—turns retrograde three times. During these periods it's wise not to sign contracts (unless you don't mind renegotiating when Mercury is moving direct), to check and recheck travel plans, and to communicate as succinctly as possible. Refrain from buying any large-ticket items or electronics during this time too. Often computers and appliances go on the fritz, cars act up, data is lost ... you get the idea. Be sure to back up all files before the dates below:

February 6–28: Mercury retrograde in Pisces, your solar ninth house. This one impacts foreign travel. Mercury slips back into Aquarius before it turns direct, so it impacts your joint resources, too. Be sure to check and re-check bank statements.

June 7–July 1: Mercury is retrograde in your sign. This retrograde may make you feel as if your personal life is in chaos. It really isn't, but the retrograde makes it impossible to ignore issues you should tackle and resolve.

October 4–25: Mercury retrograde in Scorpio, your solar fifth house. This one impacts your love life and creative work. Be sure to communicate succinctly and clearly with everyone in your work environment—employees, coworkers, bosses. If you receive a worrisome health report, get rechecked after Mercury turns direct again.

ECLIPSES

Solar eclipses tend to trigger external events that bring about change according to the sign and house in which they fall. Lunar eclipses trigger inner, emotional events according to the sign and house in which they fall. Any eclipse marks both beginnings and endings. The solar and lunar eclipse in a pair falls in opposite signs. If you're interested in detailed information on eclipses, take a look at Celeste Teal's excellent and definitive book, *Eclipses: Predicting World Events & Personal Transformation.*

If you were born under or around the time of an eclipse, it's to your advantage to take a look at your birth chart to find out exactly where the eclipses will impact you.

Most years feature four eclipses—two solar, two lunar—with the set separated by about two weeks. Let's take a closer look.

April 15: Lunar eclipse in Libra, your solar fourth house. Emotional issues surface related to your domestic situation. The emotions are positive, though!

April 29: Solar eclipse in Taurus, your solar eleventh house. New opportunities for working with groups, networking, and with friends. It's a good time to join a gym or sign up for yoga classes. With Mercury forming a close conjunction to the eclipse degree, Jupiter forming a beneficial angle to it, and both Mercury and Jupiter forming great angles to your sun sign, the opportunities will be expansive.

October 8: Lunar eclipse in Aries, your solar tenth house. Uranus is closely conjunct the moon, so you can expect sudden and unexpected emotional issues related to your career and professional life.

October 23: Solar eclipse in Scorpio, your solar fifth house. New romantic possibilities and opportunities to show off your creative abilities.

LUCKIEST DAYS OF THE YEAR

Every year there are one or two days when Jupiter and the sun meet up, and luck, serendipity, and expansion are

the hallmarks. This year those days fall on July 25–26. Circle the dates. Do whatever you enjoy!

January—Cancer

The year begins with Mercury—the planet of communication and travel—in Capricorn, your opposite sign, where it remains until January 11. This transit should facilitate communication with business and romantic partners. It's a carryover from the last part of 2013, so look back to the end of that year for clues about what to expect.

Between January 11 and 31 Mercury moves through air sign Aquarius, your solar eighth house. During this transit you're focused on things like mortgages, loans, insurance, and taxes. Pretty boring, right? Well, don't get discouraged. The eighth house is also associated with the esoteric and metaphysical—ghosts, life after death, communication with the dead. So you may be discussing these areas or having experiences with them.

Mercury enters fellow water sign Pisces on January 31, a transit we'll discuss under the February roundup.

Venus begins 2014 retrograde in Capricorn, your opposite sign. This retro can create some challenges in your personal and business partnerships, but your intuition is powerful enough to circumvent problems. One possible repercussion of a Venus retrograde is that if you buy a large-ticket luxury item, you may get a good deal, but it probably won't be exactly what you're looking for. Best to avoid such purchases until the retro is over.

Mars starts the year retrograde in Libra, your solar fourth house, and doesn't turn direct until March 1. During this retro period home-renovation projects may be delayed. It's not a good time to put your home on the market or to look for a new place to live. If you don't have a regular exercise routine yet, it's a good time to start one. Just make sure it's something you can commit to. The best way to navigate this retro is to try to go with the flow.

Jupiter begins the year retrograde in your sign and doesn't turn direct until March 6. Jupiter has been in your sign since last year, so you should be well acquainted with the kind of expansion that is happening in your life. During the retro period the expansion slows down and gives you an opportunity to explore how your life is changing and fine-tune things.

Saturn starts off the year in direct motion in fellow water sign Scorpio, your solar fifth house. During this transit Saturn forms a beneficial angle to your sun and strengthens the structures in your life, bolsters your intuition, and may bring a romantic relationship into a deeper commitment.

Uranus in Aries, Neptune in Pisces, and Pluto in Capricorn all begin the year in direct motion. These three planets have been in these signs for several years now, so you should be accustomed to their respective energies.

IMPORTANT DATES

There are three lunations in January, each with its own distinctive energy. Let's take a closer look.

January 1: The new moon in Capricorn, your opposite sign, should usher in new opportunities in personal and business partnerships. Perhaps you find the perfect agent or manager, accountant, or business partner. Pluto and

Mercury form close conjunctions to this new moon, suggesting that you're a powerful communicator and know exactly what you're looking for.

January 15: The full moon in your sign should be quite stupendous for you! Jupiter is also in your sign at this time, expanding what you feel and experience. Any news you hear around the time of this full moon—give it a couple of days on either side of this date—should be positive. Saturn forms a close, beneficial angle to the full moon, suggesting that any news you hear provides a solid foundation and structure to a romance or creative endeavor.

January 30: The new moon in Aquarius brings new opportunities to think outside the box and use what you learn in a creative way. It applies to mundane areas like joint finances but also to esoteric areas like ghosts and other things that go bump in the night.

January 31: Mercury enters Pisces. More on that in February's roundup. Venus turns direct in Capricorn.

February—Cancer

While Mercury transits Pisces, your solar ninth house, in direct motion, you enjoy a surge in intuition, your imagination is working overtime, and your communication skills are highlighted in some way. You might consider fiction writing or scriptwriting, Cancer. Your muse is ever present.

Between February 6 and 28 Mercury is moving retrograde. Before the retro starts, be sure to back up your computer files, make your travel plans for dates after

Mercury turns direct, and be sure to communicate clearly and succinctly with everyone in your environment. Reread the section about Mercury retrograde in The Big Picture section for other suggestions on how to successfully navigate this retrograde.

On January 31 Venus turned direct in Capricorn, your solar seventh house, so in February you get to enjoy Venus in all her glory. This transit could bring you and your partner closer together and you may decide to deepen your commitment to each other. If you're already married, perhaps you and your partner should get away together for a long romantic weekend.

Mars is still moving in direct motion in Libra until March 1, when it turns retrograde. This means that things at home should be quite active and social throughout February. Just don't bend over backward, Cancer, to please everyone around you. Keep some time open just for yourself.

IMPORTANT DATE
February 14: Just in time for Valentine's Day! This full moon in fire sign Leo occurs in your financial area. Expect news about money, or your finances are highlighted in some way. Mars forms a perfect, beneficial angle to this full moon, so there's plenty of action and activity.

March—Cancer

March is one of those months that may drive you half-crazy simply because you feel you have way too much to do and not enough time.

Mercury went direct on February 28 in Aquarius and now moves toward its appointment with Pisces on March 17, where it will be until April 7. While Mercury transits fellow water sign Pisces, you may be talking and thinking about your worldview, spiritual beliefs, and an overseas trip you're planning. Or you could take a class or seminar in a topic that interests you.

Between March 5 and April 5 Venus transits Aquarius, your solar eighth house. This transit could bring a special romantic interest into your life, someone who thinks differently from other people or whose work is cutting edge. This period also favors obtaining a mortgage or loan or getting a break in taxes or insurance.

Mars turns retrograde in Libra on March 1 and turns direct again on May 19. During this period life generally slows down, projects are delayed, and your physical energy may be sluggish. With Mars retro in Libra, your social life may slow down too. It's a good time to do things you've procrastinated about.

There are three lunations in March. Let's take a look. On March 1 a new moon in fellow water sign Pisces should usher in new opportunities in foreign travel, publishing, creative endeavors, and with higher education. Neptune forms a close conjunction to the new moon, indicating your ideals are somehow part of these opportunities that surface.

March 16 features a full moon in compatible earth sign Virgo. This moon illuminates the details in your life—in communication with siblings, other relatives, and neighbors. If you've been considering a move, then you may find the perfect neighborhood for you and your family.

The new moon on March 30 falls in Aries, your career area. Expect new professional opportunities to surface, and they do so suddenly and unexpectedly, thanks to a close conjunct from Uranus. Pluto forms a challenging angle to this new moon, however, so beware of power plays!

IMPORTANT DATES
March 2: Saturn turns retrograde in Scorpio, your solar fifth house, until July 20. During this period romantic relationships and creative endeavors may feel sluggish. You may be reviewing your priorities in romance and creativity.

March 5: Jupiter turns direct in your sign, a cause for celebration! So between now and July 16, when Jupiter enters Leo, you enjoy the expansion and good fortune this planet often brings.

April—Cancer

This month isn't quite as frantic astrologically as March was. For the first week Mercury continues its transit of Pisces, bolstering your imagination and intuition. Then between April 7 and 23 Mercury transits Aries, your career area. During this period talk and write about your own projects and endeavors. If you need approval to move forward with an endeavor, you should be able to get it. Your professional skills are sharp.

Between April 23 and May 7 Mercury transits Taurus, an earth sign compatible with your sun sign. This transit should increase activity in your social life. You hang out more often with friends, may join a group of like-minded individuals, or may be involved in some sort of joint creative endeavor. You tend to be more stubborn during this transit.

Between April 5 and May 2 Venus moves through fellow water sign Pisces and increases the likelihood of overseas travel. You may meet a romantic interest while traveling, could be involved in a creative endeavor while traveling, or may decide to go to college or grad school. If you're already involved, this transit should bring you and your partner more in synch with each other.

Throughout April Mars continues its retrograde movement through Libra, your solar fourth house. Don't do any home renovations right now. Wait until after Mars turns direct on May 19.

IMPORTANT DATES

April 14: Pluto turns retrograde in Capricorn, your solar seventh house, and turns direct again on September 22.

April 15: Lunar eclipse in Libra, your solar fourth house. Emotions swirl in your domestic environment. The emotions seem to be positive, though, but there's a lot of frenetic activity. Take time for yourself, Cancer.

April 29: Solar eclipse in Taurus, your solar eleventh house. New opportunities surface in friendships and with groups, and this enables you to achieve your dreams. One such opportunity may involve communication and writing.

May—Cancer

For the first week in May Mercury continues its transit of Taurus. Then between May 7 and 29 it moves through Gemini, your solar twelfth house. During this period you have easy access to your own unconscious, and your dreams and meditations contain information and insights that are helpful.

Between May 29 and July 1 Mercury transits your sign, turns retrograde, and turns direct again in Gemini. More on that transit in next month's roundup.

Between May 2 and 28 Venus transits Aries, your career area. Fantastic! You could get a raise or promotion and suddenly find yourself at the top of your game professionally. Others recognize your talents and skills. Another possibility is that a flirtation with someone you work with could escalate into a romantic relationship. Think twice before you leap in.

Mars turns direct on May 19 in Libra and now moves toward its appointment with Scorpio on September 13. Until then it's a great time to complete home renovations and to generally spiff up your house—clean out closets, your attic, your garage. You may decide to host a party or some other activity at your place.

IMPORTANT DATES
May 14 features a full moon in Scorpio, your solar fourth house. Thanks to a beneficial angle from Jupiter in Cancer, this full moon illuminates a domestic issue or brings news about a project that is important to you personally. Saturn forms a close conjunction to this moon, so any

news that you hear around this time deserves your serious consideration.

May 28 features a new moon in Gemini, your solar twelfth house. New opportunities surface in communication, writing, perhaps even in travel. Uranus forms a wide, beneficial angle to this new moon, suggesting the opportunities come out of the blue. Be prepared to seize them!

June—Cancer

The second Mercury retrograde of 2014 starts on June 7 and ends on July 1. The retro begins in your sign, Cancer, then Mercury slips back into Gemini and goes direct there. During the retrograde period follow the three Rs: revise, rethink, review. Try not to start any new projects, tie up loose ends, be sure to back up all your computer files before the retro starts. In fact you may want to try cloud backups through Drop box, icloud (if you have a Mac), or other similar services.

For the first twenty-three days of the month Venus continues its transit of compatible earth sign Taurus, your solar eleventh house. This transit could signal the beginning of a romance with a friend or with someone you meet through a group to which you belong. It also stimulates your social life. If you're single, use this favorable time to get out and about and network. If you're in a relationship, you and your partner may be spending time together with friends.

On June 23 Venus enters Gemini, your solar twelfth house, where it will be until July 18. During this period you have greater access to information and insights through dreams, meditation, and other altered states of consciousness. You may be doing a lot of writing, perhaps to meet a deadline, and do it mostly in solitude. A romance could be a secret now. But after Venus enters your sign on July 18, it's no longer a secret.

Throughout June Mars continues its transit of Libra, your solar fourth house. It keeps things lively and interesting in your domestic environment.

On June 9 Neptune turns retrograde in Pisces, your solar ninth house, and remains like that until November 15. During this period you may be deeply into spiritual studies or are on some sort of spiritual quest that takes you abroad.

IMPORTANT DATES

The full moon on June 13 falls in fire sign Sagittarius, your solar sixth house. This moon sheds light on a work issue or relationship. The insights you gain or the information or news you hear occur suddenly. Uranus forms a wide and beneficial angle to this full moon, and whenever Uranus is involved, there's an unpredictability to everything. In this instance, the news should be positive.

June 27 features a new moon in your sign. This one is something to anticipate. It happens just once a year and sets the tone for the next twelve months. So envision what you would like to accomplish in the next twelve months. Back these visions with powerful emotion, then release your desires and let the universe do the rest. You've still got expansive, lucky Jupiter in your sign too, Cancer, an additional plus.

July—Cancer

The best news this month is that Mercury turns direct on July 1 in Gemini. Look back to the patterns that were occurring in your life between May 7 and 29, when Mercury was also in Cancer, for a hint about what this transit, which lasts until July 12, may bring. Between July 12 and 31, Mercury transits your sign again in direct motion, and what a treat that should be. Your conscious mind is more intuitive and imaginative, and you may feel more creative and optimistic generally.

Venus continues its transit of Gemini, your solar twelfth house, until July 18, then it enters your sign, where it stays until August 12. This period marks one of the most romantic and creative for you all year. Others are receptive to you and your ideas and find you enormously appealing. In romance you're in top form, Cancer, with your pick of partners. If you're already involved, your partner is attentive and caring.

On July 25 Mars finally leaves Libra and enters fellow water sign Scorpio, the romance and creativity section of your chart. This transit lasts until September 13 and should galvanize your love life and all your creative endeavors. Your sexuality is heightened and so is your need for research and investigation into something that interests you. Mars corules Scorpio, and while it's in that sign it forms a beneficial angle to your sun, making it more likely that your physical energy is excellent.

July 12 features a full moon in your sign. Jupiter forms a wide conjunction to it, and Scorpio forms a beneficial angle. You should receive news that delights you or gain insights that somehow expand your understanding of a facet of your personal life.

The new moon in Leo on July 26 falls in your financial area. With Jupiter now in Leo and forming a tight conjunction to this new moon, you may receive a raise, unexpected bonus, land a new job that pays you more, or get a tax or insurance break. Regardless of the specifics, your income will now benefit.

IMPORTANT DATES
July 16: Jupiter leaves your sign and enters Leo, your financial area, where it will be until August 11, 2015. During this period your finances should improve considerably. Even if your expenses increase, you'll be making enough money to meet this. Your priorities may shift during this transit. Your spiritual beliefs could deepen.

July 20: Saturn turns direct in Scorpio. Celebrate this one. It's always best to have Saturn in direct motion, bolstering the structures in your life.

July 21: Uranus turns retrograde in Aries, your career area. You may be taking a deeper look at your profession and career direction.

July 31: Mercury enters Leo. More on that in the August roundup.

August—Cancer

Okay, Mercury first. It entered Leo on July 31, joining Jupiter in your financial area. With these two planets traveling together, your focus is on finances. You talk about money, think about money, and are trying to figure out how to earn more of it and spend less. The trick here is to not obsess, to go with the flow and take your cue from synchronicities—meaningful coincidences.

On August 15 Mercury enters Virgo, a sign that it rules, your solar third house. This transit lasts until September 2 and should galvanize your communication skills. You may be doing more public speaking, more writing, and could be updating your blog or Web site in a big way. You could be traveling more than usual too and spending more time with siblings and neighbors.

Between August 12 and September 5 Venus transits your financial area, another terrific bonus for your income. It travels for a while with Jupiter, just as Mercury did, and should help to increase your income. You may be tempted to spend on luxury items, but do so only if you pay cash.

Throughout August, Mars continues its movement through Scorpio, so be sure to reread July's overview for what that means. Take advantage of your physical energy by tackling difficult stuff that you may have placed on a back burner.

IMPORTANT DATES
August 10: The full moon in Aquarius falls in your solar eighth house. Some facet of your joint resources—partner's income, taxes, insurance, mortgage—is highlighted. Uranus forms a close, beneficial angle to this full moon, suggesting that news you hear is sudden and unexpected.

August 25: The new moon in compatible earth sign Virgo may usher in new opportunities in communication and travel. If you've been thinking about a move, this new moon could enable you to find the perfect neighborhood.

September—Cancer

It's another busy month in the zodiac, so you're apt to feel a bit nutty at times. Just remember: this too shall pass.

Between September 2 and 27 Mercury transits Libra, your daily work area, so your conscious focus is on your daily work routine. You may be spending more time hanging out with coworkers and employees during this period. Or you're networking more frequently online through Facebook, twitter, even with text messages.

On the 27 Mercury enters Scorpio. On October 4 it turns retrograde in that sign, travels back into Libra, and finally turns direct again in that sign on October 25. Whew, long retro. We'll talk more about it during next month's roundup. However, while Mercury is moving direct in fellow water sign Scorpio, you think a lot about romance and creative endeavors, and may be discussing these areas and brainstorming with a partner or friends.

Venus enters Virgo, your solar third house, on September 5, and during its transit, which ends on the 29, you may be pickier than usual when it comes to romance and creative endeavors. That said, romance may be as close as your backyard, and something may be kindled with a neighbor or someone you meet through siblings. Your relationships with siblings and other relatives as well as neighbors should be smooth and hassle free.

Mars enters fire sign Sagittarius on September 13 for a transit that lasts until October 26. During this period you may be traveling for work and seem to grasp the larger picture of your daily routine. There could be some contact with publishers or people in higher education. Or perhaps you decide to go on to college or graduate school, or your novel or book sells!

IMPORTANT DATES

September 8: The full moon in fellow water sign Pisces should be sublime for you, with news about a trip abroad or insights gained into your worldview and spiritual beliefs. The moon receives a friendly nod from Pluto, so you're in the power seat. Not a bad place to be, right?

September 22: Pluto turns direct in Capricorn, your solar seventh house. Partnerships should unfold more smoothly now.

September 24: A new moon in Libra ushers in new opportunities at home and in your domestic situation. A move is possible. Or you refurbish your home in some way. Mars forms a wide, beneficial angle to this new moon, indicating a lot of activity and forward thrust.

October—Cancer

Here comes another frantic month, Cancer, so buckle up and let's take a look at what could be a wild ride.

Bad news first: Mercury turns retrograde again, in Scorpio. The good news is that it's the last Mercury retro of 2014. By now you know the drill: rewrite, revise, review, rethink, redo, revisit. Make travel plans on either side of the retro, and try not to travel during the retrograde. If you must, however, go with the flow, and don't be surprised if your plans suddenly change. On October 10 Mercury slides back into Libra, where it turns direct again on the 25.

For the first twenty-three days of October Venus is in Libra, a sign that it rules, so the planet is quite happy there. This transit brings a greater harmony to your domestic life and could spur a more active social life. You may want to beautify your home in some way during this transit. It doesn't have to be expensive or elaborate—bright colors on the walls would work! So would indoor plants and flowers.

Between October 23 and November 16 Venus moves through Scorpio, your romance area. This period is apt to be emotionally intense but also enormously creative. In fact it's one of two periods this year that should be deliciously romantic, with your muse shadowing you constantly.

October 26 marks the day that Mars enters Sagittarius, your solar sixth house. This transit lasts until December 4 and really triggers activity in your daily work routine. You may travel more frequently for work, have your eye on the bigger picture of what you're involved in, and may even pursue some sort of spiritual quest that you manage to thread into your daily work life.

IMPORTANT DATES

October 8: A lunar eclipse in Aries, your career area, enjoys a beneficial angle from expansive Jupiter, so the news for you will be good, although sudden and unexpected because Uranus is closely conjunct to the moon. Mars also forms a tight, beneficial angle, suggesting heightened activity and movement.

October 23: A solar eclipse in Scorpio. Wow. You should love this one, Cancer. Venus is exactly conjunct the moon, so the promise here is for new opportunities in love and romance, creativity, and with children. If you and your partner have been hoping to start a family, the eclipse could bring it about!

November—Cancer

As you enter the next to last month of the year, it's to your advantage to take a little time to reflect on your life this year. Have you accomplished what you hoped? Has the quality of your life improved? What are your goals for 2015?

The month begins with Mercury in Libra until November 8, a continuation of its having turned direct on October 25. Between November 8 and 27 the planet of communication transits fellow water sign Scorpio again, as it did in late September before it turned retro. So you're back to discussing and thinking about romance, creativity, and your kids. You may decide to dust off an old manuscript that you stashed away some time ago and give it another shot!

On the 27 Mercury enters Sagittarius, where it will be until December 16. During this transit your conscious focus is on your daily work routine and the ways you maintain your health. You may decide to try a new diet or nutritional program or even a new exercise routine. Herbs, vitamins, acupuncture, yoga: you're sampling all of it.

From November 16 to December 10 Venus transits

Sagittarius, joining Mercury in your solar sixth house. Others are attracted to your ideas and enjoy your company, particularly the people with whom you work. A romance could start up with an employee or coworker. If you're already involved, you and your partner may get involved in a joint project of some sort. Or you could decide to start your own business.

Throughout November Mars continues its transit through Capricorn, your solar seventh house. This transit could stimulate your partnership area. You pour a lot of energy into your career, search for or find the ideal business partner, or you and your present romantic partner may become business partners. Just don't take on more than you can realistically handle, Cancer. With Mars in Capricorn, that tendency can be prevalent.

IMPORTANT DATES

November 6: The full moon in compatible earth sign Taurus falls in your eleventh house. With both Pluto and Mars forming beneficial angles to this full moon, but opposed to your sun sign, you could find yourself in something of a quandary as a result of news you hear. The news could involve a friend or a group to which you belong.

November 22: The new moon in Sagittarius should usher in new work opportunities. If you've been out of work or underemployed, then this new moon could bring the opportunity for a new job. Keep one eye on the future, Cancer, and your feet firmly grounded in the now.

December—Cancer

Take some time this month to look ahead to 2015. What are your goals for the coming year? What would you like to experience and achieve? If you're a list maker, create a list of your new year's resolutions! Mercury in Sagittarius until December 16 gives you the bird's-eye view for doing exactly that.

Between December 16 and January 5, 2015, Mercury moves through Capricorn, your partnership area. During this period you're thinking about and discussing partnership options in business and your personal life as well. You and your romantic partner may be hammering together ideas about launching your own business.

From December 10 to January 4, 2015, Venus also transits Capricorn, joining Mercury in your partnership area. With these two planets traveling together, your love life should be humming along at a pace that suits you, and you and your partner may decide to deepen your commitment to each other.

On December 4 Mars enters Aquarius, your solar eighth house, where it will be until January 12, 2015. This transit suggests you may be applying for a loan or mortgage or dealing with insurance and tax issues. A lot of your energy goes into resources you share with others—a partner, a child, perhaps a sibling.

The full moon on December 6 falls in Gemini and receives a beneficial angle from Uranus and a wide, beneficial angle from Jupiter. The result? The news you hear should please you enormously. Whatever it is, it enables you to expand your life in a significant way.

On December 21 the new moon in Capricorn is perfect for ushering in the new year and new opportunities in partnerships. Look to your career for starting something new and exciting, perhaps involving communication and or/travel. Five planets are in Capricorn on this date, so there's plenty of grounding to these new opportunities.

IMPORTANT DATES

The nice thing about December—other than the holidays, of course!—is that by the end of the year every planet except Jupiter is moving in direct motion.

December 8: Jupiter turns retrograde in Leo, and it lasts until April 8, 2015. This essentially means that Jupiter goes into a kind of dormant state, and your luck factor won't be moving along at the same swift click financially.

December 21: Uranus turns direct in Aries.

December 23: Saturn leaves Scorpio and enters Sagittarius, your solar sixth house, where it will be for the next two and a half years.

HAPPY NEW YEAR!

6

Leo

The Big Picture in 2014

Welcome to 2014, Leo! It's a 3 year for you, which emphasizes communication and innovation. Your creative talents are highlighted this year, your social energy is warm and generous, your intuition is powerful, and your attitude determines just about everything.

Now that you've the tumult of 2012 and the realignment of 2013 behind you, you're ready to embark on yet another journey.

So let's look at how specific areas of your life may be impacted and which dates will be of vital importance to you.

ROMANCE/CREATIVITY
One of the most romantic and creative times for you all year occurs between August 12 and September 5, when Venus transits your sign. During this period your muse shadows you like a long-lost friend. Your creative drive is so heightened that unusual solutions to challenges and issues are at your fingertips.

You feel more self-confident. Others pick up on that vibe and are attracted to you, your ideas, persona, and creative projects. So if you have these ready, start submitting and exhibiting them, doing whatever you need to do in order to advertise them.

If a relationship begins during this period, it's likely to be dramatic and theatrical. You and your partner will have similar interests and a solid base for communication. The romantic interests you attract are a reflection of who you are within the most profound depths of your soul. If you're already involved in a relationship, this transit helps to define it. You and your partner may deepen your commitment to each other.

The other terrific period for romance and creativity occurs between November 16 and December 10, when Venus transits fellow fire sign Sagittarius, your solar fifth house. This transit stimulates you to do whatever it is you most enjoy. Many Leos enjoy live theater, acting, improvisation, music, and sports and have skills in these areas. It's a perfect time to fall in love with love.

Between July 16, 2014, and August 11, 2015, Jupiter moves through your sign, and it's sure to be a fabulous thirteen months for you. Jupiter expands whatever it touches, so this entire transit expands your life in some way—a new job, promotion, love interest, raise . . . in short, it's a powerful time for you, Leo. Make the most of it.

Other excellent dates:

May 2 to 28, when Venus in fellow fire sign Aries forms a beautiful angle to your sun. You take risks now in romance and with creative projects, and they pay off.

November 22, a new moon in Sagittarius, your solar

fifth house. This one should bring new romantic possibilities and a chance to do something new creatively. You may also uncover new enjoyments and pleasures or have a chance to travel internationally.

CAREER

Jupiter's transits through both Cancer and Leo will help every facet of your life, even your career. The caveat with career matters, though, is that if you're doing something you love, you benefit tremendously. If you're working in a field that doesn't excite you, that has become rather humdrum and routine, then Jupiter, Mars, Venus, Mercury, and your ruler, the moon, could help you to break away and find something that is more aligned with your passions.

Between January 1 and July 16 Jupiter transits water sign Cancer and forms a beneficial angle to your career area. This transit, a continuation from last year, may bring some unexpected and expansive professional opportunities.

Let's take a closer look at the beneficial career times:

April 23 to May 7: Mercury is moving direct in Taurus, your career area. This period favors communication with bosses and peers. It favors pitching your ideas and moving all professional matters forward. Start a blog, put up a Web site, advertise your products/services or those of your company. Your conscious mind is quite free spirited and independent.

May 28 to June 23: During this period while Venus transits Taurus, your career area, you're working steadily and resolutely on a project. Coworkers and bosses are impressed with your ideas and the way you implement them. Others find you so appealing that you're the first to be tapped for team projects.

April 29: The new moon in Taurus, your career area, is also a solar eclipse, so you can anticipate more than one beautiful professional opportunity to surface. Mercury forms a close conjunction with this new moon, suggesting an emphasis on communication: writing, blogging, public speaking, maintaining a Web site.

Between October 26 and December 4 Mars in Capricorn forms a beneficial angle to your career area. This transit brings greater focus and clarity to your professional life and goals. Is this the time to launch your own business?

FINANCES

Let's look at Venus transits first for beneficial dates for finances. Your solar second house, which rules money, is Virgo, so mark the dates between September 5 and 29, when Venus moves through Virgo. During this period you may earn extra income, get a raise, take a second job. Your income goes up, Leo. You may feel the urge to spend on a large-ticket item, but just be sure you pay cash or have the cash in the bank to cover the credit card bill when it comes due.

Another beneficial date falls on August 25, with a new moon in Virgo, your financial area. This one should bring new financial opportunities.

MERCURY RETROGRADES

Every year Mercury—the planet of communication and travel—turns retrograde three times. During these periods it's wise not to sign contracts (unless you don't mind renegotiating when Mercury is moving direct), to check and recheck travel plans, and to communicate as succinctly as possible. Refrain from buying any large-ticket items or electronics during this time too. Often computers and appliances go on the fritz, cars act up, data is lost ... you get the idea. Be sure to back up all files before the dates below:

February 6–28: Mercury retrograde in Pisces, your solar eighth house. This one impacts your shared resources. Mercury slips back into Aquarius before it turns direct, so it impacts your partnerships too.

June 7–July 1: Mercury retrograde in Cancer, your solar twelfth house. This retrograde stirs up your personal unconscious. You have to tackle issues you thought were resolved. Great period for therapy, if you're so inclined. Your dreams are a source of insights and information.

October 4-25: Mercury retrograde in Scorpio, your solar fourth house. This one impacts your domestic environment. One possibility is problems with plumbing in your house or problems with appliances. Be sure to communicate clearly with everyone in your family. It will save you headaches later!

ECLIPSES

Solar eclipses tend to trigger external events that bring about change according to the sign and house in which they fall. Lunar eclipses trigger inner, emotional events according to the sign and house in which they fall. Any eclipse marks both beginnings and endings. The solar and lunar eclipse in a pair falls in opposite signs. If you're interested in detailed information on eclipses, take a look at Celeste Teal's excellent and definitive book, *Eclipses: Predicting World Events & Personal Transformation.*

If you were born under or around the time of an eclipse, it's to your advantage to take a look at your birth chart to find out exactly where the eclipses will impact you.

Most years feature four eclipses—two solar, two lunar—with the set separated by about two weeks. Let's take a closer look.

April 15: Lunar eclipse in Libra, your solar third house. Emotional issues surface related to siblings, communication, and travel. The emotions are positive, though!

April 29: Solar eclipse in Taurus, your career area. New professional opportunities. New job, promotion, new creative venues. With Mercury forming a close conjunction to the eclipse degree and Jupiter forming a beneficial angle to it, the opportunities headed your way will expand your professional life.

October 8: Lunar eclipse in Aries, your solar ninth house. Uranus is closely conjunct the moon, so you can expect sudden and unexpected emotional issues related to your spirituality, higher education, publishing, and overseas travel.

October 23: Solar eclipse in Scorpio, your solar fourth house. New domestic possibilities. You and your partner may move in together. You could move or buy a new home.

LUCKIEST DAYS OF THE YEAR
Every year there are one or two days when Jupiter and the sun meet up, and luck, serendipity, and expansion are

the hallmarks. This year those days fall on July 25–26. Circle the dates. Do whatever you enjoy!

January—Leo

For the first ten days of the month Mercury is moving through Capricorn, a transit that started in December 2013. It's a good transit for getting back into the swing of your work routine. On January 11 Mercury enters Aquarius, your opposite sign, and brings your conscious attention to partnerships—both business and personal. This transit lasts until January 31 and should stimulate plenty of cutting-edge ideas that you can use in your creative endeavors.

On January 31 Mercury enters Pisces, your solar eighth house, where it will turn retrograde on February 6. We'll discuss this in next month's roundup. But in preparation for the retro, it would be a good idea to read about Mercury retros in The Big Picture for your sign.

Venus begins the year in retrograde motion in Capricorn, your daily work area. Ouch! The retro started in December of last year, so you're probably accustomed to this energy by now. Until Venus turns direct, though, your personal relationships may experience some bumps and bruises, but nothing too serious. It's a good idea not to buy any large-ticket items during this period, unless you don't mind returning them later because you uncover a flaw!

On January 31 Venus turns direct in Capricorn and starts moving toward its appointment with Aquarius on March 5. Smoother sailing all the way around during this period.

Mars starts the year in direct motion in Libra, an air sign compatible with your fire-sign sun. This transit stimulates your social calendar and activities in your neighborhood, and you may be spending more time than usual with siblings, other relatives, and neighbors. Mars forms a beneficial angle to your sun during this time, so your physical energy should be excellent, and your sexuality is heightened.

Expansive Jupiter begins the year retrograde in Cancer, your solar twelfth house. It means things are moving a bit slowly, that there may be delays in your endeavors. However, this retro enables you to delve more deeply into your own unconscious, and you have easier access to information and insights contained in dreams.

Saturn begins 2014 in direct motion in Scorpio, your solar fourth house. This transit, a continuation of last year, ends on December 23, when Saturn enters fire sign Sagittarius. Until then, while Saturn is in direct motion, you may be involved in research and investigation, and there could be psychic occurrences in your home. The structure of your domestic environment is being strengthened.

Uranus, the planet of sudden, unexpected change, begins the year in direct motion in fellow fire sign Aries, where it has been since 2011. This transit is exciting for you, Leo, and helps to shake up your worldview and spiritual beliefs so that you can discard those beliefs that no longer serve your best interests.

Neptune is still in Pisces, where it has been since February 2012. By now you're accustomed to this energy. You may be experiencing psychic phenomena or delving into that field. Your spiritual beliefs may be in flux, and you are probably discovering how important these beliefs are to you. Neptune in Pisces increases imagination and intuitive ability, Leo.

Pluto continues its long transit of Capricorn, where it has been since 2008. Your career goals and strategies are undoubtedly changing, and your daily work routine is impacted in some way. By the time this transit is finished in 2024, your work life will be on a totally different trajectory.

IMPORTANT DATES

January 1: The new moon in Capricorn could usher in a whole new chapter in your job, Leo. If you've been unemployed, then you may find exactly the right job. You could get a raise or promotion, find a new job that is more in line with your values, or discover that you have new career goals. Pluto is closely conjunct this new moon, so there could be some power plays going on around you.

January 15: The full moon in Cancer occurs in your solar twelfth house. Something hidden is now illuminated. Jupiter is widely conjunct this full moon, so any news you hear should be positive and will expand your life in some way.

January 30: The new moon in Aquarius ushers in new partnership opportunities—in business and your personal life. With Uranus forming a close, beneficial angle to this new moon, opportunities will surface suddenly. Be ready to seize them!

February—Leo

Let's talk first about the Mercury retrograde and get the bad news out of the way! Between February 6 and 28 Mercury is retro in Pisces, but because it turns in the early degrees of Pisces, it slips back into Aquarius on February 12 and turns direct in that sign on the 28.

Before the retro begins, be sure to back up your computers on a flash drive, an external hard drive, and even on a free service like Drop box. Make travel plans on either side of the retro, and if you absolutely must travel during the retrograde, go with the flow even if your itinerary changes suddenly. Reread the section on Mercury retrograde under The Big Picture for your sign.

While Mercury is retro in Pisces, be sure to check and double-check your financial statements, and go with your hunches. Your intuition should be quite powerful now. While Mercury is retro in Aquarius, you and your partner may be rehashing old issues.

For all of February Venus continues its transit of Capricorn. Since it turned direct on January 31, your work environment is now much more conducive to harmonious professional relationships. Peers and bosses look to you for answers. An office flirtation could start up. Be careful before you leap into a relationship. If things don't work out, you still have to work with this individual.

Mars continues its forward movement through Libra, your solar third house. It means your social life continues to be active and you may be looking for a neighborhood that would be more suitable for you and your family.

IMPORTANT DATES

February 14: The full moon in your sign should be dramatic, filled with news, activity, and a lot of socializing. You'll have a chance to strut your stuff, Leo, and display your considerable talents!

February 28: Mercury turns direct in Aquarius.

March—Leo

March is an active month astrologically, so it may be a wild month, Leo. Let's take a closer look.

For the first seventeen days of the month Mercury is moving through Aquarius, your opposite sign, and stimulates conversations and discussions with partners—romantic and business. Your conscious mind is filled with cutting-edge ideas that you can use in a creative endeavor of some kind.

Between March 17 and April 7 Mercury transits Pisces, your solar eighth house. During this period your mind is deeply intuitive and imaginative, so follow your hunches in all things. Listen to your intuition particularly when it comes to your creative endeavors and the mundane stuff—mortgages, loans, your shared finances.

Venus transits Aquarius between March 5 and April 5, a beautiful time to be with the one you love. If possible, get out of town together for a long, romantic weekend in an exotic location. Create memories that you'll one day look back on!

Mars turns retrograde in Libra on March 1 and remains that way until May 19. During this lengthy retro your social life may feel sluggish, and relationships with siblings and neighbors may feel the same way. It's a good idea to maintain your exercise routine when Mars is retrograde.

The month's three lunations are sure to keep you hopping. On March 1 the new moon in Pisces enjoys a close conjunction with Neptune, creating a kind of dreamy, intuitive feel to everything. New opportunities surface in resources you share with others or with creative endeavors that require imagination.

March 16 features a full moon in Virgo, your financial area. Something connected to money is illuminated. Saturn forms a beneficial angle to this full moon, suggesting that any news you hear strengthens a structure in your life.

On March 30 a new moon in Aries should bring in new opportunities for foreign travel and in education and publishing. Your worldview may figure into the equation too.

IMPORTANT DATES
March 1: Mars turns retro in Libra until May 19

March 2: Saturn turns retro in Scorpio, your solar fourth house, and remains there until July 20.

March 6: Jupiter turns direct in Cancer, your solar twelfth house. It's always preferable to have this planet's luck and expansion functioning at optimum levels.

April—Leo

Compared to March, April is an easy month, more laid back. You'll enjoy Mercury's transit of fellow fire sign Aries between April 5 and 23. It stimulates your mind, and you reach out in new directions to express yourself. Publishing, foreign travel, and your spirituality are highlighted in some way. Your communication skills are sharp, so take advantage of that.

Between April 23 and May 7 Mercury transits Taurus, your career area. This period should enable you to push your own ideas and endeavors forward. You're quite stubborn during this transit and insist on doing things your way. Good thing too. A boss or peer may be trying to push you around.

From April 5 to May 2 Venus transits Aries, so for a while it's traveling with Mercury, a nice combo of energies. With Venus in the picture, a flirtation or romance at work could heat up. You're more impetuous now when it comes to both romance and creative endeavors. You brainstorm with trusted coworkers, family, or friends.

For all of April Mars continues its retrograde motion in Libra, your solar third house. Things overall may seem somewhat sluggish now. Just try to go with the flow, and don't try to push ideas or relationships. Things will unfold in their own time.

On April 15 there's a lunar eclipse in Libra, your solar third house. News you hear around the time of this eclipse is positive and uplifting and could involve a friendship, a creative endeavor, or something connected to a sibling or your neighborhood.

Two weeks later on April 29 the solar eclipse in Taurus, your career area, is one to anticipate. This eclipse ushers in new professional opportunities. You could land the job of your dreams, get promoted, receive a great raise. Make a list of what you hope for in your career, and then step aside and let the universe make it happen.

IMPORTANT DATE
April 14: Pluto turns retrograde in Capricorn until September 22.

May—Leo

From May 7 to 29 Mercury moves through compatible air sign Gemini, your solar eleventh house. This transit should be delightful for you, Leo. It ramps up your social life and increases the likelihood of meeting someone special. Your gift of gab now means you can talk to anyone about virtually anything. If you've got a manuscript stashed away somewhere, now is the time to dust it off, polish it up, and submit it.

On the 29, Mercury enters Cancer, and next month it will turn retrograde in that sign, which we'll talk about more in next month's roundup.

Between May 2 and 28 Venus moves through fellow fire sign Aries, which should be a pleasant transit for you. You may travel abroad, could meet a romantic interest from a foreign country, and are impetuous when it comes to romance. On the creative front, you're not hesitant to take risks and may tackle something new with enormous passion.

Between May 19 and July 25 Mars is finally in direct motion again, and things overall should begin gaining momentum. Just be patient. Yes, that can be difficult for a Leo, but in the long run things are unfolding according to schedule.

Look to the full moon in Scorpio on May 14 to light up some facet of your home life. There could be news concerning your domestic situation, and thanks to a close conjunction with Saturn, the news deserves your serious consideration and thought.

On May 28 the new moon in Gemini should be terrific. It falls in your solar eleventh house, so new friendships may be entering your life, and there could be new opportunities in communication and travel. Combined with Venus entering Taurus on this same day, there could be new professional opportunities and perhaps a romance in the offing!

IMPORTANT DATE
May 28: Mercury enters water sign Cancer, your solar twelfth house.

June—Leo

Okay, let's talk about Mercury first. Until June 7 it's moving in direct motion in water sign Cancer, so the contents of your unconscious should be more readily available to you through dreams, meditation, and any altered state. Between June 7 and July 1 Mercury is retrograde—first in Cancer, then it slides back into Gemini and goes direct in that sign.

This is the second Mercury retro of the year, so you undoubtedly have figured out on your own how to successfully navigate these periods. Follow the three Rs—revise, rethink, and review, and then reread the Mercury retro section in The Big Picture for your sign. Regardless of what sign the retro is in, it's always smart to back up your computer files—a flash drive, external hard drive, even on an external service like Drop box.

While Mercury is retro in Cancer, you could encounter old friends, former lovers, or spouses whom you haven't seen in years. Old issues may surface too, particularly concerning power you have disowned over the years.

Until June 23 Venus continues its transit through Taurus, the career area of your chart. Take advantage of this transit by garnering support from coworkers and bosses for your projects and endeavors. People are open and receptive now to you and your ideas.

Once Venus enters Cancer on June 23, you and your partner may be spending more time alone together. You could be involved in a creative endeavor, working in solitude much of the time. That transit ends on July 17.

On May 19 Mars finally turns direct in Libra and moves toward its appointment with Scorpio on July 25. Now that Mars is moving direct again, momentum is the name of the game!

IMPORTANT DATES

June 9: Neptune turns retrograde in Pisces, your solar eighth house, until November 15. While retro, you're taking a deeper look at your spiritual values and what you expect and want in terms of resources you share with others. Your imagination is a powerful tool.

June 13: The full moon in fellow fire sign Sagittarius illuminates or brings news about a romantic relationship or creative endeavor. Your kids may be highlighted in some way too. Uranus forms a wide, beneficial angle to this moon, suggesting that news and events are sudden and unexpected.

June 27: The new moon in water sign Cancer brings

opportunities to work behind the scenes in some capacity. The insights and information you gain through your own dreams are valuable.

July—Leo

Good news first—Mercury turns direct on July 1 in Gemini. So now it's safe to pack your bag and hit the road. If you have delayed signing a contract, wait a few more days for Mercury to stabilize before doing so. Send out résumés, queries, and submissions. Life is now in forward motion again, and Mercury is moving toward its appointment with Cancer on July 12, where it will remain until the 31.

While the planet transits Cancer, your solar twelfth house, your intuition and imagination are powerful. You have greater access to information and insights in your dreams, while meditating, and in other altered states. On the 31 Mercury enters your sign, where it will remain until August 15. We'll discuss that transit under next month's roundup.

Venus moves through Cancer from July 18 to August 12, so for part of this time it will be traveling with Mercury. This duo suggests discussion with a partner or romantic interest that helps to define your relationship. You may be working in solitude on a creative endeavor, perhaps because you're up against a deadline.

For the first twenty-five days of the month Mars continues its transit of Libra, an air sign compatible with your fire-sign sun. This transit's energy is similar to what was going on for the first two months of 2014, before

Mars turned retro. Your social life is more active, you feel more artistic and creative, and you could be looking for a neighborhood that would be better for you and your family.

Now for the really fantastic news: on July 16 expansive Jupiter enters your sign, Leo, and it's going to be there until August 11, 2015. For the next thirteen months your personal life will expand in ways you haven't seen for the last twelve years. In fact, look back to the period between August 2002 and August 2003. What kinds of things were going on in your life then? Was your life expanding in a significant way? Take advantage of all opportunities that come your way. Jupiter in Leo is moving in direct motion until December 8.

IMPORTANT DATES

July 12: The full moon in Capricorn brings career news or news related to your daily work or health. Pluto is widely conjunct this moon, and Uranus forms a close and challenging angle to it. The news you hear may not be exactly what you had hoped for, but just remember the adage about silver linings.

July 25: Mars enters Scorpio.

July 26: The new moon in Leo should be fantastic for you. This moon happens just once a year and sets the tone for the next twelve months. Focus on what you would like to do and achieve in the next year, make a list, meditate on it. Then release the desires, and let the universe do its work. With Jupiter only a degree from this new moon, your luck right now is extraordinary.

August—Leo

August is a fairly tame month astrologically. Now that Jupiter is in your sign, you're feeling more upbeat, optimistic, cheerful, generous. For the first fifteen days of August Mercury travels with Jupiter, and your mind overflows with ideas. You may decide to launch a business, write a book, move, get married, start a family. No telling exactly how Jupiter's expansiveness touches your life. But when it's paired with Mercury, your consciousness is like a sponge, absorbing everything.

Between August 15 and September 2 Mercury transits Virgo, a sign that it rules, your financial area. During this period you're fiddling around with your money—perhaps creating a budget, keeping close tabs on what you earn and spend. You may look for another job that pays more.

From August 12 to September 5 Venus transits your sign, one of the most spectacularly creative and romantic periods for you all year. With Jupiter also in your sign and Mercury too, for a few days, the odds are all stacked in your favor. Your muse tags you like a friendly ghost, your love life is wonderful, and life overall seems magnificent.

For all of August Mars continues its transit of emotionally intense Scorpio, your solar fourth house. You may be doing a lot of stuff around your home during the month of August, be involved in research of some kind, or could have some psychic experiences that blow you away! Mars is always a motivator.

IMPORTANT DATES

August 10: The full moon in Aquarius occurs in your partnership sector. News that you hear could catch you off guard. Uranus forms a beneficial angle to this full moon, but Saturn forms a challenging angle. Perhaps the news is sobering in some way.

August 25: The new moon in Virgo falls in your financial area. This one should usher in new opportunities with money. You might land a job that pays you much more than you currently earn, or you could get a significant raise. Regardless of how the specifics unfold, this new moon brings plenty to celebrate.

September—Leo

September is a busy month in the zodiac and could leave you feeling somewhat frazzled if you try to take on too much. That said, your finances should be improving. Let's take a closer look.

From September 2 to 27 Mercury transits Libra, your solar third house. During this period you communicate or hang out with siblings more frequently, may be more involved in your community in some way, or could be traveling and socializing more. You think creatively now, so be sure to jot down ideas when they occur to you. You'll be able to use them later.

On September 27 Mercury enters Scorpio, where it's going to turn retrograde on October 4. We'll discuss this in next month's roundup.

In September Venus occupies three signs—Leo, Virgo, and Libra. For the first four days of the month you enjoy the tail end of Venus' transit through your sign, Leo, so make the most of it.

Then between September 5 and 29 Venus moves through Virgo, your financial area. You may be spending more, but your income should increase too. There's a tendency with this transit to be lured by big-ticket items. If you're lured, forget using a credit card; pay cash. In terms of romance, this transit could bring someone into your life whose values are similar to your own. You may be more discriminating now about who you get involved with.

Venus enters Libra on September 29 and remains there until October 23, a transit we'll discuss in next month's roundup.

Mars changes signs on September 13. It enters fellow fire sign Sagittarius, your solar fifth house. Your love life and creative flow really accelerate until October 26, when Mars enters Capricorn. The other part of this equation is that with Mars in Sadge, your enjoyment of life is paramount.

IMPORTANT DATES

September 8: The full moon in Pisces falls in your career area. This moon should bring professional news, and it looks to be positive. Pluto forms a beneficial angle to this moon, so you're in the driver's seat professionally. A good place to be!

September 22: Pluto turns direct in Capricorn.

September 24: A new moon in Libra, your solar third house, ushers in new opportunities with your community and neighborhood, with creative endeavors, and in your social life!

October—Leo

Mercury retrograde alert! For the first four days of the month Mercury continues its journey through Scorpio, your domestic area. Then on October 4 it moves retrograde, slides back into Libra on the 10, and turns direct again in that sign on the 25. So two areas of your life are impacted by this retro: your domestic environment and communication and travel. Reread the section on Mercury retrograde under The Big Picture for your sign for tips on how to successfully navigate this retrograde.

Venus continues its journey through Virgo, your financial area, until October 23. This transit should be increasing your income and clarifying what you value. In terms of romance, you may meet someone who shares your values, particularly with Mars still in fellow fire sign Sagittarius until the 26. If the relationship takes off, it should be romantic and fun. Then between October 23 and November 16 Venus enters Scorpio, your solar fourth house. During this period romance has an edgy intensity to it, and your sexuality is heightened. Due to the Mercury retro, you and your partner may be at odds about something, but as long as your discuss your relationship openly and honestly, the disagreements are just minor blips in an otherwise intensely romantic period.

Between October 26 and December 4 Mars moves through Capricorn, your solar sixth house. During this period your daily work routine ramps up. You may take on additional responsibilities and work longer hours. Your focus is strong and certain, and your career goals possess more clarity now too. During this period Mars travels with Pluto, a powerful combination for getting things done!

IMPORTANT DATES
October 8: A lunar eclipse in Aries, a fellow fire sign, brings sudden and unexpected insights and news concerning overseas travel, education, or publishing. Mars forms a close, beneficial angle to the eclipse degree, suggesting a lot of activity and commotion. You may be feeling the urge to try something radically new and different — a risk.

October 23: The solar eclipse in Scorpio ushers in new opportunities in your home life and, thanks to an exact conjunction from Venus, romance and your creative endeavors.

November—Leo

As you enter the final two months of the year, take a few minutes to look ahead to 2015. What would you like to achieve and experience next year? What habits do you want to break or cultivate? Start your list of new year's resolutions.

On November 8 Mercury enters Scorpio once again, so some of the same themes that were prevalent in late September may repeat. Your mind is intensely focused during this transit, and your power of concentration is excellent. During part of this transit, which lasts until November 27, Venus will be traveling with Mercury. This duo increases the likelihood of discussions with your partner about your relationship, love, and life.

For the first sixteen days of the month Venus moves through Scorpio. You can see by the dates that Venus and Mercury travel together for about eight days, an intense period. Then between November 16 and December 10 Venus moves through fellow fire sign Sagittarius, marking one of the most romantic and creative periods for you this year. There could be some foreign travel during this period too, or perhaps you and your partner embark on a joint creative endeavor.

For the month of November, Mars continues its journey through Capricorn, so you may be working diligently on a project for work. If your physical energy doesn't feel quite up to par, you might consider experimenting with different nutritional programs and exercise routines. Be sure to get plenty of sleep during this transit—i.e., resist the temptation to burn your candle at both ends!

IMPORTANT DATES

November 6: The full moon in Taurus occurs in your career area. This lunation could be quite powerful for you. A project culminates, and accolades flow your way. You're recognized by bosses and peers for your skills and talents. Pluto and Mars both form beneficial angles to this full moon, suggesting a flurry of activity and power plays—that you win!

November 22: A new moon in fellow fire sign Sagittarius should be glorious. New opportunities are ushered in with romance, your creative endeavors, and everything you do for fun and pleasure. Venus forms a wide conjunction with this new moon, suggesting a beautiful harmony between you and the one you love.

December—Leo

As we enter December, every planet except Uranus is moving direct, so life in general unfolds with greater ease and smoothness. Let's look more closely.

Mercury spends the first sixteen days of the month in Sagittarius, and for part of that time it's still traveling with Venus in the same sign in the love and romance area of your chart. This period should be especially enjoyable.

Between December 16 and January 5, 2015, Mercury transits Capricorn, your solar sixth house. Even though the holidays are just around the corner, you may be focused on work and completing something before they are really upon you. You may be spending more time with employees and bosses, perhaps at Christmas and New Year's parties?

On December 10 Venus enters Capricorn, where it will be until January 4, 2015. For a time Venus will be traveling with Mercury, so it looks as if there's a possibility that an office flirtation heats up. Things with coworkers and employees go well, and you may land a nice end-of-the-year bonus. You could be looking for end-of-the-year tax breaks too, and these items could be included as Christmas gifts.

On December 4 Mars enters Aquarius, your opposite sign, where it will be until January 12, 2015. This transit could bring exactly the right business partner, manager, agent, accountant, or financial backer and can also bring in people with vision and imagination.

Jupiter turns retrograde in your sign on December 8 and remains that way until April 8, 2015. This may slow things down somewhat, but use the time to look within at your priorities for next year.

IMPORTANT DATES

December 6: The full moon in Gemini brings news about a friendship or a group to which you belong. It highlights communication and travel too. Don't be surprised if your inbox fills with emails inviting you to this party and that function. It's the season, after all, for feeling good, generous, and happy!

December 21: The new moon in Capricorn could bring new opportunities in your career—a promotion? raise? new job? With Mercury forming a wide conjunction to this new moon, at least one opportunity dealing with communication and travel could surface.

On this same day Uranus turns direct in Aries, taking you into the new year with unexpected surprises.

December 23: Saturn enters Sagittarius, your love and romance area, for a transit that will last about two and a half years. This transit could signal that a romantic relationship becomes more serious and your creative endeavors are grounded and taking on a solid, structured form.

HAPPY NEW YEAR!

7

Virgo

The Big Picture in 2014

Welcome to 2014, Virgo! It's a 4 year for you, so the emphasis is on the development of your intuition, nurturing yourself and others, and creating foundations upon which you can build your life.

Now that you've the tumult of 2012 and the realignment of 2013 behind you, you're ready to embark on yet another journey.

So let's look at how specific areas of your life may be impacted and which dates will be of vital importance to you.

ROMANCE/CREATIVITY
One of the most romantic and creative times for you all year occurs between September 5 and 29, when Venus transits your sign. During this period your muse tags your heels like a beloved pet. Your creative drive is so heightened that you find unusual solutions and ideas simply by paying attention to your environment. Use synchronicity as a guidance system.

You feel more self-confident. Others pick up on that vibe and are attracted to you, your ideas, persona, and creative projects. So if you have these ready, start submitting and exhibiting them, doing whatever you need to do in order to advertise them.

If a relationship begins during this period, it's likely to start first in the intellectual realm, with ideas and communication. You might meet this individual through Facebook or Twitter or some other social media site. Perhaps you and this individual work in the same profession or have careers that are allied in some way. You and your partner will have similar interests and a solid base for communication. If you're already involved in a relationship, this transit helps to define it. You and your partner may deepen your commitment to each other.

The other terrific period for romance and creativity occurs between December 10 and January 4, 2015, when Venus transits fellow earth sign Capricorn, your solar fifth house. This transit stimulates you to do whatever it is you most enjoy. Many Virgos are ardent readers, enjoy movies, and love to travel. But whatever it is you enjoy, you do more of it during this transit.

Creatively you're at the top of your game, and anything you tackle works effortlessly. Romantically you're interested in having fun and probably aren't in the frame of mind for anything serious. If you're involved already, this transit stimulates the relationship in such a way that you two rediscover what drew you together in the first place.

Between January 1 and July 15 Jupiter continues its transit through compatible water sign Cancer. It's been going on since last year, so by now you undoubtedly have a good grasp of how this transit is expanding some facet of your life. You feel lucky, and those feelings draw more experiences that bolster that luck. You may meet someone special through friends or through a group to which you belong. Or maybe you've already met that special person. You're more nurturing of yourself and others. Your intuition deepens.

Other excellent dates:

January 1, the new moon in fellow earth sign Capricorn, your solar fifth house, brings in new romantic opportunities. A great way to start the new year. Look for new opportunities in your creative endeavors.

May 28 to June 23, when Venus in fellow earth sign Taurus forms a terrific angle to your sun. You may be a tad more cautious now about getting romantically involved, but once you do, it all feels right.

CAREER

Jupiter's transits through both Cancer and Leo will help every facet of your life, even your career. The caveat with career matters, though, is that if you're doing something you love, you benefit tremendously. If you're working in a field that doesn't excite you, that has become rather humdrum and routine, then Jupiter, Mars, Venus, Mercury, and your ruler, the moon, could help you to break away and find something that is more aligned with your passions.

Between July 16, 2014, and August 11, 2015, Jupiter transits fire sign Leo and forms a beneficial angle to your career area. This transit may bring some unexpected and expansive professional opportunities.

Let's take a closer look at the beneficial career times:

May 7 to 29: Mercury is moving direct in Gemini, your

career area. This period favors communication with bosses and peers. Pitch your ideas and move all professional matters forward. Start a blog, put up a Web site, advertise your products/services or those of your company. Your conscious mind is quite versatile during this transit.

June 23 to July 18: During this period, while Venus transits your career area, you're working steadily and resolutely on a project. Coworkers and bosses are impressed with your ideas and the way you implement them. Others find you so appealing that you're the first to be tapped for team projects.

May 28: The new moon in Gemini should usher in new professional opportunities. You land a new job, get the interview you've hoped for, are promoted, move into a larger office, or sell your book or novel. Mars forms a close, beneficial angle to this new moon, suggesting a lot of activity.

Between December 4 and January 12, 2015, Mars in Capricorn forms a beneficial angle to your career area. This transit brings greater focus and clarity to your professional life and goals. Is this the time to launch your own business?

FINANCES
Let's look at Venus transits first for beneficial dates for finances. Your solar second house, which rules money, is Libra, so mark the dates between September 29 and October 23, when Venus moves through Libra. During this period you may earn extra income, get a raise, or take a second job. Your income rises, but your expenses may too. Just be sure to pay cash for everything. That way you'll know when you can't afford something!

Another beneficial date falls on September 24, with a new moon in Libra. This one should bring new financial opportunities.

MERCURY RETROGRADES

Every year, Mercury—the planet of communication and travel—turns retrograde three times. During these periods it's wise not to sign contracts (unless you don't mind renegotiating when Mercury is moving direct), to check and recheck travel plans, and to communicate as succinctly as possible. Refrain from buying any large-ticket items or electronics during this time too. Often computers and appliances go on the fritz, cars act up, data is lost . . . you get the idea. Be sure to back up all files before the dates below:

February 6–28: Mercury retrograde in Pisces, your partnership area. Ouch! It slips back into Aquarius before it turns direct, so it also impacts your solar sixth house—daily work.

June 7–July 1: Mercury retrograde in Cancer, your solar eleventh house. This retrograde affects your friendships, wishes, dreams. You have to tackle issues you thought were resolved.

October 4–25: Mercury retrograde in Scorpio, your solar third house. This one involves your neighbors and neighborhood, communication, travel, siblings.

ECLIPSES

Solar eclipses tend to trigger external events that bring about change according to the sign and house in which they fall. Lunar eclipses trigger inner, emotional events according to the sign and house in which they fall. Any eclipse marks both beginnings and endings. The solar and lunar eclipse in a pair falls in opposite signs. If you're interested in detailed information on eclipses, take a look at Celeste Teal's excellent and definitive book, *Eclipses: Predicting World Events & Personal Transformation.*

If you were born under or around the time of an eclipse, it's to your advantage to take a look at your birth chart to find out exactly where the eclipses will impact you.

Most years feature four eclipses—two solar, two lunar—with the set separated by about two weeks. Let's take a closer look.

April 15: Lunar eclipse in Libra, your solar second house. Emotional issues surface related to finances. The emotions are positive, though!

April 29: Solar eclipse in Taurus, your solar ninth house. New opportunities surface in education, overseas travel, spirituality, and publishing. With Mercury forming a close conjunction to the eclipse degree and Jupiter forming a beneficial angle to it, the opportunities headed your way will expand your life in some way.

October 8: Lunar eclipse in Aries, your solar eighth house. Uranus is closely conjunct the moon, so you can expect sudden and unexpected emotional issues related to shared resources, your partner's income, and metaphysics.

October 23: Solar eclipse in Scorpio, your solar third house. New possibilities in communication.

LUCKIEST DAYS OF THE YEAR

Every year there are one or two days when Jupiter and the sun meet up, and luck, serendipity, and expansion are

the hallmarks. This year those days fall on July 25–26. Circle the dates. Do whatever you enjoy!

January—Virgo

Mercury begins this year in Capricorn, a fellow earth sign, your solar fifth house, a continuation of its transit from 2013. For the first ten days of this new year your focus is on romance and love, your creative endeavors, and having fun. But since Capricorn is involved in this equation, you may also be hammering together some sort of professional strategy.

On January 11 Mercury begins its transit of Aquarius, your solar sixth house. This movement lasts until January 31 and triggers a flurry of discussions and communication about your daily work routine. Your ideas are edgy and trend setting now, Virgo, so be sure to keep track of them.

Venus begins the year retrograde in Capricorn, your love and romance area. You and your romantic partner may not be seeing eye to eye on the details of your relationship. Don't squabble about it, though. Resume the discussion when Venus turns direct on January 31. Things will look considerably brighter then.

Mars, the planet that symbolizes physical energy and sexuality and acts as your booster rocket, starts the year retrograde in Libra, your financial area. Finances may be moving at a snail's pace, with delays in receiving money you're owed. This starts to clear up on March 1, when Mars turns direct again.

Jupiter starts the year retrograde in Cancer, your

solar eleventh house. This retro motion is also a continuation of something that started at the end of 2013. It simply means that you may be taking a deeper look at your various friendships and what you're seeking in these relationships. Your social life may not be as active now as it usually is. But all this changes on March 6, when Jupiter turns direct again in Cancer. In the meantime, take advantage of the slower pace to nurture the friendships you have.

Saturn begins the year in direct motion in Scorpio, a water sign compatible with your earth-sign sun. This transit lasts until December 23 and brings greater stability and structure to your relationships with siblings, other relatives, and neighbors. The transit began in October 2012.

Uranus begins the year direct in Aries, where it has been since March 2011. This transit lasts until early January 2019 and brings sudden, unexpected changes to some area of your life. It falls in your solar ninth house, so one area could be your partner's income or any resources you share with another. Uranus' job is to shake up the status quo, to get rid of stuff in your life that no longer works.

So that brings us to Neptune and Pluto. Neptune continues its transit of Pisces, your solar seventh house, where it has been since 2012. This transit lasts until early 2026 and can bring confusion to personal partnerships. It can also prompt you to seek a deeper spiritual connection in your partnerships.

Pluto has been in earth sign Capricorn since 2008 and will be there until early 2024, transforming your creative endeavors and love life. It forms a beneficial angle to your sun and puts you in the power seat, Virgo.

IMPORTANT DATES

There are three lunations in January, and each one holds something unique and special for you.

January 1: The new moon in Capricorn, your solar fifth house, should usher in new romantic and creative opportunities. The fifth house also concerns what you do for fun and pleasure, so you can expect new opportunities in that area too. Pluto and Mercury both form close conjunctions to this new moon, suggesting that one possible opportunity could involve communication—writing, public speaking—and travel.

January 15: The full moon in Cancer enjoys a wide conjunction with Jupiter and a beneficial angle from Saturn, so you can expect positive news about a friendship or some dream or wish that you have. Your social calendar should heat up for several days on either side of this full moon.

January 30: The new moon in Aquarius falls in your solar sixth house. This moon should bring new opportunities in your daily work routine—a promotion, perhaps, with greater responsibility, a new job, or some new approach to your job.

January 31: Mercury enters Pisces, your solar seventh house, and Venus turns direct in Capricorn. We'll talk about these in next month's roundup.

February—Virgo

Mercury is now moving through Pisces, your opposite sign, so you and your partner should be enjoying lively discussions about your relationship. The same could be true for any business partners you have. You may be involved in joint creative projects of some kind, and there's an intuitive flow to what you're doing. However, on February 6 Mercury turns retrograde for the first time this year. Since your sign is ruled by Mercury, these retro periods may impact you and Gemini, the other sign Mercury rules, more than most people.

First reread the section on Mercury retrograde in The Big Picture for your sign, then be sure to follow the rules of the three Rs: revise, review, rethink. Since Mercury is in the early degrees of Pisces when it turns retro, it slips back into Aquarius on February 12 and turns direct in that sign on February 28.

Now that Venus has turned direct on January 31, it spends until March 5 in Capricorn, marking a romantic and creative period for you, one of the best all year in fact. Everything in your life seems to run with greater smoothness and ease, but your love life, creative drive, and what you do for pleasure are highlighted.

Mars continues its journey through Libra until March 1, when it turns retrograde in that sign. It turns direct again on May 19. During February you pour a lot of time and energy into finances—earning money, spending it, budgeting it. You may be applying for jobs too, sending out résumés and scheduling interviews, or you could be hammering together the final pieces of your own business. It all depends on what you want to do to earn your living, Virgo.

IMPORTANT DATE

February 14: The full moon in Leo occurs in your solar twelfth house. Expect news about or insights into something in your life that's hidden — an issue, relationship, or even creative endeavor. Mars forms an exact and beneficial angle to this full moon, so a financial issue could be involved too.

March—Virgo

Compared to February, March is a wild roller coaster ride, so hang on tightly, Virgo!

Mercury is in Aquarius, your daily work area, until March 17. It continues to keep your conscious focus on your daily work routine. You may be socializing more with coworkers and employees and networking with individuals who work in related fields. Between March 17 and April 7 Mercury transits Aries, your solar eighth house. This transit may prompt you to take risks with investments. If you know what you're doing, fine. But if you're short on money, stick to what's safe. Your partner's income enters into the discussions for some reason. Perhaps he or she lands a raise?

Venus moves through Aquarius from March 5 to April 5, a period that should create greater harmony in your daily work life and the way you maintain your health. You may experiment with various nutritional programs or diets or try alternative therapies for health stuff. Romance is possible in the workplace. If you're already involved with someone, you and your partner may work on a joint project together.

Mars turns retrograde on March 1 in your financial area. Between now and May 19 when it turns direct again, money you're owed may be slow to arrive. Be sure to check bank statements carefully. It may be difficult to obtain a mortgage or loan. Life generally slows down when Mars is retro, so go with the flow, Virgo.

Jupiter turns direct on March 6 in Cancer, a major plus. Your social life now picks up momentum again, you make new friends and connections, and Jupiter expands your life in positive, beneficial ways.

Saturn turns retro in Scorpio, your solar third house, on March 2 and stays that way until July 20. During the retro period you may be rethinking and reevaluating your relationships with siblings and neighbors. You may feel dissatisfaction with your neighborhood. Don't make any hard and fast decisions until after Saturn turns direct.

IMPORTANT DATES

It's another month, like January, with three lunations. March 1 features a new moon in Pisces, your partnership area. Neptune forms a five-degree conjunction to the new moon, so there's going to be a kind of dreamy flavor to opportunities that surface. These new opportunities occur in the areas of partnership, creative endeavors, and intuitive development.

March 16 features a full moon in your sign, which illuminates an issue in your personal life or brings news that impacts you personally. Saturn retrograde forms a close, beneficial angle to this moon, so any news you hear deserves your serious consideration.

On March 30 the new moon in Aries brings new opportunities in shared resources. You might get a break in your mortgage or with taxes and insurance. You have a chance now to become an entrepreneur!

April—Virgo

Mercury is bouncing around this month, occupying three signs, which may leave you feeling somewhat harried. During the first week Mercury winds up its transit through Pisces, and between April 7 and 23 it transits Aries, your solar eighth house. During this period you may be discussing joint finances—with your partner, kids, parents. This transit isn't particularly comfortable to you as an earth sign, but it has its place in that it prompts you to look at things differently. Your perceptions change; you're more daring.

On the 23 Mercury enters fellow earth sign Taurus, your solar ninth house. This transit lasts until May 7 and should be much more comfortable for you than Mercury's transit of Aries. You may be exploring various spiritual belief systems or could be planning a trip abroad or traveling abroad. You might sign up for a workshop or seminar or college or graduate level classes. Your conscious mind is stubborn and resolute.

From April 5 to May 2 Venus moves through Pisces, your solar seventh house. During this period your most intimate partnership should be more harmonious. You and your partner may decide to deepen your commitment to each other by moving in together or getting engaged or married. If you're not involved, the energy may pertain to business partnerships. This transit favors all your creative endeavors. Your muse is right in step with you.

Throughout April Mars continues its retrograde through Libra, your financial area. You may feel frustrated about the delays in receiving money that's owed you. Sit tight, Virgo. Financial matters straighten out after May 19.

Pluto turns retro in Capricorn on April 19. Yes, that occurs in your romance and creativity area. But don't fret about it. This retro gives you greater access to your own unconscious, and you have greater insights into what you're really seeking in a romantic relationship and your creative endeavors. You have tremendous regenerative powers now. Pluto turns direct again on September 22.

IMPORTANT DATES
April features two eclipses—a lunar eclipse in Libra, your financial area, and a solar eclipse in fellow earth sign Taurus, your solar ninth house.

April 15: The lunar eclipse in Libra looks positive. You hear news about finances, a creative endeavor, or friends. Or you gain insights into these areas.

April 29: The solar eclipse in Taurus should usher in new opportunities for foreign travel and in publishing or higher education and the exploration of your worldview and spiritual beliefs. Mercury is closely conjunct to the eclipse degree, suggesting that one of the opportunities may involve some facet of communication.

May—Virgo

Mercury occupies three signs again this month. For the first week it continues its transit of Taurus. Then between May 7 and 29 it transits Gemini, your career area.

This period favors communication in all its forms, discussions and meetings with bosses and coworkers, and garnering the support you may need for your own projects and endeavors. Travel may be related to career matters.

On the 29 Mercury enters Cancer, your eleventh house. But because this transit involves a retrograde from June 7 to July 1, we'll discuss it in next month's roundup.

Between May 2 and 28 Venus moves through Aries, your solar eighth house. If you apply for a mortgage or loan during this period, this process should go smoothly. Just don't sign any papers during the retro period next month. You may take some emotional risks or be more impulsive in romance during this transit.

On May 29 Venus enters Gemini, your career area. We'll discuss this important transit in next month's roundup.

On May 19 Mars finally turns direct again in Libra and now moves toward its appointment with Scorpio in mid-September. Your financial situation should improve now. Money you're owed begins to arrive. You may still be working longer hours, and the payoff will start showing up in your bank account.

IMPORTANT DATES
After last month's two eclipses, May's lunations may seem fairly tame in comparison. The full moon on May 14 falls in Scorpio, a water sign compatible with your earth-sign sun. Any news you hear deserves your serious consideration, thanks in part to the fact that Saturn is closely conjunct this full moon. The other plus for this

full moon is that Jupiter forms a beneficial angle to it. So this news or the insights you gain expand your life in a significant way.

The new moon on May 28 falls in Gemini, your career area. This one ushers in professional opportunities of some kind. Perhaps you land your dream job, get a significant raise or promotion, or change careers altogether. Mars, now in direct motion, makes a close and beneficial angle to this new moon, indicative of accelerated activity and a forward thrust to events.

June—Virgo

On May 29 Mercury entered Cancer, your solar eleventh house. Until June 7 your social life picks up, and your conscious mind is powerfully intuitive, leading you in new directions toward new friends and acquaintances. On June 7 Mercury turns retrograde in Cancer, slides back into Gemini on June 17, then turns direct in that sign on July 1. While it's retro in Cancer, your social life may slow down, your intuitive ability may feel sluggish, and all the other attributes of a Mercury retro apply.

Once Mercury slides back into Gemini, it will be in your career area. Be sure to communicate clearly with bosses and coworkers, lessening the chances of miscommunication. Of course as for any Mercury retro, follow the rules of the three Rs: revise, review, rethink.

On May 28 Venus entered Taurus, a fellow earth sign, and it will be there until June 23. As a sign that Venus rules, the planet is happy here and functions well. This transit should be pleasurable for you. You could take a workshop or class in something that fascinates you, find romance while traveling, or may become involved in a creative endeavor that deals with spiritual beliefs or different worldviews.

For the month of June Mars continues its transit through Libra, your financial area, so there's plenty of activity involving money.

Circle June 9 on your calendar. Neptune turns retrograde in Pisces that day, so if life begins to feeling foggy, confusing, and dreamy, that's why. This retro lasts until November 15.

IMPORTANT DATES
June 13: The full moon in Sagittarius occurs in your solar fourth house. This moon should illuminate something in your domestic environment or bring news related to home, parents, or family. Thanks to a favorable angle from Uranus, the news comes out of the blue, and it looks positive.

June 27: The new moon in Cancer should be a good one for you, ushering in new friendships or new opportunities to achieve your wishes and dreams or with your family.

July—Virgo

It's going to be a crazy month, with planets changing signs and directions left and right! The best news: Mercury turns direct on July 1 in Gemini. Pack your bags, send out your résumés, submit manuscripts, make your travel plans, sign those contracts. Life now moves forward again, and Mercury heads toward its appointment with Cancer once again.

Between July 12 and 31 Mercury transits Cancer, your solar eleventh house, once more. This transit also occurred in early June, so think back to what was going on then. Possibilities? You spend more time with friends, get involved with group endeavors that involve like-minded individuals, and consciously work toward achieving your wishes and dreams.

Mercury transits Leo from July 31 to August 15, and we'll talk about that in next month's roundup.

Until July 18 Venus continues its transit of Gemini, your career area. Lucky you! This transit facilitates all your professional endeavors, puts you in the good graces of your boss and fellow workers, and sweetens everything about your career. From July 18 to August 12 Venus transits Cancer, your solar eleventh house. Hmm, Virgo. You may have a romantic encounter with someone you meet through friends or through a group to which you belong. This period favors all endeavors that enable you to reach for your dreams.

On July 25 Mars enters Scorpio, your solar third house. This transit is probably going to be intense, but in a positive way. Scorpio, a water sign, is compatible with your earth-sign sun and forms a beneficial angle to it. During this transit, which lasts until September 13, your physical energy is strong, your sexuality is heightened, and you're after the absolute bottom line in everything you do.

IMPORTANT DATES

July 12: The full moon in Capricorn, a fellow earth sign, occurs in that part of your chart that governs romance and creativity. Something in these areas is illuminated, or there's news in one of these areas. Pluto forms a wide conjunction to this moon, suggesting power plays and profound insights.

July 16: Expansive Jupiter enters Leo, your solar twelfth house, where it will be until August 11, 2015. During this transit your creative abilities expand in some way, and you have ample opportunities to show them off. You also have greater access to your own subconscious. Dreams and meditative states hold information and insights.

July 20: Saturn turns direct in Scorpio.

July 21: Uranus turns retrograde in Aries.

July 26: The new moon in Leo occurs in your financial sector. Fantastic for you, Virgo. New financial opportunities are headed your way. And with Jupiter closely conjunct this new moon, your financial base is expanded.

July 31: Mercury enters Leo, a transit we'll discuss in next month's roundup.

August—Virgo

Now that Mercury has joined Jupiter in your solar twelfth house, you may be involved in a writing endeavor that demands more solitude and focus. It's a good time to do things like clean out closets and attics and get rid of stuff you no longer use. In a sense, you're clearing the deck for when Mercury enters your sign on August 15.

Once Mercury enters your sign, you're in much more comfortable territory. Your communication skills are stellar, ideas come to you fast and furiously, and you may travel simply because the spirit moves you. This transit lasts until September 2.

Between August 12 and September 5 Venus moves through Leo, your solar twelfth house. This transit could bring a romance that takes place mostly in secret, or perhaps you and your partner are spending more time alone together. This transit also favors therapy, meditation, and dream work.

For the entire month of August Mars continues its transit of Scorpio, a sign it corules. This transit galvanizes your search for the ideal neighborhood for yourself and your family. It also brings a kind of intensity to everything you do and undertake. You won't settle for easy answers.

IMPORTANT DATES

August 10: The full moon in air sign Aquarius brings something to light about your daily work routine or health. Thanks to a beneficial angle from Uranus, any news you hear is sudden and unexpected and should be good.

August 25: The new moon in your sign is something to celebrate. It happens just once a year and sets the tone for the next twelve months. Decide what you would like to experience and achieve in the next year, back those desires with powerful emotion, then release them and let the universe bring the right circumstances your way.

September—Virgo

It's a busy month astrologically, with Mercury in four signs, Venus in three signs, and Mars changing signs. Let's take a closer look.

Until September 2 Mercury is in Virgo, finishing its transit through that sign, then between September 2 and 27 it moves through Libra, your financial area. On September 27 it enters Scorpio, where it will turn retrograde on October 4. We'll discuss this transit in next month's roundup.

During the period Mercury is in Libra your conscious focus is on financial matters. You may be discussing budgets with family members, applying for a second job, or doing something in your regular job that will bring in more money. It could be that you need to put your priorities in order!

Venus starts off the month by completing its transit of Leo. Between September 5 and 29 it moves through your sign, and what a fabulous period this will be. Romance and creativity are highlighted, and life generally unfolds with a harmony and ease. Others are receptive to you, your presence and ideas, and your muse is eager and willing to help with all your creative endeavors.

Between September 29 and October 23 Venus moves through Libra, which we'll discuss in next month's roundup.

Mars enters Sagittarius, your solar fourth house, on September 13 and remains there until October 26. This transit is sure to trigger a lot of activity in your domestic environment. If you have children, they and their friends are coming and going constantly. You may be doing renovations on your home and could be trying to squeeze travel into your busy schedule.

IMPORTANT DATES

September 8: The full moon in Pisces occurs in your solar seventh house of partnerships. This moon illuminates or brings news about the romantic and business partnerships in your life. Pluto forms a wide, beneficial angle to this full moon, suggesting that you're in control.

September 22: Pluto turns direct in fellow earth sign Capricorn, which should be good news for your love life and creative endeavors.

September 24: The new moon in Libra should usher in new financial opportunities. Mars forms a wide, beneficial angle to this new moon, so there's going to be a flurry of activities and forward thrust that somehow benefits your pocketbook.

October—Virgo

The stars are incredibly busy this month, and all the activity could leave you feeling somewhat frazzled, so be sure to get plenty of rest, eat well, and maintain your exercise program.

Let's start with the Mercury retrograde, the last one this year. On September 27 Mercury entered Scorpio, your solar third house, an intense transit that really deepens your focus, intentions, and intuitive skills. Between October 4 and 25 Mercury will be moving retrograde. Because the retro begins in the early degrees of

Scorpio, Mercury slips back into Libra, your financial area, on October 10 then turns direct in that sign. So two areas of your life are impacted by this retro. Follow the usual three Rs advice—revise, review, rethink. Since part of the retro occurs in your financial area, be sure to re-check bank and investment statements. Once Mercury turns direct again, it heads for its second appointment with Scorpio on November 8.

Venus entered Libra, your financial area, on September 29 and remains there until October 23. Usually this transit increases your income and perhaps your spending, too and also enhances your social life and artistic endeavors. But from October 4 to 29 Mercury is retrograde in your financial area, which mitigates some of the Venus transit benefits. If a romantic relationship starts during the Venus transit, be sure to communicate clearly and take nothing for granted!

Until October 26 Mars continues to travel through Sagittarius, your domestic area. This transit definitely stirs up frenetic activity at home. Then things begin to calm down between October 26 and December 4, when Mars transits fellow earth sign Capricorn. During this period your sexuality is heightened, and your muse sticks to you like Velcro.

IMPORTANT DATES

October 8: The lunar eclipse in Aries occurs in your solar eighth house. Resources you share with others are highlighted. Your partner's income figures into this equation. Thanks to a close conjunction from Uranus, news about your partner's income comes out of the blue and should be positive!

October 23: The new moon in water sign Scorpio occurs in your solar third house. This one ushers in new opportunities in communication, travel, research, and psychic development.

November—Virgo

Between November 8 and 27 Mercury transits Scorpio and until the 16 is traveling with Venus. This very nice combo favors your love life, heightens your sexuality, and brings a bottom-line intensity to any romantic relationship in which you're involved. Your conscious mind is extremely intuitive, and if you listen to that inner voice, your choices are smarter and your decisions happen more quickly.

On November 27 Mercury enters Sagittarius, your domestic area, and remains there until December 16. During this transit you can expect a lot of conversation and discussions with your partner, kids, and anyone else in your personal environment. Travel could figure in, particularly long-distance travel. Perhaps you and your family are planning a vacation during the December holidays. Venus joins Mercury in Sagittarius on November 16, so once again these two planets travel together for a spell—until the 27. It all makes for a pleasant Thanksgiving, regardless of who you're with or where you are. Venus remains in Sadge until December 10.

Now that Mars is in Capricorn until December 4, you've got a booster rocket that enables you to accomplish twice what you usually do. This transit heightens your sexuality and ambition and improves your physical energy.

On November 15 Neptune turns direct in Pisces, your solar seventh house. Now you can move forward with integrating your spirituality into your business and romantic partnerships.

IMPORTANT DATES
November 6: The full moon in earth sign Taurus should be particularly nice for you, Virgo. It sheds light on a trip abroad that you would like to take or are enjoying now and brings news about education and/or publishing. Thanks to beneficial angles from Pluto and Mars, you're in the driver's seat and loving it.

November 22: The new moon in Sagittarius ushers in all sorts of new opportunities connected to home and hearth, foreign travel, and publishing. Venus forms a wide conjunction to this new moon, suggesting that romance and creativity are definitely highlighted too.

December—Virgo

It's hard to believe it's December already, right? Each year seems to fly by, which underscores the importance of living in the now and appreciating everything and everyone in your life. You may want to take some time this month to focus on what you would like to experience and achieve in 2015.

Until December 16 Mercury continues its transit of Sagittarius. Then it enters Capricorn, and that carries you into the new year—until January 5, 2015. While Mercury is in Capricorn your conscious focus is on pleasurable pursuits (it's the holidays, after all!) romance, and creativity. However, because Capricorn is involved, you could also be spinning possible strategies related to your career. Even if you can't implement these strategies until next year, you'll be ready!

From December 10 to January 4, 2015, Venus also transits Capricorn, your solar fifth house. This should be one of the most romantic and creative periods for you all year and practically guarantees that your holidays and New Year's celebrations go very well.

On December 4 Mars enters air sign Aquarius and prompts you to really reach outside the box in your daily work. This will become a tad more difficult as the holidays get closer and you're distracted by office parties and social gatherings. But you deftly gather your ideas and supporters so that as soon as the new year rolls around, you can start implementing your plans. The transit lasts until January 12, 2015.

On July 8 Jupiter turns retrograde in Leo and remains that way until April 8, 2015. During this period you have greater access to your own unconscious and dreams, and meditative states hold information and insights.

On December 21 Uranus turns direct in Aries. So you go into the new year with all planets in direct motion, functioning exactly as they should.

IMPORTANT DATES

December 6: The full moon in Gemini lights up your career area. News arrives, and thanks to a wide, beneficial angle from Jupiter, this news will expand your professional opportunities in some way. Also—an additional bonus—the North Node of the moon forms a beautiful angle to the full moon too.

December 21: The new moon in Capricorn is a beauty that ushers in new opportunities in romance and creativity and with children. Mercury forms a wide conjunction to this new moon, so some new opportunity may surface in communication.

HAPPY NEW YEAR!

8

Libra

The Big Picture in 2014

Welcome to 2014, Libra! It's a 5 year for you. This suggests a year in which your personal freedom and creativity are important to you. New ideas are highlighted. You develop new ways of looking at things, delve into a variety of new areas that interest you and are gearing up for big changes. Travel is favorable this year too, and the more exotic it is, the better.

Now that you've the tumult of 2012 and the realignment of 2013 behind you, you're ready to embark on yet another journey. So let's look at how specific areas of your life may be impacted and which dates will be of vital importance to you.

ROMANCE/CREATIVITY

One of the most romantic and creative times for you all year occurs between September 29 and October 23, when Venus transits your sign. During this period your muse shadows you everywhere, and your creative drive is powerful and on target. New ideas come to you easily, so be sure to have a recorder or pen and paper handy regardless of where you are.

You feel more self-confident. Others pick up on that vibe and are attracted to you, your ideas, persona, and creative projects. So if you have these ready, start submitting and exhibiting them, doing whatever you need to do in order to advertise them.

Romantically you're in love with love during this transit. If you're involved in a relationship already, your relationship with your partner simply improves. You appreciate the qualities that brought you together to begin with.

If a relationship begins during this period, it's likely to begin in a social atmosphere. You might be at a party, an art exhibit, traveling. This stranger catches your eye; something clicks before you even speak to each other. Or you could meet this person through Facebook or Twitter or some other social media site. Perhaps you and this individual work in the same profession or have careers that are allied in some way. You and your partner will have similar interests and a solid base for communication. If you're already involved in a relationship, this transit helps to define it. You and your partner may deepen your commitment to each other.

The other terrific period for romance and creativity occurs between March 5 and April 5, when Venus transits fellow air sign Aquarius, your solar fifth house. This transit urges you to enjoy yourself. What a concept, right? Many Libras enjoy art, music, photography, writing, anything artistic, so it's possible that during this transit you become more engaged in these pursuits.

Creatively you're at the top of your game, and anything you tackle works effortlessly. Romantically you're interested in having fun and probably aren't in the frame of mind for anything serious. If you're involved already, you and your partner enjoy a period of near bliss!

Between July 16, 2014, and August 11, 2015, Jupiter moves through compatible fire sign Leo. You feel lucky, and those feelings draw more experiences that bolster that luck. You may meet someone special through friends or through a group to which you belong.

Other excellent dates:

January 30, the new moon in Aquarius, your solar fifth house, brings in new romantic opportunities. A great way to start the new year. Look for new opportunities in your creative endeavors.

June 23 to July 18, when Venus in fellow air sign Gemini forms a terrific angle to your sun. This transit enhances your communication abilities and curiosity. You can talk to anyone about anything.

CAREER

Jupiter's transits through both Cancer and Leo will help every facet of your life, even your career. The caveat with career matters, though, is that if you're doing something you love, you benefit tremendously. If you're working in a field that doesn't excite you, that has become rather humdrum and routine, then Jupiter, Mars, Venus, Mercury, and your ruler, the moon, could help you to break away and find something that is more aligned with your passions.

Between January 1 and July 15 Jupiter transits Cancer, your career area. This transit may bring some unexpected and expansive professional opportunities.

Let's take a closer look at the beneficial career times:

May 29 to June 7: Mercury is moving direct in Cancer through your career area. This period favors communication with bosses and peers. Pitch your ideas and move all professional matters forward. Start a blog, put up a Web site, advertise your products/services or those of your company. Your conscious mind is versatile and lightning quick during this transit.

July 18 to August 12: During this period while Venus transits your career area you're working steadily and resolutely on a project. Coworkers and bosses are impressed with your ideas and the way you implement them. Others find you so appealing that you're the first to be tapped for team projects. Venus in Cancer confers intuitive and nurturing qualities.

June 27: The new moon in Cancer should usher in new professional opportunities. You land a new job, get the interview you've hoped for, are promoted, move into a larger office, or sell your book or novel. Neptune forms a close, beneficial angle to this new moon, suggesting opportunities that enable you to integrate your idealism and spiritual beliefs into your professional life.

Between July 25 and September 13 Mars in Scorpio forms a beneficial angle to your career area. This transit brings greater focus to your professional life and goals and enhances your research and investigative abilities.

FINANCES

Let's look at Venus transits first for beneficial dates for finances. Your solar second house, which rules money, is

Scorpio, so mark the dates between October 23 and November 16, when Venus moves through Scorpio. During this period you may earn extra income, get a raise, or take a second job. Your income rises, but your expenses may too. Keep track of your finances.

Another beneficial date falls on October 23, with a new moon in Scorpio, your financial area. This one should bring new financial opportunities.

MERCURY RETROGRADES

Every year Mercury—the planet of communication and travel—turns retrograde three times. During these periods it's wise not to sign contracts (unless you don't mind renegotiating when Mercury is moving direct), to check and recheck travel plans, and to communicate as succinctly as possible. Refrain from buying any large-ticket items or electronics during this time too. Often computers and appliances go on the fritz, cars act up, data is lost . . . you get the idea. Be sure to back up all files before the dates below:

February 6–28: Mercury retrograde in Pisces, your solar sixth house of daily health and work. It slips back into Aquarius before it turns direct, so your romantic and creative life are also affected.

June 7–July 1: Mercury retrograde in Cancer, your solar tenth house. This retrograde affects your career.

October 4–25: Mercury retrograde in Scorpio, your solar second house. This one impacts your finances.

ECLIPSES

Solar eclipses tend to trigger external events that bring about change according to the sign and house in which they fall. Lunar eclipses trigger inner, emotional events according to the sign and house in which they fall. Any eclipse marks both beginnings and endings. The solar and lunar eclipse in a pair falls in opposite signs. If you're interested in detailed information on eclipses, take a look at Celeste Teal's excellent and definitive book, *Eclipses: Predicting World Events & Personal Transformation.*

If you were born under or around the time of an eclipse, it's to your advantage to take a look at your birth chart to find out exactly where the eclipses will impact you.

Most years feature four eclipses—two solar, two lunar—with the set separated by about two weeks. Let's take a closer look.

April 15: Lunar eclipse in your sign. Emotions surface related to your personal life, but the emotions are positive.

April 29: Solar eclipse in Taurus, your solar eighth house. New opportunities surface with mortgages, insurance, taxes, inheritances. Your partner may have a new source of income. You may have a chance to delve into some facet of metaphysics. Mercury is closely conjunct the eclipse degree, suggesting news and a new venue for communication.

October 8: Lunar eclipse in Aries, your solar seventh house. Uranus is closely conjunct the moon, so you can expect sudden and unexpected emotional issues related to both personal and professional partnerships.

October 23: Solar eclipse in Scorpio, your solar second house. New financial opportunities!

LUCKIEST DAYS OF THE YEAR

Every year there are one or two days when Jupiter and the sun meet up, and luck, serendipity, and expansion are the hallmarks. This year those days fall on July 25–26. Circle the dates. Do whatever you enjoy!

January—Libra

The year begins with Mercury in Capricorn, your solar fourth house, a continuation from 2013. On the 11, Mercury enters fellow air sign Aquarius, your solar fifth house. This transit should be enjoyable. Your conscious mind is focused on romance, creativity, and whatever you do for fun and enjoyment. This transit lasts until January 31, when Mercury moves into Pisces. Since this transit leads into the first Mercury retrograde of the year, we'll discuss it in next month's roundup.

Venus begins the year retrograde in Capricorn, your solar fourth house. This retro is also a continuation from 2013. Any Venus retro can cause bumps and bruises in a relationship. However, one of the more likely scenarios is that something in your home or personal environment creates physical discomfort. Maybe your heat or air conditioning (depending on where you live!) goes out. Or your hot water heater quits. Venus moves direct on January 31 and heads toward its appointment with Aquarius on March 5. We'll talk more about that in the February roundup.

Mars starts the year in your sign. Aren't you the lucky one! This transit galvanizes you, acts as your booster rocket. You have more physical energy, may not need as much sleep, and are able to accomplish more than usual. Your social life probably picks up too, with people getting in touch left and right and inviting you here and there.

Jupiter starts off the year retro in Cancer, your career area. Professional matters move more slowly, but you now have a chance to appraise what you're doing professionally and whether it suits your temperament. The retro period lasts until March 6.

Saturn begins the year in direct motion in your financial area. This transit should be helping you to stick to a budget, perhaps because your income has been curtailed in some way. Or it may be enabling you to establish a firm foundation for your finances. It turns retro on March 2.

Uranus begins the year in direct motion in Aries, your opposite sign. Neptune begins the year in direct motion in Pisces, and Pluto is also moving direct, in Capricorn. For information on how these transits may impact your life, reread The Big Picture section for your sign.

IMPORTANT DATES

January 1: The new moon in Capricorn falls in your solar fourth house. This new moon is a great way to start the new year and should usher in new opportunities in your domestic area. You might sell your home and move, for instance. You could find the perfect roommate. Or perhaps you start refurbishing your home.

January 15: The full moon in Cancer occurs in your career area. This one illuminates something in your profession that may have been hidden from your view. Since Jupiter forms a wide conjunction to this full moon, the news is positive and expands your professional venues in some way.

January 30: The new moon in Aquarius occurs in your solar fifth house. This one ushers in a new romance or opportunity to express yourself creatively or could result in a pregnancy.

February—Libra

Okay, let's discuss this Mercury retro, the first of the year. It occurs in Pisces, your solar sixth house, from February 6 to 28. Since it turns retro in the early degrees of Pisces, Mercury slides back into Aquarius on February 12 and then turns direct in that sign on the 28. The impact?

While Mercury is retrograde in Pisces, things in your daily work routine may not go as smoothly as you like. Be sure to communicate clearly with employees and co-workers, so there's no misunderstanding about what you want or expect. Back up all computers. While Mercury is retro in Aquarius, you may be going over old issues in a romantic relationship and could be revising a creative endeavor. Just remember: this too shall pass!

For the entire month of February Venus transits Capricorn, your domestic area. This should be a pleasant transit for your home life. Since Venus is in Capricorn, there may be a career bonus to the transit as well. Possibilities? You and your sweetheart tie the knot, find the perfect home, or perhaps move. You land a nice bonus at work, get a raise, or find the support you need for a creative endeavor.

Mars continues its transit through your sign in direct motion, so you've got the entire month to keep pushing forward, accomplishing whatever is on your agenda. The risk is that you take on too much and don't have enough time for yourself to recharge your batteries. It's important to maintain your exercise routine, make sure you eat well, and get enough sleep.

IMPORTANT DATES
February 14: The full moon in Leo on Valentine's Day should be a perfect recipe for enjoying the one you love. If you aren't involved, you celebrate with your friends and any groups to which you belong. Mars in your sign forms an exact, beneficial angle to this full moon, so don't be surprised if events take you by storm!

February 28: Mercury turns direct in Aquarius.

March—Libra

It's a hectic month astrologically, so be sure to get enough sleep, carve out time for yourself, and pace yourself.

On February 28 Mercury turned direct in Aquarius, your solar fifth house. That's cause for celebration. You and your romantic partner now communicate well and can agree on just about everything. Whatever you do for fun and enjoyment should unfold with greater ease now.

On March 17 Mercury enters Pisces once again, so some of the same patterns you experienced between January 31 and February 6 may be repeated. Your daily work routine takes center focus. This transit ends on April 7.

Between March 5 and April 5 you enjoy one of the most romantic and creative times all year: Venus transits Aquarius, your solar fifth house. During this month-long period your muse whispers in your ear 24/7, urging you to dive into your creative endeavors. Your romantic partner is attentive, and everything you do for pleasure unfolds smoothly. The other period like this occurs when Venus transits your sign between September 29 and October 23. Circle those dates!

On March 1 Mars finally turns direct in your sign, and oh wow, you are moving forward with excitement, energy, and enthusiasm. Your booster rocket is pushing you in new, unprecedented directions. Mars in your sign makes things happen. This transit lasts until May 19.

On March 6 Jupiter turns direct in Cancer, your career area, a huge bonus for your professional life. Expect expansion to occur rapidly in unexpected ways.

IMPORTANT DATES

In addition to three lunations, there are some other noteworthy dates. Let's take a closer look:

March 1: The new moon in Pisces receives an exact, beneficial angle from expansive Jupiter, so this new moon should be exceptionally good for you and your daily work and health. Neptune is conjunct this new moon, which suggests your spirituality and ideals may be integral to the new opportunities that surface. The new opportunities should surface with creative endeavors, in your daily work, and with your intuition.

March 2: Saturn turns retrograde in Saturn, your financial area. Ouch. Okay, it's not great, but it's not awful either. You may be rethinking your financial strategies, budget, and ability to earn. The retro lasts until July 20.

March 16: The full moon in Virgo occurs in your solar twelfth house and illuminates something in your life that has been hidden. Saturn forms a beneficial angle to this full moon, suggesting that whatever you discover, whatever news you hear, helps to provide a stronger structure in your finances.

March 30: The new moon in Aries occurs in your partnership area. Very nice, Libra. You and your partner enter new realms in your relationship. Perhaps you commit more deeply to the relationship by getting engaged, moving in together, or getting married.

April—Libra

This month is somewhat calmer astrologically than March. Between April 7 and 23 Mercury transits Aries, your opposite sign. During this period you can expect discussions with business and romantic partners. You may be redefining expectations, goals, and strategies. Your conscious mind will be edgy, seeking new venues for self-expression.

From April 23 to May 7 Mercury transits Gemini, a fellow air sign, your solar ninth house. This transit could take you overseas or attract individuals in higher education or publishing. Or you may be taking a workshop in intuitive development to explore your spiritual beliefs.

Your ruler, Venus, moves through water sign Pisces between April 5 and May 5, highlighting your daily work routine and schedule and the way you maintain your health. You may go for a whole new work look—new clothes, new hairstyle, a new you. Or you may experiment with a different nutritional program or try alternative treatments for an ailment.

For all of April you're enjoying Mars in your sign, Libra. Take advantage of it. Stick to your exercise routine, tackle challenging projects at home and at work, and take advantage of social networking, something at which you probably excel.

Circle April 14. Pluto turns retro in Capricorn that day, in your solar fourth house. This movement, which lasts until September 22, may cause delays in home projects, or things may not be moving along as quickly as you would like.

IMPORTANT DATES

April 15: A lunar eclipse in your sign brings good news and may do so rather suddenly. You gain insight into a personal issue. Mars forms a wide conjunction to the eclipse degree, so you've still got all this great physical energy in your court. Make use of it!

April 29: The solar eclipse in Taurus ushers in new opportunities in resources you share with others. You obtain the mortgage or loan you need, your spouse or partner lands a bonus or raise, or you sell a creative project. Mercury forms a close conjunction with the eclipse degree, so one of the opportunities could be related to writing and communication.

May—Libra

May is a surprisingly busy month astrologically, so there may be times that you feel especially frazzled or overwhelmed. Just breathe through it, and be sure to leave time for yourself.

Between May 7 and 29 Mercury moves through Gemini, your solar ninth house. This transit should be plenty of fun, with lively discussions, even some travel. If you travel, it could be abroad, or perhaps you're planning a trip abroad. Either way, the planning and the travel itself are equally enjoyable for you.

From May 29 to June 7 Mercury is moving direct in Cancer. We're going to discuss this transit in June's roundup, as the transit leads into the next Mercury retro.

Your ruler, Venus, starts the month in Pisces, a continuation of a transit that began in April. Then on May 2 it enters Aries, your opposite sign, and things with your partner heat up. Romance, high passions, risks, and dares: sounds like a romantic adventure. You two may decide to deepen your commitment to each other. The transit lasts until May 28.

Between May 28 and June 23 Venus moves through Taurus, another sign it rules, so the planet is quite happy here. We'll talk about this transit in the June roundup.

Finally on May 19 Mars turns direct in your sign, and it will be moving toward its appointment with Scorpio on July 25. Until then you enjoy another period when your physical energy is excellent, and you can accomplish more than usual.

IMPORTANT DATES

May 14: The full moon in Scorpio falls in your financial area. Something about your finances is illuminated, or there's news about your money situation. Saturn forms a close conjunction to this full moon, so the news may be sobering, or it may provide a structure to your finances. Pluto forms a wide and beneficial angle to this full moon, suggesting that you're in the power seat.

May 28: The new moon in Gemini falls in your solar ninth house, and what a good one this will be! It ushers in new opportunities in travel, higher education, publishing, and communication.

May 29: Mercury enters Cancer. Since it leads into a Mercury retrograde next month, we'll discuss it in the June roundup.

June—Libra

The second Mercury retrograde occurs this month. Mercury entered Cancer on May 29, your professional sector. Until June 7 you're on a fast track in promoting your agenda. Engage in discussions with bosses, coworkers, employees. On June 7 Mercury turns retrograde in Cancer, your career area. Because it turns retro in the early degrees of Cancer, Mercury slides back into Gemini on June 17 and turns direct in that sign on July 1. Follow the three Rs during this period: revise, review, rethink. Reread the section on Mercury retros in The Big Picture section for your sign.

Your ruler, Venus, spends the first three weeks of the month in Taurus, your solar eighth house, a continuation of last month's transit. For the first week of this transit Venus should facilitate obtaining a loan or mortgage. However, once Mercury turns retro, Venus loses some of her punch in this area. Best to wait until after July 1. Between June 23 and July 18 Venus moves through fellow air sign Gemini, your solar ninth house. This transit stimulates the possibility of foreign travel and/or dealings with foreigners. You may also take a seminar, sign up for college or graduate school classes, or submit a manuscript for publication. All forms of communication are highlighted.

Mars remains in your sign for the entire month of June and doesn't hit Scorpio until July 25. Lucky you! This gives you another seven weeks or so to get things done. Mars is your booster rocket, remember? It makes stuff happen.

IMPORTANT DATES

June 13: The full moon in compatible fire sign Sagittarius highlights that area of your chart dealing with communication, travel, siblings, and your neighborhood. Any news that comes your way should be positive and unexpected.

June 27: The new moon in Cancer occurs in your solar tenth house. This moon should usher in new career opportunities—a raise, a promotion, a new career path altogether.

July—Libra

Mercury turns direct in Gemini on July 1. Time to celebrate! Pack your bags, get out of town for a few days, send out résumés and job applications—move forward again with all your endeavors. On July 12 Mercury enters Cancer, your career area, again and will be there until July 31. During this period you're able to garner the support you need for all your professional endeavors and can sell just about anything to anyone. Your conscious mind is more intuitive, and if you heed that inner voice, you won't go wrong.

Between July 31 and August 15 Mercury transits fire sign Leo. We'll talk about that transit in the August roundup.

Between July 18 and August 12 Venus transits Cancer, your solar tenth house. This one is great for professional accomplishments. Peers, bosses, and employees are open and receptive to your ideas and endeavors; things flow your way. A flirtation could start up at work or with someone you meet through work.

Between July 25 and September 13 Mars transits Scorpio, a sign it corules, your financial area. During this period you may be working harder to make ends meet, your hard works pays off, or you're working to finish something by a certain deadline. You may be shuffling around the financial priorities in your life.

IMPORTANT DATES

July 12: The full moon in Capricorn lights up your domestic area. Something comes to light in this area, or there's news that is powerfully transformative. Pluto forms a close conjunction to this full moon, and Saturn forms a beneficial angle to it, so any news you hear helps to stabilize something in your domestic environment.

July 16: Jupiter enters fire sign Leo and will be there until August 11, 2015. This transit forms a beneficial angle to your sun and should bring an element of luck and opportunity with it. You gain now through friends, group activities, publishing, or higher education. Foreign travel is a distinct possibility too.

July 20: Saturn turns direct in Scorpio. Major plus. Any delays you've been dealing with in finances should now straighten out.

July 21: Uranus turns retrograde in Aries, your solar seventh house. This movement can prompt you to become compulsive, or you may find certain partnership issues repeating themselves.

July 26: The new moon in compatible fire sign Leo should be great for you. It ushers in new opportunities for creative endeavors and in friendships and group activities. Jupiter forms a close conjunction, suggesting expansion and luck in all these areas.

August—Libra

Mercury entered Leo on July 31 and will be there until August 15. During this transit your social life should pick up significantly. You may join a group whose ideals or activities interest you, or you could team up with a friend for some sort of creative endeavor. Mercury forms a beneficial angle to your sun now, so you're in your element, Libra.

Between August 15 and September 2 Mercury moves through Virgo, your solar twelfth house. You may seek more privacy now. Dreams and meditative states may hold vital information and insights. If you're so inclined, therapy could be helpful. If you don't already meditate, then by all means start a meditation practice during this transit.

Venus transits Leo, your solar eleventh house, from August 12 to September 2. During this period your social life really takes off. Everyone seeks you out, Libra. Your inbox fills up with invitations to social functions; your Facebook friends increase. Romance could be sparked with a friend or someone you meet through friends. Your muse is shadowing you.

For all of August Mars continues its journey through Scorpio, your financial area. Your research and investigative skills are well honed during this transit. You're after the absolute bottom line.

IMPORTANT DATES

August 10: The full moon in fellow air sign Aquarius lights up the romance and creativity area of your chart. Any news you hear will be totally unexpected and sudden and should be quite positive. You and a romantic partner may discuss your respective visions and hopes for the relationship.

August 25: The new moon in Virgo occurs in your solar twelfth house. It ushers in new opportunities to work behind the scenes in some capacity. You have a chance to explore your own unconscious, perhaps through dream work or hypnosis.

September—Libra

It's a busy month in the zodiac. Mercury occupies three signs, Venus occupies three signs, Mars changes signs, and Pluto turns direct. In other words, Libra, buckle up for a wild, unpredictable ride!

September 1 marks the end of Mercury's transit through Virgo, your solar twelfth house. Between September 2 and 27 Mercury moves through your sign. This transit should be very much to your liking. Your mind hums along totally in synch with your desires and aspirations. You're in a very social and artistic mood too, so indulge your creative side.

On September 27 Mercury enters Scorpio, but this leads into the final Mercury retro of 2014, so we'll discuss it under the October roundup.

Venus spends the first four days of September in Leo, then it enters Virgo, where it will be until September 29. It's easier during this period to access your own unconscious through dream work, meditation, even conventional therapy. If a romance begins during this transit, it's probably occurring in secret, and that will continue until Venus enters your sign, Libra. Then you'll be announcing the relationship to the rest of the world.

From September 29 to October 23 Venus transits your sign. This is one of the best transits for you all year, so we'll discuss it under October's roundup.

Between September 13 and October 26 Mars moves through Sagittarius, your solar third house. This transit should be a good one for you. It boosts your communication skills, and you may be traveling more than usual. You could have contact with educators, attorneys, and people in publishing. Mars is always your booster rocket, the planet that makes stuff happen.

On September 22 Pluto turns direct in Capricorn, your solar fourth house. Any home-improvement projects that have been delayed should now move forward again. In fact with Pluto moving direct, your domestic situation generally should be more comfortable.

IMPORTANT DATES
September 8: The full moon in Pisces occurs in your solar sixth house. Expect news related to your daily work routine and/or your health or a creative endeavor. Pluto forms a beneficial angle to this full moon, so you're in the power seat, a very nice place to be.

September 24: A new moon in your sign is something to plan for and anticipate. Make a list of what you would like to achieve or experience in the next twelve months. Be realistic, but creative! Then step back and let the universe answer your desires. New opportunities surface quickly, so be prepared to seize them.

October—Libra

This month is busy astrologically, so be sure you get enough rest and pace yourself in all your activities.

On October 4 Mercury turns retro in Scorpio. On the

10 it slides back into Libra and turns direct in your sign on October 25, then moves toward its appointment with Scorpio again on November 8. So two areas of your chart are impacted—your finances and then your personal life. By now you know the drill on these retrograde periods—revise, review, rethink. Be sure to check and recheck bank accounts. Old lovers/spouses and friends may surface.

Your ruler, Venus, is in your sign for the first twenty-two days of the month, a major bonus. This period is one of the most romantic and creative times for you all year. Your muse shadows you, your love life soars, and life in general, despite Mercury's trickery, is quite satisfying. It would be better of course if Mercury weren't retro during this transit, but even so, put the time to good use.

Between October 23 and November 16 Venus transits Scorpio, your financial area. You may have more expenses, but you also have more income coming in. Try to pay cash for big-purchase items. Stick to your budget. On the other hand, don't deny yourself something that you truly want.

Until the 26 Mars continues its transit of Sagittarius, then it moves through Capricorn from October 26 to December 4. During this period stuff is happening in your domestic environment—a lot of people coming and going, a plethora of activity. Perhaps you're refurbishing your place or adding an addition to your home. This period should be quite productive regardless of the specifics.

IMPORTANT DATES
October 8: A lunar eclipse in Aries, your opposite sign, brings news or insights into a partnership—business or

romantic. Thanks to a close conjunction from Uranus, this eclipse and the several days on either side of it are likely to be extremely busy and active. You may feel a little nuts too, so try to go with the flow.

October 23: A solar eclipse in Scorpio ushers in new financial opportunities. They could come through research, investigative work, or even intuitive development. Mercury is exactly conjunct the eclipse degree, suggesting that one possible opportunity could involve communication.

November—Libra

With Mercury now moving in direct motion again, it remains in your sign until November 8, so you may experience a repeat of some of the same wonderful patterns that occurred between September 2 and 27.

While Mercury transits Scorpio from November 8 to 27, your conscious attention is quite focused on finances. You may be taking a closer look at your budget or entrepreneurial ways to increase your income and could be using your communication skills in some way to earn additional money. It's likely that you're doing research into a variety of methods for earning more.

Venus moves through Sagittarius, your solar third house, between November 16 and December 10. If you're planning to move, this transit could help you to find the right neighborhood for yourself and your family. You may be hanging out with siblings and neighbors more often than you usually do. If you're not in a relationship right now, this transit may bring a romance with someone who lives in your neighborhood or whom you meet through siblings.

Mars spends the entire month of November in Capricorn, your domestic area. This transit promises a continuation of what began late last month in terms of home projects. However, because Capricorn is involved, there are career considerations too. Maybe you're setting up a home office.

On November 15 Neptune turns direct in Pisces, your solar sixth house. Now your imagination is moving in the right direction, and you're able to successfully integrate your spirituality into your daily work life.

IMPORTANT DATES
November 6: The full moon in Taurus sheds light on a partner's income or brings news about a mortgage or loan for which you've applied. Pluto forms a beneficial angle to this full moon, so it looks as if the news is powerful.

November 22: The new moon in compatible fire sign Sagittarius ushers in new opportunities regarding your neighborhood, a move, travel, or your relationships with siblings and neighbors.

December—Libra

For the first two weeks or so of December Mercury continues its movement through Sagittarius, your solar third house. Then between December 16 and January 5 it transits Capricorn, your solar fourth house. This transit is actually where Mercury began the year, so there's a sense of things coming full circle. While Mercury is in this sign your home is a hub of activity and lively discussions. You might consider a new year's celebration at your place.

Between December 10 and January 4 Venus moves through Capricorn, your solar fourth house. For a time then it travels with Mercury, and this duo ushers in 2015. The combination of the two planets suggests that your creative ventures go well and you and your partner are able to discuss your relationship clearly and realistically.

Mars enters fellow air sign Aquarius, your solar fifth house, on December 4 and remains there until January 12, 2015. This transit suggests that you are actively seeking romance and involved in creative endeavors. A lot of your energy goes into these pursuits. You're also focused on what you do for fun and enjoyment, certainly a good thing for the holidays!

On December 8 Jupiter turns retro in Leo, which lasts until April 8, 2015. This movement prompts delays in social plans, but nothing that's insurmountable.

Uranus turns direct in Aries on December 21. Now *that* is something to celebrate with your partner. Forward movement is guaranteed in all your partnerships.

IMPORTANT DATES

December 6: The full moon in Gemini should be very much to your liking. It illuminates or brings news about your worldview, publishing endeavors, or communication projects. You may also hear news about an upcoming trip abroad you're taking.

December 21: The new moon in Capricorn, your solar fourth house, ushers in new opportunities in your domestic situation. Someone moves in or out; you move or put your home on the market; one of your parents has an opportunity to improve his or her life. With Mercury widely conjunct, one of the opportunities may involve a writing or communication project.

December 23: Saturn enters Sagittarius, where it will be for the next two and a half years. This transit should be good for you. It stabilizes your daily life.

HAPPY NEW YEAR!

9

Scorpio

The Big Picture in 2014

Welcome to 2014, Scorpio! It's a 6 year for you. This suggests a year in which diplomacy takes you farther than confrontation, when you should strive to make others happy. It could also indicate that a change of some kind is needed at home. Travel is favorable this year too.

Now that you've the tumult of 2012 and the realignment of 2013 behind you, you're ready to embark on yet another journey. So let's look at how specific areas of your life may be impacted and which dates will be of vital importance to you.

ROMANCE/CREATIVITY

One of the most romantic and creative times for you all year occurs between October 23 and November 16, when Venus transits your sign. During this period your muse is at your beck and call 24/7, and your creative drive is powerful, a magnet that draws the people you need when you need them. New ideas come easily, so be sure to have a recorder or pen and paper handy regardless of where you are. You feel more self-confident during this transit. Others pick up on it and are attracted to you, your ideas, persona, and creative projects. So if you have these ready, start submitting and exhibiting them, doing whatever you need to do in order to advertise them.

Your sexuality is heightened during this transit and so is your need for love and romance. If you're involved in a relationship already, your relationship with your partner simply improves. You appreciate the qualities that brought you together to begin with.

If a relationship begins during this period, it's likely to begin in a social atmosphere. You might be at a party, an art exhibit, traveling. This stranger catches your eye; something clicks before you even speak to each other. Or you could meet this person through Facebook or Twitter or some other social media site. Perhaps you and this individual work in the same profession or have careers that are allied in some way. You will have similar interests and a solid base for communication. If you're already involved in a relationship, this transit helps to define it. You and your partner may deepen your commitment to each other.

The other terrific period for romance and creativity occurs between April 5 and May 2, when Venus transits fellow water sign Pisces, your solar fifth house. This transit urges you to enjoy yourself. What a concept, right? Pisces is an imaginative, artistic sign, so it's likely that you'll become engaged in pursuits like music, photography, writing, and art. Creatively you're at the top of your game, and anything you tackle works effortlessly.

Romantically you're interested in having fun and

probably aren't in the frame of mind for anything serious. If you're involved already, you and your partner enjoy a period of near bliss!

Between January 1 and July 16 Jupiter transits fellow water sign Cancer. You feel lucky, and those feelings draw more experiences that bolster that luck. You may meet someone special through friends or a group to which you belong.

Other excellent dates:

March 1, the new moon in Pisces, your solar fifth house, brings in new romantic opportunities. A great way to greet the spring. Look for new opportunities in your creative endeavors.

July 18 to August 12, when Venus transits fellow water sign Cancer and forms a terrific angle to your sun. This transit enhances your spirituality and hunger for travel. The travel may involve a spiritual or creative quest of some kind.

CAREER

Jupiter's transits through both Cancer and Leo will help every facet of your life, even your career. The caveat with career matters, though, is that if you're doing something you love, you benefit tremendously. If you're working in a field that doesn't excite you, that has become rather humdrum and routine, then Jupiter, Mars, Venus, Mercury, and your ruler, the moon, could help you to break away and find something that is more aligned with your passions.

Between January 16, 2014, and August 11, 2015, Jupiter transits Leo, your career area. This transit may bring some unexpected and expansive professional opportunities.

Let's take a closer look at the beneficial career times:

July 31 to August 15: Mercury is moving direct in Leo, your career area. This period favors communication with bosses and peers. Pitch your ideas, and move all professional matters forward. Start a blog, put up a Web site, advertise your products/services or those of your company. Your communication skills are powerful now.

August 12 to September 5: During this period, while Venus transits your career area, you're working steadily and resolutely on a project. Coworkers and bosses are impressed with your ideas and the way you implement them. Others find you so appealing that you're the first to be tapped for team projects. Venus in Leo encourages you to strut your professional stuff. Don't be shy.

July 26: The new moon in Leo should usher in new professional opportunities. You land a new job, get the interview you've hoped for, are promoted, move into a larger office, or sell your book or novel. Jupiter forms a close, beneficial angle to this new moon, suggesting the opportunities are expansive, big.

Between September 13 and October 26 Mars in Sagittarius forms a beneficial angle to your career area. This transit suggests that foreign travel may be connected to your career.

FINANCES

Let's look at Venus transits first for beneficial dates for finances. Your solar second house, which rules money, is Sagittarius, so mark the dates between November 16 and December 10, when Venus moves through that sign. During this period you may earn extra income, get a raise, or take a second job. Your income rises, but your expenses may too. Keep track of your finances.

Another beneficial date falls on November 22, with a new moon in Sagittarius, your financial area. Venus forms a wide conjunction to this new moon, so it should be exceptionally beneficial for you financially.

MERCURY RETROGRADES

Every year Mercury—the planet of communication and travel—turns retrograde three times. During these periods it's wise not to sign contracts (unless you don't mind renegotiating when Mercury is moving direct), to check and recheck travel plans, and to communicate as succinctly as possible. Refrain from buying any large-ticket items or electronics during this time too. Often computers and appliances go on the fritz, cars act up, data is lost . . . you get the idea. Be sure to back up all files before the dates below:

February 6–28: Mercury retrograde Pisces, your solar fifth house of love and romance. It slips back into Aquarius before it turns direct, so your domestic environment is also impacted.

June 7–July 1: Mercury retrograde in Cancer, your solar ninth house. This retrograde affects overseas travel, education, publishing. Since it's in Cancer, it may also impact the people who nurture you and those whom you nurture.

October 4–25: Mercury retrograde in your sign. This one impacts your personal life.

ECLIPSES

Solar eclipses tend to trigger external events that bring about change according to the sign and house in which they fall. Lunar eclipses trigger inner, emotional events according to the sign and house in which they fall. Any eclipse marks both beginnings and endings. The solar and lunar eclipse in a pair falls in opposite signs. If you're interested in detailed information on eclipses, take a look at Celeste Teal's excellent and definitive book, *Eclipses: Predicting World Events & Personal Transformation.*

If you were born under or around the time of an eclipse, it's to your advantage to take a look at your birth chart to find out exactly where the eclipses will impact you.

Most years feature four eclipses—two solar, two lunar—with the set separated by about two weeks. Let's take a closer look.

April 15: Lunar eclipse in Libra, your solar twelfth house. Emotions surface about information you have buried, experiences you have pushed aside, and perhaps about your social circles.

April 29: Solar eclipse in Taurus, your solar seventh house. New opportunities surface with business and romantic partnerships. You and your partner may decide to get engaged or married. If you're involved already, you and your partner may have a chance to work jointly on a project.

October 8: Lunar eclipse in Aries, your solar sixth house. Uranus is closely conjunct the moon, so you can expect sudden and unexpected emotional issues related to your daily work routine and health.

October 23: Solar eclipse in your sign. Wow! No telling what magnificent opportunities may come your way.

LUCKIEST DAYS OF THE YEAR

Every year there are one or two days when Jupiter and the sun meet up, and luck, serendipity, and expansion are

the hallmarks. This year those days fall on July 25–26. Circle the dates. Do whatever you enjoy!

January—Scorpio

Mercury begins the year in Capricorn, your solar third house. This transit is a continuation of one that began at the end of 2013 and heightens your communication abilities. You may also have more contact than usual with neighbors and siblings. On January 11 Mercury enters Aquarius, where it remains until the 31. This transit brings an edginess to your conscious mind, and it's easier for you to spot future trends on which you can capitalize. You are more independent now too. On January 31 Mercury enters Pisces, the romance area of your chart. Since this leads into the first Mercury retrograde of the year, we'll discuss it in February's roundup.

Venus begins the year retrograde in Capricorn, your solar third house. This movement is also a holdover from the end of 2013. It can create difficulties in personal relationships, but these difficulties are usually minor scuffles and disagreements about silly things! More likely is that there're physical discomforts during this transit. Maybe the heat or air conditioning (depending on where you live) in your car or home goes on the fritz. Maybe the windshield wipers on your car stop working while you're driving through a thunderstorm. Venus retro prompts us to look inward at what we really want in a romantic relationship. On the 31, Venus turns direct in Capricorn and now heads toward its appointment with Aquarius on March 5.

Mars begins the year in Libra, your solar twelfth house. This transit suggests activity behind the scenes. You may be pushing against a looming deadline on a project and are in a work-intensive mode. This transit favors therapy, meditation, and dream-recall work. It's a good transit for clearing out psychic debris. You're preparing for Mars' transit of your sign.

IMPORTANT DATES
There are three lunations this month, which keeps things hopping, Scorpio. Let's take a look.

January 1: The new moon in Capricorn ushers in new opportunities in communication and travel. With Pluto and Mercury both forming close conjunctions to this new moon, your communication skills are heightened, and you're in the power seat, exactly where you like to be.

January 15: The full moon in fellow water sign Cancer illuminates your spiritual beliefs and brings news about higher education or publishing. Jupiter forms a wide conjunction to this full moon, suggesting expansion and luck.

January 30: The new moon in Aquarius ushers in new opportunities related to your home and domestic situation.

February—Scorpio

For the first six days of the month Mercury is in Pisces, your solar fifth house. This transit brings your conscious attention to romance, creativity, and everything you do for fun and pleasure. On February 6 Mercury turns retro for the first time this year, in Pisces, then slides back into

Aquarius on February 12 and turns direct again in that sign on February 28. Follow the three Rs during this retrograde: revise, review, rethink. Make your travel plans on either side of the retrograde, and if you need to travel during this period, don't be surprised if your itinerary changes unexpectedly. Go with the flow. Be sure to communicate succinctly and clearly with the people around you.

For the month of February Venus moves through Libra, your solar twelfth house. This transit suggests that a romance remains hidden and private and that you maybe doing creative work behind the scenes. Once Venus enters your sign on March 5, however, all the energy changes, and you enter once of the most romantic and creative periods for you all year.

In February your coruler, Mars, continues its retrograde transit through Libra, your solar twelfth house. While Mars is traveling with Venus, your sexuality will be heightened, and your love life should be quite exciting. You and your partner may be dealing with old issues in your relationship.

Saturn is still in your sign, Scorpio, moving direct until March 2. It's helping you to solidify existing foundations in your life. You may experience some delays, but Saturn's transit through your sign prompts you to meet your obligations and responsibilities.

IMPORTANT DATE
Since there were three lunations in January, there's only one this month. On February 14 the full moon in Leo occurs in your career area. This moon illuminates a professional concern, issue, or relationship. Expect a lot of activity.

March—Scorpio

Now that Mercury is moving direct again, it continues its movement through Aquarius, headed for its appointment with Pisces on March 17. While it's in Aquarius, your home is a hub of activity and discussions. You may be working out of your home part of the time or could be having discussions with contractors, plumbers, workmen.

Between March 17 and April 7 Mercury transits Pisces, your solar fifth house. During this period you and your romantic partner are discussing your relationship, and you may be in discussions with a partner about a creative endeavor. Your conscious mind is deeply intuitive during this transit. Listen to your hunches.

From March 5 to April 5 Venus transits Aquarius, your solar fourth house. You may feel the urge to beautify your home in some way—a new paint job, an addition to your home, new furniture. Practice Feng Shui on your home to maximize the flow of energy.

On March 1 Mars turns retro in Libra, your solar twelfth house. This period lasts until May 19 and favors anything you do behind the scenes or in privacy. It's an excellent period for working actively with your dreams, to practice meditation, or to take up yoga or some other mind/body activity.

On March 6 Jupiter turns direct in Cancer, your ninth house. Now you are about to enjoy expansion in the areas of your spirituality, foreign travel, higher education, and publishing. Read more about Jupiter's transit through Cancer in The Big Picture section for your sign.

IMPORTANT DATES

In March three lunations may leave you feeling sort of crazy, but once you get past that, you'll uncover some hidden gems. Let's take a look.

March 1 features a new moon in fellow water sign Pisces, your solar fifth house. This new moon ushers in new opportunities in romance and creativity and with kids. If you and your partner have been considering starting a family or expanding your current family, this new moon could make it happen. Another possibility is a new creative endeavor that thrills and excites you. With Jupiter forming an exact and beneficial angle to this new moon, these new opportunities expand your horizons in every way.

March 16 features a full moon in compatible earth sign Virgo, your solar eleventh house. Expect news about a friend or a group to which you belong. Saturn forms a beneficial angle to this full moon, indicating that the news you hear or the insights you gain help to stabilize and ground some area of your life.

On March 30 the new moon in fire sign Aries brings new opportunities in your daily work routine and with your health. Uranus forms a close conjunction to this new moon, so these opportunities come fast and furiously. Be prepared to seize them!

Another date to watch for this month? March 2. Saturn turns retrograde in your sign, leading to delays in your personal life.

April—Scorpio

April is a calmer month astrologically than March, and there're some pleasant transits to look forward to. For the first week of the month Mercury continues to move through Pisces, the romance and creativity sector of your chart. Be sure to take full advantage of this by discussing your ideas and endeavors with others, particularly in your profession. You and your partner should enjoy lively discussions about your relationship and may even have a meeting of the minds about where things go from here.

Between April 7 and 23 Mercury transits Aries, your solar sixth house. You now explore new areas in your daily work routine. You may alter the way you do things, could change your work schedule, or perhaps try doing something new with your daily work. Perhaps you're trying to add some excitement to what you do each day. Follow your instincts. Don't hesitate to branch out.

From April 23 to May 7 Mercury moves through Taurus, your opposite sign. This transit should make it easier to discuss things with your partners—both business and professional. You may be more stubborn now than usual but may need that stubbornness to find a resolution.

Between April 5 and May 2 you experience one of the most romantic and creative periods for you all year. Why? Venus transits Pisces, your solar fifth house, that area of your chart that rules romance, love, creativity, children, and everything you do for fun and pleasure. Indulge your creative interests; your muse is supportive. Do whatever brings you enjoyment. Love the one you're with!

Mars continues to move retrograde through Libra

until May 19. This movement slows things down but gives you a chance to review your priorities and explore your own unconscious.

On April 14 Pluto turns retro in Capricorn, your solar third house. This retrograde lasts until September 22 and simply means that in the areas of communication, travel, and relationships with siblings, things move more slowly.

IMPORTANT DATES
April 5: The lunar eclipse in Libra occurs in your solar twelfth house. Your inner world, your emotions, are galvanized by a wide conjunction with retrograde Mars. You may discover something within that demands action.

April 29: The solar eclipse in Taurus ushers in new opportunities with partnerships.

May—Scorpio

It's another busy month in the zodiac. Both Mercury and Venus occupy three signs apiece, so your head is sure to be spinning.

For the first week of the month Mercury continues its journey through Taurus, your opposite sign. Then between May 7 and 29 it transits Gemini. On May 29 it enters Cancer, where it turns retrograde on June 7. We'll talk about that transit in next month's roundup, so let's focus on Mercury's transit through Gemini, your solar eighth house.

During this period your conscious focus is on resources you share with others. You may be thinking about or applying for a mortgage or loan or could be refinancing your present mortgage. There's also a strong communication component with this transit and a psychic quality because it's the eighth house. Things that go bump in the night, anyone?

Venus spends just one day in Pisces, the tail end of its journey through your romance and creativity area. Then between May 2 and 28 it transits Aries, that area of your chart that rules your daily work routine and the maintenance of your daily health. During this period work matters and relationships flow your way. An office flirtation could turn into something more, and you may be socializing more frequently with coworkers and employees.

Between May 28 and June 23 Venus transits Taurus, your opposite sign. This transit favors an intimate partnership and business partnerships too. If you're involved, then you and your partner may deepen your commitment to each other. You might get married, move in together, decide to start a family.

On May 19 Mars turns direct in Libra, and until July 25 it continues its transit through that sign. This transit activates your solar twelfth house, the most private part of your chart. You may be working behind the scenes in some capacity or could be involved in dream work or therapy. Paradoxically there's a social component to this transit because Libra is involved.

IMPORTANT DATES

May 14: The full moon in your sign highlights something in your personal life or brings news that helps to stabilize and ground your life. Jupiter forms a strong, beneficial angle to this full moon, indicating that any news you hear or insights you gain expand your world in a significant way.

May 28: The new moon in Gemini should usher in new opportunities in communication in things like mortgages, insurance, and taxes, and also metaphysical areas.

June—Scorpio

For the first six days of June Mercury's transit through Cancer ignites your itch to hit the open road, to hop a plane for some exotic destination, or to just get out and about. You may delve more deeply into your spiritual beliefs or be getting ready for college or grad school. Then Mercury turns retrograde on the 7, and forward motion screeches to a halt. Mercury slips back into Gemini on June 17 and turns direct in that sign on July 1. This means that two areas of your life are impacted. As usual, follow the three Rs—revise, review, rethink—and stick to projects that are already underway rather than starting anything new.

Venus continues its transit through Taurus, your partnership area, until June 23, when it enters Gemini. During this transit, which lasts until July 28, you may be writing about and exploring the mysterious aspects of life—ghosts, past lives, communication with the dead, mythological creatures . . . you get the idea! Your conscious mind is particularly lively during this transit. Be sure to keep a pen and paper or your iPad handy at all times for jotting down ideas.

For the entire month of June Mars continues its journey in direct motion through Libra, your solar twelfth house. It's time to clear the decks, Scorpio—tie up loose ends and get rid of beliefs that no longer serve your best interests. You're preparing for Mars' transit of your sign.

On June 9 Neptune turns retrograde in Pisces, your solar fifth house. This movement allows you time to assess what you want in a romantic relationship and what you should strive for in your creative endeavors. Neptune turns direct again on November 15.

IMPORTANT DATES
June 13: The full moon in Sagittarius occurs in your solar second house and illuminates something to do with your finances. Uranus forms a wide, beneficial angle to this full moon, so insights or news you hear about your finances, publishing, higher education, and foreign travel will be sudden and unexpected.

June 27: A new moon in Cancer should attract new opportunities in foreign travel and, because it's in Cancer, your domestic environment. Neptune forms a close, beneficial angle to this new moon, suggesting a spiritual or imaginative component to the new opportunities.

July—Scorpio

The best news this month? Mercury turns direct in Gemini on July 1. So pack your bags and take off for parts unknown; send out your résumés; tackle new creative endeavors. Life is now moving forward again. On July 12 Mercury enters Cancer again, and until July 31 you enjoy some of the same energy you did between May 29 and

June 7. It's in your romance and creativity area, so make good use of it, Scorpio! Talk, discuss, brainstorm.

Until July 18 Venus continues its journey through Gemini, your solar eighth house. Refer to June's roundup about this transit. Between July 18 and August 12 and 31 Venus moves through Cancer, your solar fifth house. This period is one of the most creative and romantic for you all year. Your creative adrenaline is pumping hard and fast, and your muse shadows you 24/7. If you're not involved in a romantic relationship when this transit begins, you probably will be by the time it ends.

Your coruler, Mars, enters your sign on July 25 and remains there until September 13. During this period your life really picks up speed and momentum. Mars is your booster rocket and enables you to get things done quickly, efficiently, thoroughly. Mars is the planet that makes stuff happen, so take full advantage of this transit to tackle difficult or challenging issues and endeavors.

IMPORTANT DATES

July 16: Jupiter enters fire sign Leo, your career area, where it will be until August 11, 2015. During this magnificent period your professional life expands, and new career opportunities surface. You're in the right place at the right time.

July 12: The full moon in compatible earth sign Capricorn occurs in your solar third house. This one lights up your communication and travel area. News you hear could relate to your neighborhood, siblings, and neighbors.

July 20: Saturn turns direct in your sign. Go celebrate!

July 26: The new moon in Leo ushers in new career opportunities. With Jupiter closely conjunct to this new moon, these opportunities will expand your professional life in significant ways.

July 31: Mercury enters Leo, your career area.

August—Scorpio

The month begins with Mercury in Leo, your professional area. This transit, which lasts until August 15, is excellent for professional communication. If you're sending out résumés, be sure your résumé shines. Don't hesitate to toot your own horn, Scorpio! Communicate with employees, bosses, and coworkers in a succinct, clear way. Focus on your own work and gathering support for your endeavors.

Between August 15 and September 2 Mercury moves through compatible earth sign Virgo, your solar eleventh house. This transit should activate your social life and attract opportunities that enable you to work toward achieving your wishes and dreams. You pay particularly close attention to details.

For the first twelve days of the month Venus is in Leo, facilitating all your professional concerns, relationships, and endeavors. Things unfold so smoothly that you may be tempted to sit back and chill. Resist that urge and make every moment count. Show off your talents and skills. Romance with a coworker, peer, or boss is possible. If you're already in a relationship, perhaps you and your partner team up for a project.

Between August 12 and September 5 Venus moves through earth sign Virgo, your solar eleventh house. For part of this transit, then, Venus and Mercury will be traveling together, a great recipe for your social life. You'll be hanging out more with friends and could meet someone special through them. Life is generally quite pleasing.

For the month of August Mars continues its journey through your sign. With the support of Mercury and Venus, you should be able to achieve just about anything. So move full steam ahead, Scorpio. You're primed for success in all areas of your life.

IMPORTANT DATES
August 10: The full moon in Aquarius occurs in your solar fourth house. This moon shines a light on your domestic environment. Some issue or concern surfaces fully so that you can resolve it.

August 25: The new moon in Virgo falls in your solar eleventh house. This new moon brings opportunities for new friendships and social activities. Think as far outside the box as possible.

September—Scorpio

As you enter the last quarter of the year, it would be to your advantage to take stock of where you've been so far and where you are headed for the rest of the year. Are you achieving your goals? The period from September 2 to 27, while Mercury is in Libra, your solar twelfth house, is an excellent time for this kind of introspection. You have greater access to your own unconscious, dreams, stuff you have buried in your psyche. Friends may prove helpful.

On September 27 Mercury enters your sign. It turns

retrograde there on October 4, so we'll discuss this transit in more depth in October's roundup.

From September 5 to 29 Venus moves through Virgo, your solar eleventh house. This lovely transit spiffs up your social life, others are eager to spend time with you, and you could meet someone special through friends. You may be fussier about your romantic interests but are honing your desires about what you seek in a partner.

From September 29 to October 23 Venus journeys through Libra. We'll discuss this in October's roundup.

On September 13 Mars enters Sagittarius, your financial area. During this period you may be fired up about a new way to earn additional income, could be branching out on your own in some capacity, and have a firmer grasp on the larger picture concerning your finances.

Pluto turns direct in Capricorn on September 22, a change that will help you out considerably when Mars moves through Capricorn between October 26 and December 4. More on that in next month's roundup.

IMPORTANT DATES
September 8: The full moon in Pisces occurs in the romance and creativity section of your chart. Something in those areas is illuminated, or you hear news. Pluto forms a beneficial angle to this full moon, so any news you hear should be transformative!

September 24: The new moon in Libra occurs in your solar twelfth house. Get ready for a new opportunity to work behind the scenes in some capacity, perhaps on an artistic endeavor. This new moon should also usher in new friendships and group associations.

October—Scorpio

All right, it's a busy month that includes two eclipses and the last Mercury retro of 2014. On September 27 Mercury entered your sign, and until October 4 you enjoy a pleasant week in which you are in complete synch. Your mind is sharp, your research skills are impeccable, and your intuition is greatly heightened.

Then between October 4 and 10 Mercury is retrograding in your sign, slides back into Libra, and turns direct in that sign on October 25. While retro in Scorpio, you may be revisiting old issues in your personal life, and something you researched or investigated in the past may resurface. While Mercury is retrograding through Libra, friends or former partners you haven't seen in months or years may resurface. You may be revisiting power issues that you thought were resolved. Stick to the three Rs: revise, review, rethink.

Until October 23 Venus continues its transit of Libra, your solar twelfth house. For part of this transit Venus travels with Mercury retro, so it's possible that you'll be revisiting romance and creativity issues and concerns. If you're involved in a relationship, you and your partner are apt to be spending a lot of time alone together.

From October 23 to November 16 Venus transits your sign, and what fun this will be! This period is one of two this year when your love life and creativity hum along at a perfect pitch. Other people find you attractive and seek out your company. You exude sex appeal. Your sexuality is heightened; you're a seductive and magnetic presence.

Your coruler, Mars, continues its journey through

Sagittarius, your financial area, until October 26, when it enters Capricorn. This transit lasts until December 4 and galvanizes your communication skills. It may prompt you to look for a neighborhood that suits you and/or your family. You could be putting your place on the market once you find the perfect neighborhood.

This transit should also help you to accomplish more professionally. You're incredibly motivated now. Nothing stands in your way.

IMPORTANT DATES

October 8: The lunar eclipse in Aries brings sudden, unexpected news concerning your daily work that may cause you some concern. Pluto forms a challenging angle to the eclipse degree, so power plays may be involved.

October 23: The solar eclipse in your sign should be spectacular! Venus is exactly conjunct, and Neptune forms a beautiful angle to the eclipse degree. This combination should usher in new opportunities in romance, creative endeavors, and finances.

October 25: Mercury turns direct in Libra.

November—Scorpio

With Mercury now moving direct again in Libra, it's headed toward its appointment with your sign on November 8. Between November 8 and 16 Mercury and Venus are traveling together in your sign, a great combination for romance, communication, research, and investigation. Mercury remains in your sign until November 27, and Venus remains there until November 16.

When Mercury and Venus travel together in your sign, you and your significant other should be getting along famously, communicating honestly and openly about your relationship.

Between November 27 and December 16 Mercury moves through Sagittarius, your solar second house. This transit brings your conscious focus to finances—what you earn and spend, how or if you budget. You may be looking for a part-time job to pay for holiday gift-buying or could ask for a raise at work—and get it!

Between November 16 and December 10 Venus moves through Sagittarius, your financial area. You may be spending more, but your income could increase too. In the romance department, you could meet someone whose values and priorities differ from yours but complement them.

On October 26 Mars entered Capricorn, your solar third house, and it remains there until December 4. This transit galvanizes your professional ambition and urges you to move forward with all your career endeavors. It sharpens your communication skills too.

Neptune turns direct in Pisces on November 15, which should benefit your love life and creative endeavors. You now are able to integrate your spirituality and imagination into all areas of your life.

IMPORTANT DATES

November 6: The full moon in Taurus, your opposite sign, sheds light on a partnership—romantic or business. Pluto forms a beneficial angle to this full moon, suggesting that if power plays enter the picture, you're able to hold your ground.

November 22: A new moon in Sagittarius could usher in new financial opportunities. You might sell a novel, book, even a screenplay. Communication somehow fits into whatever unfolds.

December—Scorpio

As you enter the final month of the year, take a few moments to look back and then forward to 2015. Where would you like to be in your life at this time next year? It's not too early to come up with your new year's resolutions!

Until December 16 Mercury remains in Sagittarius, your financial area, so your conscious focus is on money. When you're out and about, buying gifts for the holidays, be sure to pay cash so that you don't go into credit card shock when the bills come due in January! Between December 16 and January 5, 2015, Mercury transits compatible earth sign Capricorn and travels with powerful Pluto, your ruler. This transit favors travel and communication. You may have more contact than usual with neighbors, siblings, and other relatives.

From December 10 to January 4, 2015, Venus transits Capricorn too and hooks up with Pluto and then Mercury. This powerful trio packs a wallop. If you're job hunting, polish up your résumé and send it off. If you're launching your own business, set up your Web site, create your business cards and flyers, and get moving! The stars are on your side.

Between December 4 and January 12 Mars moves through Aquarius, your solar fourth house. This transit promises an active holiday, with your home as the hub of parties and celebrations.

Jupiter turns retro on December 8 in Leo, your career area, and goes direct again on April 8, 2015. During this period things in your career may feel sluggish, but you'll have an opportunity to review your career and professional goals. Every retrograde serves a purpose.

Uranus turns direct in Aries on December 21, certainly a cause for celebration! Now you can clean off your desk, tie up loose ends at work, and sail into the new year with everything in order.

IMPORTANT DATES

December 6: The full moon in Gemini shines a light on resources you share with others. Your partner's income, for instance, comes under scrutiny for some reason. Or perhaps your partner lands a raise! Or is paid a hefty bonus. If there's news, it comes out of the blue.

December 21: The new moon in Capricorn is a beautiful way to get started with the new year. This one ushers in new opportunities for travel and communication. Mercury forms a wide conjunction to this new moon, indicating that writing/communication plays a major role in whatever surfaces.

HAPPY NEW YEAR!

10

Sagittarius

The Big Picture in 2014

Welcome to 2014, Sagittarius. It's a 7 year for you. This
suggests a year in which you explore the unknown, journey into your own unconscious, and are involved in research and investigation. As a Sadge, you'll be doing
your share of actual physical traveling as well.

Now that you've the tumult of 2012 and the realignment of 2013 behind you, you're ready to embark on yet
another journey. So let's look at how specific areas of
your life may be impacted and which dates will be of
vital importance to you.

ROMANCE/CREATIVITY
One of the most romantic and creative times for you all
year occurs between November 16 and December 10,
when Venus transits your sign. During this period your
muse is at your beck and call 24/7, and your creative
drive is powerful, a magnet that draws the people you
need when you need them. New ideas come easily, so be
sure to have a recorder or pen and paper handy regard-

less of where you are. You feel more self-confident during this transit. Others pick up on it and are attracted to you, your ideas, persona, and creative projects. So if you have these ready, start submitting and exhibiting them, doing whatever you need to do in order to advertise them.

You're in a romantic mood during this transit, and that's true whether you're involved or not. If you're already in a relationship, things between you and your partner should be quite pleasurable, fun, and loving. If you're not involved when the transit begins, you probably will be before the transit ends.

If a relationship begins during this period, it's likely to begin in a social atmosphere. You might be at a party, an art exhibit, traveling. This stranger catches your eye; something clicks before you even speak to each other. Or you could meet this person through Facebook or Twitter or some other social media site. Perhaps you and this individual work in the same profession or have careers that are allied in some way. You will have similar interests and a solid base for communication. If you're already involved in a relationship, this transit helps to define it. You and your partner may deepen your commitment to each other.

The other terrific period for romance and creativity occurs between May 2 and 28, when Venus transits fellow fire sign Aries, your solar fifth house. This transit urges you to enjoy yourself. What a concept, right? Aries is something of a thrill-seeker and very definitely takes risks. So you may be taking emotional/romantic risks during this period. You dive into a new relationship and worry about the consequences later.

Romantically you're interested in having fun and probably aren't in the frame of mind for anything serious. If you're involved already, you and your partner enjoy a period of near bliss!

Creatively you're at the top of your game, and anything you tackle works effortlessly.

Between July 16, 2014, and August 11, 2015, Jupiter transits fire sign Leo. You feel lucky, and those feelings draw more experiences that bolster that luck. You may meet someone special through friends or a group to which you belong. You could also meet someone special while traveling abroad.

Other excellent dates:

March 30, the new moon in Aries, your solar fifth house, brings in new romantic opportunities. A great way to greet the spring. Look for new opportunities in your creative endeavors too.

August 12 to September 5, when Venus transits fire sign Leo and forms a terrific angle to your sun. This transit enhances your spirituality and hunger for travel. The travel may involve a spiritual or creative quest of some kind.

CAREER

Jupiter's transits through both Cancer and Leo will help every facet of your life, even your career. The caveat with career matters, though, is that if you're doing something you love, you benefit tremendously. If you're working in a field that doesn't excite you, that has become rather humdrum and routine, then Jupiter, Mars, Venus, Mercury, and your ruler, the moon, could help you to break away and find something that is more aligned with your passions.

Between January 1 and July 16 Jupiter transits water sign Cancer and forms a dynamic angle to your career area. You can expect great expansion in your professional opportunities, relationships, and responsibilities.

Between July 16, 2014, and August 11, 2015, Jupiter transits fellow fire sign Leo and forms a terrific angle to your sun sign. During this thirteen-month period your life expands in positive ways and brings greater self-confidence, opportunities that thrill you, and a sense that your life is headed in the right direction.

Let's take a closer look at the beneficial career times:

August 15 to September 2: Mercury is moving direct in Virgo, your career area. This period favors communication with bosses and peers. Pitch your ideas, and move all professional matters forward. Start a blog, put up a Web site, advertise your products/services or those of your company. Your communication skills are powerful now.

September 5 to 29: During this period, while Venus transits your career area, you're working steadily and resolutely on a project. Coworkers and bosses are impressed with your ideas and the way you implement them. Others find you so appealing that you're the first to be tapped for team projects. Venus in Virgo prompts you to pay close attention to details and perfect whatever you do.

August 25: The new moon in Virgo should usher in new professional opportunities. You land a new job, get the interview you've hoped for, are promoted, move into a larger office, or sell your book or novel.

Between September 13 and October 26 Mars transits your sign, bringing abundant physical energy and drive. It's the perfect time to tackle challenges.

FINANCES

Let's look at Venus transits first for beneficial dates for finances. Your solar second house, which rules money, is Capricorn, and there are two periods this year to look for. The first, when Venus is moving direct through Capricorn, occurs between January 31 and March 5. The second period occurs between December 10, 2014, and January 4, 2015.

During these two transits you may earn extra income, get a raise, or take a second job. Your income rises, but your expenses may too. Keep track of your finances.

Another beneficial date falls on January 1, with a new moon in Capricorn. Venus forms a wide conjunction to this new moon, so it should be exceptionally beneficial for you financially. And how nice that it falls on the first day of the new year!

MERCURY RETROGRADES

Every year Mercury—the planet of communication and travel—turns retrograde three times. During these periods it's wise not to sign contracts (unless you don't mind renegotiating when Mercury is moving direct), to check and recheck travel plans, and to communicate as succinctly as possible. Refrain from buying any large-ticket items or electronics during this time too. Often computers and appliances go on the fritz, cars act up, data is lost ... you get the idea. Be sure to back up all files before the dates below:

February 6–28: Mercury retrograde in Pisces, your solar fourth house—your domestic environment. It slips back into Aquarius before it turns direct, so your third house of travel and communication is also impacted.

June 7–July 1: Mercury retrograde in Cancer, your solar eighth house. This retrograde affects shared resources—your partner's income, mortgages, loans, insurance. In other words, don't apply for loans during this retrograde. Since the retro is in Cancer, it may also impact the people who nurture you and those whom you nurture.

October 4–25: Mercury retrograde in Scorpio. This one impacts your solar twelfth house, so don't be surprised if old issues—and relationships—surface.

ECLIPSES

Solar eclipses tend to trigger external events that bring about change according to the sign and house in which they fall. Lunar eclipses trigger inner, emotional events according to the sign and house in which they fall. Any eclipse marks both beginnings and endings. The solar and lunar eclipse in a pair falls in opposite signs. If you're interested in detailed information on eclipses, take a look at Celeste Teal's excellent and definitive book, *Eclipses: Predicting World Events & Personal Transformation.*

If you were born under or around the time of an eclipse, it's to your advantage to take a look at your birth chart to find out exactly where the eclipses will impact you.

Most years feature four eclipses—two solar, two lunar—with the set separated by about two weeks. Let's take a closer look.

April 15: Lunar eclipse in Libra, your solar eleventh house. Friendships, relationships, wishes, and dreams stir up your emotions.

234

April 29: Solar eclipse in Taurus, your solar sixth house. New opportunities surface in your daily work life. You might get promoted, move to a new office, hire new employees, or land a new job that suits you better.

October 8: Lunar eclipse in Aries, your solar fifth house. Uranus is closely conjunct the moon, so you can expect sudden and unexpected emotional issues related to your love life, creativity, and children.

October 23: Solar eclipse in Scorpio, your solar twelfth house. New opportunities surface to work behind the scenes in some capacity and access personal power you have buried.

LUCKIEST DAYS OF THE YEAR

Every year there are one or two days when Jupiter and the sun meet up, and luck, serendipity, and expansion are the hallmarks. This year those days fall on July 25–26. Circle the dates. Do whatever you enjoy!

January—Sagittarius

2014 begins with Mercury in Capricorn, your financial area. This means that until January 11 your conscious focus is on money—what you earn, spend, how you budget (or don't), and your attitudes and beliefs about money.

Between January 11 and 31 Mercury moves through air sign Aquarius, your third house, a transit that is compatible with your fire-sign sun. During this period you may be traveling more than usual and communicating frequently through email, Twitter, or texting. You may be spending more time than usual with siblings and neighbors.

On January 31 Mercury enters Pisces, where it will turn retrograde on February 6. We'll discuss this in the February roundup.

Venus starts the year retrograde in Capricorn, a carryover from 2013, so it won't come as any great shock to you. There may be misunderstandings in intimate relationships, and something could go haywire in your home or at work—no heat, no AC (depending on where you live!)—that creates physical discomfort. Your finances may be confusing; money you're owed doesn't arrive. On January 31 Venus turns direct in Capricorn, and things begin to turn around financially and romantically.

Mars begins the year in Libra, your solar eleventh house. This transit certainly triggers activity in your social life. You're suddenly the person everyone wants to hang out with; people gravitate toward you. You're the one who gets things done, and people recognize that.

Your ruler, Jupiter, begins the year retrograde in Cancer, your solar eighth house. It's a carryover from last year, so you already understand the impact of this energy on your joint finances—slow, slow, slow. Things will change after March 6, when Jupiter turns direct again.

IMPORTANT DATES

January 1: The new moon in Capricorn ushers in new financial opportunities, which is a terrific way to start the new year! Pluto, Mercury, and Venus are also in Capricorn, so at least one of these opportunities involves writing/communication and the creative arts. You're in the driver's seat, Sadge.

January 15: The full moon in Cancer occurs in your solar eighth house. This one illuminates finances and resources you share with others.

January 30: The new moon in compatible air sign Aquarius ushers in new opportunities in communication and travel. Uranus forms a close, beneficial angle to this new moon, so these opportunities arrive suddenly and unexpectedly. Be ready to seize them!

February—Sagittarius

Mercury begins the month in Pisces, your solar fourth house, a continuation of a transit that started last month. On February 6 it turns retrograde, on February 12 it slips back into Aquarius, and on February 28 it turns direct in that sign. While Mercury is retro in Pisces, things in your domestic area may be somewhat bumpy and unsettled. Your intuition is certainly heightened, though, which helps you to solve problems that may arise. Once Mercury slides back into Aquarius, travel plans may get fouled up, and it's easy to be misunderstood. So communicate clearly, and follow the three Rs: revise, review, rethink.

Venus spends the month of February in Capricorn, your financial area, a major bonus. Financial matters ease up now. Even if you're spending more, you're also earning more. Perhaps someone repays a loan, an unexpected check could arrive, or you land a raise or find a part-time job. Whenever Capricorn is in the picture, your career and ambition enter into the flow of events. Perhaps now is the time to tackle a challenge at work.

Mars spends the month of February in Libra, your

solar eleventh house, so your social life continues to pick up momentum. You may be meeting a lot of different kinds of people who may be helpful to you in some capacity. Keep your business cards handy. Don't be shy about talking to strangers.

IMPORTANT DATE
February 14: The full moon in Leo is perfect for Valentine's Day! You grasp this energy and run with it. With Mars forming an exact and beneficial angle to this moon, any news you hear should be positive and exciting. This full moon illuminates your worldview, Sagittarius. Now you grasp the truly big picture.

March—Sagittarius

March is an incredibly busy month in the zodiac, with three lunations and a number of planets changing signs or turning direct or retrograde. Let's take a closer look.

Since Mercury turned direct on February 28, it's now moving through Aquarius, your solar third house. This transit brings a certain edginess to your conscious thoughts, a need to peek into the future at what may be headed toward you. If you don't have a meditation practice already, get started. It will not only benefit you physically, but will heighten your intuitive awareness.

Between March 17 and April 7 Mercury moves through Pisces, your solar fourth house, once again. This transit brings a nice intuitive flow to your domestic environment, and it's easy to use your imagination to manifest your desires. Get busy with the manifestations, Sadge!

Between March 5 and April 5 Venus moves through Aquarius, your solar third house. This transit should be pleasant for you. Aquarius is an air sign compatible with your fire-sign sun, and it helps to attract people into your life who are eager to get to know you, to spend time with you. If you're not involved right now, you may meet someone in your neighborhood who interests you romantically, or a sibling or neighbor could introduce you to someone special.

Mars has been moving direct in Libra since the first of the year. On March 1 it turns retrograde in that sign, your solar eleventh house, and remains that way until May 19. A Mars retro definitely slows things down, and you'll feel it in your social life. But some down time may be just what you need right now.

Your ruler, Jupiter, turns direct on March 6 in Cancer, your solar eighth house. This is great news for your joint finances. Now your partner should see significant momentum in income.

Saturn turns retrograde in Scorpio on March 2 and remains that way until July 20. During this period your focus turns inward. You may be involved in therapy, working actively with your dreams, and could expand your meditation practice.

IMPORTANT DATES

March 1: The new moon in Pisces, your solar fourth house, receives an exact and beneficial angle from Jupiter, so new opportunities that surface are going to expand your world significantly. One possible opportunity that surfaces could be a creative endeavor.

March 16: The full moon in Virgo occurs in your career sector and sheds light on a professional matter. You now are able to see the details related to your career path.

March 30: The new moon in Aries is a beauty. It occurs in the romance and creativity sector of your chart and should usher in new opportunities in both those areas.

April—Sagittarius

Mercury transits Aries from April 7 to 23, a beautiful period for you. You and your romantic partner discuss your relationship openly and clearly. You're both intent on enjoying yourselves and discover you have more in common than you thought. Between April 23 and May 7 Mercury transits Taurus, your solar sixth house. This transit brings your conscious focus to your daily work routine and the ways in which you maintain your health. You might try a new nutritional program or diet, take up meditation or expand your practice, or try a new exercise routine or alternative therapy.

Between April 5 and May 2 Venus transits Pisces, your solar fourth house. This period favors love and romance in your domestic area. You and your partner may team up for a creative endeavor, your kids could be particularly loving and compassionate, and your home is definitely your sanctuary. You may decide to beautify the rooms in some way or to refurbish the house.

Throughout April, Mars continues its retrograde motion through Libra. Even though your social life may not be as active as you like, you've got plenty to keep you busy. You're essentially planning and strategizing, figuring the angles as only a Sadge can do, and are preparing to implement things when the time is right!

IMPORTANT DATES
There are two eclipses this month. Keep in mind that eclipses usually bring stuff to light and also initiate new opportunities.

April 14: Pluto turns retro in Capricorn, your financial area, and remains that way until September 22. During this retro your financial matters move more slowly. There are delays.

April 15: The lunar eclipse in Libra should be quite good for you, despite the fact that Mars is still retro. You hear news about a friend or about an opportunity that enables you to further your dreams.

April 29: The solar eclipse in Taurus brings in new opportunities in your daily work that may involve travel and using your communication abilities in a more powerful way. Jupiter forms a wide, beneficial angle to the eclipse degree, suggesting expansion and luck. You're in the right place at the right time.

May—Sagittarius

From May 7 to 29 Mercury moves through Gemini, your opposite sign. Your conscious focus during this period is on straightforward communication of all kinds, travel, and discussions with partners, both business and romantic. Your lively wit charms everyone around you, and people clamor for your attention.

On May 29 Mercury enters Cancer, then it turns retrograde on June 7, so we'll discuss this in next month's roundup. Before the retro comes around, though, be sure to reread the section on Mercury retrogrades in The Big Picture for your sign.

Between May 2 and 28 Venus moves through Aries, your solar fifth house. This period is one of the most romantic and creative for you all year. If you're not involved when the transit starts, you probably will be by the time it ends. And if you're not, it won't matter because you're having way too much fun to worry about it. Your muse shadows you constantly, urging you to get to work on whatever you're passionate about. And get started before that Mercury retro begins on June 7.

A date to circle: May 19. Mars finally turns direct again, in Libra, and until July 25 your social life heats up again. Things happen; life moves forward at a pace that suits you. You're in your element again. Feels great, doesn't it?

IMPORTANT DATES

May 14: The full moon in Scorpio may be intense. Saturn forms a close conjunction to it, suggesting that any news you hear deserves your serious consideration and thought.

May 28: The new moon in Gemini ushers in new partnership opportunities. If you're involved already, you and your partner may deepen your commitment to each other. You could find the ideal business partner.

June—Sagittarius

On May 29 Mercury entered Cancer, your solar eighth house. Until June 7 this transit brings your conscious attention to resources you share with others, your home and domestic environment, and perhaps one or both of your parents. Then on June 7 Mercury turns retro in Cancer, slides back into Gemini on June 17, and turns direct in that sign on July 1. Two areas of your chart will be impacted by the retrograde—resources you share with others and your partnerships.

While Mercury is retro in Cancer there could be some issues with a mortgage, loan, insurance, or taxes. While it's retro in Gemini there could be miscommunication in partnerships. Regardless of which sign retro Mercury is in, though, it's best to review, revise, and rethink projects rather than launching something new. If you have to travel during the retro period, be prepared for unexpected changes in your itinerary.

Until June 23 Venus continues its transit of Taurus, a sign that it rules, your solar sixth house. During this period things in your daily work routine unfold smoothly. You become more conscious of health matters and may change your diet or nutritional program. A flirtation at work could lead to a full-blown romance, if that's what you desire. If you're already involved, you and your partner may embark on an exercise routine together.

Between June 23 and July 18 Venus transits Gemini, your partnership area. This transit spices up your love life and may prompt you and your partner to deepen your commitment to each other. You might decide to move in together or get engaged or married. You're able to communicate well now, with charm and wit that captivate others.

For all of June Mars continues its journey through Libra, your solar eleventh house, so your social life is moving at a pace that suits you. For part of this transit Mars forms a beneficial angle to transiting Venus, which bolsters your partnership area. If you're launching your own business, you find the ideal partner or clients or both!

On June 9 Neptune turns retrograde in Pisces, your solar fourth house. This movement, which lasts until November 15, may slow down home-improvement projects and things generally in your domestic area. You have an opportunity, however, to take a deeper look at what you would like from your home life. You may scrutinize your neighborhood in a new way. Is it perhaps time to move?

IMPORTANT DATES

June 13: The full moon in your sign illuminates something in your personal life. A creative endeavor or project reaches completion. Uranus in Aries forms a wide, beneficial angle to this full moon, suggesting that any news you hear comes out of the blue. You don't see it coming.

June 27: The new moon in Cancer occurs in your solar eighth house and ushers in new opportunities with resources you share with others. There could be new opportunities in your home life too. With Jupiter still in Cancer, these new opportunities expand your life in a significant way.

July—Sagittarius

On July 1 Mercury turns direct in Gemini and moves toward its appointment with Cancer on July 12. While it's in Gemini you may experience some of the same things you did when Mercury was in this position between May 7 and 29. For clues about Mercury's transit through Cancer, look back to the period between May 29 and June 7. The difference is that there's more going on this month, with planets changing signs and turning retro or direct. Let's take a closer look.

Until July 18 Venus is in Gemini, bringing good communication and general smoothness to your partnerships. A commitment may be deepened; the knot could be tied. From July 18 to August 12 Venus moves through water sign Cancer, your solar eighth house. This transit should facilitate obtaining a mortgage or loan or could bring a break in insurance or taxes. Another possibility is that your partner lands a nice raise or bonus. You may be delving into esoteric areas—life after death, communication with the dead, reincarnation.

Circle July 16. Jupiter enters fellow fire sign Leo, where it remains until August 11, 2015. This wonderful transit should expand many areas of your life, bring new opportunities, and could result in your going to college or grad school or traveling more frequently abroad. Another possibility is that your manuscript is published.

On July 21 Uranus turns retrograde in Aries, your solar fifth house. This movement, which lasts until December 21, suggests that you may be taking a second look at what you want romantically and from your creative endeavors.

Between July 25 and September 13 Mars transits your sign, a period to anticipate! Mars is your booster rocket, the planet that makes things happen. When it's in your sign, your physical energy increases, and the momentum of life generally picks up considerable speed.

IMPORTANT DATES
July 12: The full moon in Capricorn illuminates something in your finances. With Pluto forming a wide conjunction to this full moon, power plays and transformation are guaranteed. Certain bills could come due that prompt you to tighten your belt and stick to your budget.

July 26: The new moon in Leo should be magnificent for you. It enjoys a close conjunction with Jupiter, so opportunities that surface will expand your venues in different ways.

August –Sagittarius

Mercury continues its transit of fellow fire sign Leo, your solar ninth house, until August 15, when it enters Virgo, your career area. This transit lasts until September 2 and galvanizes your professional life. You can now pitch your agenda with ease and certainty that it will be well received. You are attentive to details and pay close attention to what bosses and coworkers have to say. Even though Mercury in Virgo forms a challenging angle to your sun during this transit, you are challenged to extend your talents and communication abilities.

For four days, from August 12 to 15, Venus and Mercury are traveling together in Leo, your solar ninth house. If this duo brings romance into your life, you and your partner certainly communicate well. You're warm and caring with each other and support each other's creative abilities. Then Mercury moves on into Virgo, and Venus continues its transit of Leo until September 5. You may travel abroad, take a seminar or workshop in something that interests you, or actively pursue a creative endeavor.

For the entire month of August Mars continues its transit of your sign. Lucky you! With so many planets in your court, you can do no wrong! Take advantage of this Mars transit by tackling challenging endeavors and issues. You'll be able to resolve them in no time!

IMPORTANT DATES

August 10: The full moon in compatible air sign Aquarius illuminates your solar third house of travel, communication, and siblings. Any news you hear around the time of this full moon will be sudden and unexpected, thanks to a beneficial angle from Uranus. Saturn forms a challenging angle to this full moon, so there could be some stress today in your personal life.

August 25: The new moon in Virgo, your career area, is something to plan for. Make a list of what you would like to experience and achieve professionally, and then release the desires and let the universe deliver.

September—Sagittarius

From September 2 to 27 Mercury transits Libra, your solar eleventh house. This movement should bring your focus to achieving your wishes and dreams. You may find help through friends and groups to which you belong. Be sure to use social media in your planning—Facebook, Twitter—and to visualize the end result you desire.

On September 27 Mercury enters Scorpio. Since this transit leads into the last Mercury retro of the year, we'll talk about it in October's wrap-up.

From September 5 to 29 Venus transits Virgo, your career area. This transit should bring a smoothness to your professional life. In fact, things may be humming along so nicely that you are tempted to kick back. Instead, take advantage of this transit by pushing your own agenda forward, gathering support from coworkers and bosses for your creative endeavors. Romance with a coworker or someone in your professional environment could be in the air.

On September 13 Mars enters Sagittarius—that's your sun sign! Lucky you. This transit is your booster rocket and enables you to accomplish stuff in half the time. It prompts you to move ahead in any endeavor you take on, and because your own momentum picks up, you attract the help you need. You may be traveling more frequently during this transit, which ends on October 26.

On September 22 Pluto turns direct in Capricorn, your financial sector. Now *that* is news to celebrate. Any financial matters that have stalled or were delayed will now move forward again.

IMPORTANT DATES

September 8: The full moon in Pisces illuminates a domestic matter or brings news about someone or something in your personal environment. With Pluto forming a beneficial angle to this full moon and Neptune widely conjunct to it, there may be an element of confusion, but you come out ahead.

September 24: The new moon in Libra occurs in your solar eleventh house. This one ushers in new friendships and new opportunities for achieving your wishes and dreams.

October—Sagittarius

There's a lot going on this month astrologically, including two eclipses and a Mercury retro. Let's talk about this retrograde—the last of 2014!

On October 4 Mercury turns retro in Scorpio, your solar twelfth house, slips back into Libra on the 10, and turns direct again in that sign on the 25. While Mercury is retro in Scorpio, people from the past may resurface in your life—former lovers, spouses. You may be revisiting issues you thought were resolved long ago and will have the opportunity to deal with and resolve them now. While Mercury is retro in Libra, your relationship with friends may get confusing due to miscommunication. Then, of course, there are the other elements to consider—reread the section on Mercury retrogrades in The Big Picture for your sign.

Venus enters Scorpio on September 29 and remains there until October 23—i.e., for most of Mercury's retro.

Still, Venus in Scorpio heightens your sexuality, investigative skills, and intuition. You have greater access to your unconscious now and to insights and information in your dreams. If you become involved romantically during this transit, the relationship may remain secretive—until Venus enters your sign on November 16.

Mars finally leaves your sign on October 26, so before that happens make that additional push to finish up whatever you're working on. While Mars is in Capricorn from October 26 to December 4, you're working like crazy to increase your income, and the results may surprise you. Remember: Mars equals booster rocket!

IMPORTANT DATES
October 8: The lunar eclipse in fellow fire sign Aries should be plenty exciting for you, Sadge. Uranus forms a close conjunction to the eclipse degree, indicative of news that comes out of nowhere and sweeps you up.

October 23: The new moon in Scorpio ushers in new opportunities in research and intuitive development. It's also possible that a sexual relationship gets off the ground.

November—Sagittarius

As you enter the tail end of 2014, you've got a lot going for you. Take a few minutes this month to reflect on where you've been this year, what you have achieved, and where you would like to be by this time next year. It's not too early to start considering your new year's resolutions!

Mercury moves through Scorpio between November

8 and 27, an intense transit that stirs up your unconscious and prompts you to deal with stuff you may have buried over the years. You have plenty of intuitive help and may enlist the aid of a psychologist or therapist or even a trusted friend or family member. You're essentially clearing the inner decks and closets, nooks and crannies in preparation for Mercury's transit through your sign from November 27 to December 16. We'll talk about that at length in December's roundup.

Now *here's* something to anticipate: from November 16 to December 10 Venus moves through your sign, and what fun this will be for you! In romance and creative endeavors things flow your way. Others seek your company; they're attracted to your ideas and your magnetic personality. Your muse shadows you 24/7, eager and ready to help you in whatever way possible.

Mars entered Capricorn on October 26, so for the entire month of November it continues its journey through that sign. This transit ramps up your professional ambition. You work harder to earn more money and may even take a second job or work out of your home in some capacity in order to make additional money, perhaps for holiday buying.

On November 15 Neptune turns direct in Pisces, your solar fourth house. Now it's easier for you to integrate your spiritual beliefs into your daily, domestic life. You may decide to spiff up your home in some way too. Perhaps you create a sanctuary for yourself?

IMPORTANT DATES
November 6: The full moon in Taurus brings something in your daily work routine to light. With Pluto forming a

beneficial angle to it, the news you hear or insights you gain put you in a more powerful position to negotiate.

November 22: The new moon in your sign happens just once a year, and this one looks magnificent. New personal opportunities surface in romance, creativity, and perhaps even in finances, thanks to a wide conjunction with Venus.

December—Sagittarius

The countdown to 2015 begins!

Mercury continues its transit through your sign until December 16, when it enters Capricorn, your solar second house of finances. It will be there until January 5, 2015, and brings your conscious focus to money. Perhaps the financial area is ripe for a new year's resolution? You're thinking about and discussing money or may be writing about it too. Your conscious focus is also on your professional ambition. What do you need to complete by the end of the year? By the holidays?

Between December 10 and January 4 Venus also transits Capricorn. So for part of this period Venus will be teamed up with Mercury, a nice combination that facilitates your earnings. You may be spending more, perhaps as a result of the holidays, but it looks as if you've got the money to do that.

Mars changes signs on December 4, moving into Aquarius, where it will be until January 12, 2015. This transit galvanizes your communication abilities and, just in time for the holidays, suggests you'll be spending more time with siblings and other relatives. You may be checking out new neighborhoods too, perhaps in anticipation of a move.

On December 8 Jupiter turns retrograde in fire sign Leo, your solar ninth house. It turns direct again on April 8, 2015. Essentially, Jupiter snoozes during this period. It can be a period of great inner expansion, though.

Saturn enters your sign on December 23, where it will be for the next two and a half years. Read about that impact under The Big Picture section for your sign.

IMPORTANT DATES

December 6: The full moon in Gemini, your opposite sign, sheds light or brings news about a partnership. Uranus forms a beneficial angle to this full moon, suggesting excitement and surprise!

December 21: The new moon in Capricorn ushers in new financial opportunities. And you, as the nomad of the zodiac, may immediately book a trip to some exotic locale. Mercury forms a wide conjunction to this new moon, so communication/writing may be part of the new opportunities.

HAPPY NEW YEAR!

11

Capricorn

The Big Picture in 2014

Welcome to 2014, Capricorn! It's an 8 year for you. This suggests a year of prosperity and financial gain—a power year.

Now that the tumult of 2012 and the realignment of 2013 are behind you, you're ready to embark on yet another journey. So let's look at how specific areas of your life may be impacted and which dates will be of vital importance to you.

ROMANCE/CREATIVITY

Aren't you lucky! Due to a retrograde of Venus early in the year, 2014 brings you two periods when Venus transits your sign: January 31 to March 5 and December 10, 2014, to January 4, 2015. Venus is retrograde in your sign between January 1 and 31. Let's take a closer look at what all this means.

The Venus retrograde at the beginning of the year is a continuation from what was going on in December 2013. It suggests some bumps in a romantic relationship—

perhaps confusion about finances—and snafus with creative projects. But Venus retros can also bring about physical discomforts in the environment—the heat in your office or home stops working, for instance. Or your new shoes don't fit right. Whatever you do during this period, don't purchase art or jewelry.

During this period your muse is at your beck and call 24/7, and your creative drive is powerful, a magnet that draws the people you need when you need them. New ideas come easily, so be sure to have a recorder or pen and paper handy regardless of where you are. You feel more self-confident during this transit. Others pick up on it and are attracted to you, your ideas, persona, and creative projects. So if you have these ready, start submitting and exhibiting them, doing whatever you need to do in order to advertise them.

You're in a romantic mood during this transit, and that's true whether you're involved or not. If you're already in a relationship, things between you and your partner should be quite pleasurable, fun, and loving. If you're not involved when the transit begins, you probably will be before it ends.

If a relationship begins during this period, it may begin at work or in a work-related setting. This stranger catches your eye; something clicks before you even speak to each other. Perhaps you and this individual work in the same profession or have careers that are allied in some way. You will have similar interests and a solid base for communication. If you're already involved in a relationship, this transit helps to define it. You and your partner may deepen your commitment to each other.

The other terrific period for romance and creativity occurs between May 28 and June 23, when Venus transits fellow earth sign Taurus, your solar fifth house. This transit urges you to enjoy yourself. What a concept, right? Taurus is a sensual, grounded sign that moves at its own pace, so the relationship may unfold slowly.

Romantically you're interested in having fun and probably aren't in the frame of mind for anything serious. If you're involved already, you and your partner enjoy a period of near bliss!

Creatively you're at the top of your game, and anything you tackle works effortlessly.

Other excellent dates:

April 29 features a solar eclipse in Taurus, your solar fifth house. Mercury is closely conjunct the eclipse degree, suggesting new opportunities to flex your creativity in some form of communication—writing, public speaking. New opportunities surface in romance too. If you're not involved, be sure to get out and socialize and network. That's how you'll meet this new romantic interest.

September 5 to 29, when Venus transits earth sign Virgo and forms a beneficial angle to your sun. This transit enhances your spirituality and hunger for travel. The travel may involve a spiritual or creative quest of some kind.

CAREER

Jupiter's transits through both Cancer and Leo will help every facet of your life, even your career. The caveat with career matters, though, is that if you're doing something you love, you benefit tremendously. If you're working in a field that doesn't excite you, that has become rather humdrum and routine, then Jupiter, Mars, Venus, Mercury, and your ruler, the moon, could help you to break away and find something that is more aligned with your passions.

Between January 1 and July 16 Jupiter transits Cancer, your solar seventh house. This transit favors an expansion of your partnerships, both business and personal. In your professional life, this transit could bring the right partner at the right time for a business venture. In love and romance, you and your partner may decide to move in together or get engaged or married.

Between July 16, 2014, and August 11, 2015, Jupiter transits fire sign Leo, your solar eighth house. This could increase your partner's income or result in breaks for you in taxes, insurance, mortgages, or loans. It could also indicate an inheritance.

Let's take a closer look at the beneficial career times:

September 2 to 27: Mercury is moving direct in Libra, your career area. This period favors communication with bosses and peers. Pitch your ideas, and move all professional matters forward. Start a blog, put up a Web site, advertise your products/services or those of your company. Your communication skills are powerful now.

September 29 to October 23: During this period, while Venus transits your career area, you're working steadily and resolutely on a project. Coworkers and bosses are impressed with your ideas and the way you implement them. Others find you so appealing that you're the first to be tapped for team projects. Venus in Libra prompts you to network, socialize, make contacts.

September 24: The new moon in Libra should usher in new professional opportunities. You land a new job, get the interview you've hoped for, are promoted, move into a larger office, or sell your book or novel.

Between October 26 and December 4 Mars transits your sign, bringing abundant physical energy and drive. It's the perfect time to tackle challenges.

FINANCES

Let's look at Venus transits first for beneficial dates for finances. Your solar second house, which rules money, is Aquarius, and there are two periods this year to look for. The first, when Venus is moving direct through Aquarius, occurs between March 5 and April 5. The second period occurs between August 12 and September 5, when Venus transits Leo, your eighth house of shared resources.

During these two transits you may earn extra income, get a raise, take a second job. Your income rises, but your expenses may too. Keep track of your finances. During the second transit your partner's income may increase, which benefits you as well, and you could get breaks with loans, mortgages, taxes, or insurance.

Another beneficial date falls on January 30, with a new moon in Aquarius, your financial area. Uranus forms a close, beneficial angle to this new moon, suggesting a suddenness to events. Maybe a financial windfall? It's a good day to buy a lottery ticket!

MERCURY RETROGRADES

Every year Mercury—the planet of communication and travel—turns retrograde three times. During these periods it's wise not to sign contracts (unless you don't mind renegotiating when Mercury is moving direct), to check and recheck travel plans, and to communicate as succinctly as possible. Refrain from buying any large-ticket items or electronics during this time too. Often computers and appliances go on the fritz, cars act up, data is lost . . . you get the idea. Be sure to back up all files before the dates below:

February 6–28: Mercury retrograde in Pisces, your solar third house of travel and communication. It slips back into Aquarius before it turns direct, so your financial area is also impacted.

June 7–July 1: Mercury retrograde in Cancer, your solar seventh house of partnerships. Since this retrograde impacts both personal and professional relationships, be careful to say what you mean. Don't sign any contracts during this retrograde.

October 4–25: Mercury retrograde in Scorpio. This one impacts your solar eleventh house. You may be reviewing your goals and what you would like to achieve in your life. Friendships may be impacted by misunderstandings.

ECLIPSES
Solar eclipses tend to trigger external events that bring about change according to the sign and house in which they fall. Lunar eclipses trigger inner, emotional events according to the sign and house in which they fall. Any eclipse marks both beginnings and endings. The solar and lunar eclipse in a pair falls in opposite signs. If you're interested in detailed information on eclipses, take a look at Celeste Teal's excellent and definitive book, *Eclipses: Predicting World Events & Personal Transformation.*

If you were born under or around the time of an

eclipse, it's to your advantage to take a look at your birth chart to find out exactly where the eclipses will impact you.

Most years feature four eclipses—two solar, two lunar—with the set separated by about two weeks. Let's take a closer look.

April 15: Lunar eclipse in Libra, your solar tenth house. Your career or professional life stirs up emotions.

April 29: Solar eclipse in Taurus, your solar fifth house. New opportunities surface in your creativity and romance.

October 8: Lunar eclipse in Aries, your solar fourth house. Uranus is closely conjunct the moon, so you can expect sudden and unexpected emotional issues related to your domestic environment.

October 23: Solar eclipse in Scorpio, your solar eleventh house. New opportunities surface with friends and your wishes and dreams.

LUCKIEST DAYS OF THE YEAR
Every year there are one or two days when Jupiter and the sun meet up, and luck, serendipity, and expansion are the hallmarks. This year those days fall on July 25–26. Circle the dates. Do whatever you enjoy!

January—Capricorn

The year begins with Mercury in your sign, Capricorn, so for the first eleven days of the month you're in your element. Your communication skills are strong, your mind is focused, and you know exactly where you're headed.

On the 11 Mercury enters Aquarius, your financial sector, where it will be until the 31. This transit brings your conscious focus to money—what you earn and spend, how or if! you budget, and what you believe about money.

On the 31 Mercury enters water sign Pisces and leads us into the first Mercury retrograde of the year. We'll discuss this in February's roundup.

Venus begins the year in your sign too, but it's retrograde. You already have a sense of the repercussions of this retro since it's a holdover from last year. Relationships may not move along as smoothly as you would like, there can be physical discomforts due to lack of AC or heat, and your feelings are easily hurt. On the 31 Venus turns direct again and heads for its appointment with Aquarius on March 5. We'll discuss this in February's roundup.

Mars starts the year in Libra, your career sector. Lucky you! This transit makes things happen professionally. It's your booster rocket and helps you to get things done. Your motivation and drive are impressive. Take advantage of this transit because in March Mars turns retrograde and essentially goes into a dormant state.

Your ruler, Saturn, begins the year in compatible water sign Scorpio. This transit has been going on since October 2012, so you already have a clear sense of how it impacts your life. It's a stabilizing influence that brings greater structure and grounding.

IMPORTANT DATES
January 1: The new moon in your sign is a wonderful start for 2014. This moon sets the tone for the next

twelve months and ushers in many new opportunities in your personal life. With Pluto and Mercury closely conjunct, you're in the power seat, Capricorn, exactly where you like to be. One of the opportunities could involve writing or other forms of communication and perhaps even travel.

January 15: The full moon in Cancer occurs in your partnership sector. With Jupiter widely conjunct, any news you hear will expand your partnerships in significant ways.

January 30: The new moon in Aquarius occurs in your financial area. This should be welcome news, Cappy. New financial opportunities are headed your way and come at you out of the blue, so be prepared to seize them.

February—Capricorn

On January 31 Mercury entered compatible water sign Pisces, your solar third house, where it remains direct until February 6. During this week your imagination soars and your intuition is sharp, right on target. You may be involved in artistic or creative endeavors, something new, perhaps? Then on February 6 Mercury turns retrograde for the first time this year, slides back into Aquarius on February 12, and turns direct in that sign on February 28. This means that two different areas of your life are impacted—your solar third house of travel and communication and your second house of finances. Reread the Mercury retro section in The Big Picture for your sign, then follow the three Rs: revise, review, and rethink. Don't launch any new projects.

For the entire month of February Venus continues its transit of Capricorn, but some of its benefits are mitigated by Mercury's retro. Still your love life, creativity, and finances can be positively impacted if you communicate clearly and carefully check bank statements. In romance you could meet someone whose values are similar to yours.

Mars also continues its present run through Libra, your career area. On March 1, though, it turns retrograde, so get everything done this month!

IMPORTANT DATES

February 14: The full moon in fire sign Leo brings a financial issue to light. You might discover something about your partner's income that you didn't know. This full moon can also prompt you to show off your creative talents in some way.

February 28: Mercury turns direct in Aquarius. We'll talk about this transit in March's roundup.

March—Capricorn

It's a busy month astrologically, and your head may be spinning at times. Just remember to breathe through it, Cappy, and you'll come out ahead.

On March 1 Mars turns retrograde in Libra, your career area, and won't turn direct again until May 19. It means that professional matters slow down and you won't be able to push ahead as quickly as you would like on your projects. This retro period favors introspection, and you may be taking a close look at what you want from your career.

Until March 17 Mercury moves through Aquarius, where it was between January 11 and 13. You may discover that some of the same patterns are repeated. You certainly will be thinking and talking about finances—what you earn and spend, how you can earn more—and may uncover some innovative ways to increase your income.

Between March 17 and April 7 Mercury moves through Pisces once again, your solar third house. This transit brings a beautiful intuitive flow to your conscious mind, fires up your imagination, and could have you traveling more often. Mercury forms a beneficial angle to your sun sign now, so make good use of this time.

Between March 5 and April 5 Venus transits Aquarius, your solar second house. This transit should bring plenty of romance into your life, and it will be close to home! You might meet someone through a sibling or neighbor, and the chemistry is just right. Your finances should improve too, perhaps as the result of a loan that is repaid or an unexpected check that arrives.

On March 6 Jupiter turns direct in Cancer, your opposite sign. Delays that have plagued your partnerships over the past several months now drop away. Expansion is the name of the game—in business and personal partnerships.

Saturn turns retro in Scorpio on March 2 and doesn't turn direct again until July 20. During this period there are delays in achieving your wishes and dreams, and you may be adjusting your plans and strategies for doing so.

IMPORTANT DATES

March features three lunations. Let's take a closer look:

March 1: The new moon in Pisces occurs in your solar

third house, and you can expect new opportunities to surface in travel and communication. Neptune is closely conjunct to the new moon, suggesting that at least one of these opportunities will involve a creative endeavor.

March 16: The full moon in fellow earth sign Virgo illuminates or brings news about a trip abroad, higher education, publishing, or your worldview.

March 30: The new moon in Aries occurs in your solar fourth house. This one could bring new opportunities in your domestic environment. Perhaps someone moves in or out. You and your partner may decide to move in together. Uranus is closely conjunct this new moon, so expect the unexpected.

April—Capricorn

It's a calmer month, and you have a chance to use the excellent energies in April to push ahead with whatever your passions are.

Between April 7 and 23 Mercury transits Aries, your solar fourth house. You're now reaping the benefits of that new moon in Aries on March 30 and are discussing it with family and friends. You may be involved in home-improvement projects now too, or at least thinking about them!

Between April 5 and May 2 Venus transits compatible water sign Pisces, your solar third house. This transit may prompt you to check out various neighborhoods in anticipation of a move. You could be gardening, perhaps planting some vegetables and fruits that you will be able to harvest this summer.

For the month of April Mars continues its journey through Libra in retrograde motion. It can be frustrating when life doesn't move along at the pace you would like, but take the time to get your priorities in order. Prepare for when Mars turns direct next month.

On April 14 Pluto turns retro in your sign. Now you have an opportunity to reflect on your personal life and make adjustments. This movement lasts until September 22.

IMPORTANT DATES
April 15: The lunar eclipse in Libra, your career area, could bring news you've been hoping for. Retrograde Mars is widely conjunct the eclipse degree, so it's possible that you're experiencing something from the past in a new way.

April 29: The solar eclipse in Taurus, your solar fifth house, ushers in new opportunities in love and romance, creative endeavors, and everything you do for fun and pleasure. Mercury is closely conjunct the eclipse degree, suggesting that at least one of these opportunities involves communication.

May—Capricorn

May is a busy month—though not quite as frantic as March was. Until May 7 Mercury continues its transit through Taurus, your romance sector. So things in romance should hum along at a good pace for you, with you and your partner able to communicate well with each other. Then between May 7 and 29 Mercury moves through air sign Gemini, your solar sixth house. This transit brings your conscious awareness to communication, your daily work routine, and the way in which you maintain your health. You may be talking about different nutritional or exercise programs and could try one or two. Your mind is active and restless; you're in need of a change.

On May 29 Mercury enters water sign Cancer, in which it turns retro next month. We'll discuss this in the June roundup.

Venus enters fire sign Aries on May 2 and remains there, your solar fourth house, until the 28. You're eager to beautify your home and domestic environment in some way. If you're in a relationship, things should be quite passionate between you and your partner. If you're not in a relationship, that fire and passion may be poured into a home-based business or some other creative endeavor in which you're involved.

Between May 28 and June 23 Venus transits earth sign Taurus, your romance sector. Wow. This is one of the best periods for you all year. Your love life is near perfect, your muse is at your beck and call, and life generally flows your way. Others are charmed by your presence, and you may decide to change your appearance in some way. New hairstyle, clothes, new makeup, new *you*!

Mars turns direct on May 19 in Libra, your career area. It remains there until July 25 and becomes your career booster rocket. Now is the time to get things done professionally, cement relationships with coworkers and bosses, and push your professional agenda forward. Figure out what you really want to do with your career, and make things happen.

IMPORTANT DATES

May 14: The full moon in compatible water sign Scorpio brings a fundamental issue to light. It may concern power plays in a friendship or other relationship. You could find certain information you've been looking for, and it proves enormously helpful. Saturn forms a close conjunction to this full moon, so any news that you hear deserves your serious consideration.

May 28: The new moon in air sign Gemini should attract new opportunities in your daily work routine. An exact and challenging angle from Neptune could confuse the picture initially, but you're able to figure things out by brainstorming with others.

June—Capricorn

On May 29 Mercury entered Cancer, your partnership area. Until June 7 this movement continues in direct motion, and you and your partners—business and personal— have a meeting of the minds. You're able to discuss things clearly. Then on June 7 Mercury turns retrograde for the second time this year, slides back into Gemini on the 17, and turns direct again on July 1. During the retro period your partnerships and daily work are affected.

Be sure to communicate clearly and succinctly with the people around you; the probability for miscommunication is high. This advice is particularly relevant when Mercury is retro in Gemini, a sign it rules. Follow the three Rs: revise, review, and rethink. If you have to travel during this period, try to go with the flow. Your itinerary may take unexpected turns.

Venus continues its transit through Taurus, so you have twenty-three days in June that are glorious for your love life and creative endeavors. Then between June 23 and July 18 Venus transits Gemini. During this period your daily work moves along well, and things unfold with relative smoothness. You may be doing more writing or communicating with coworkers and employees or could be socializing with them. A flirtation could start up with someone at work. If it develops into a full-blown romance, things may heat up quickly.

In June Mars continues its journey through Libra, headed for its appointment with Scorpio on July 25. Use this month to make professional progress.

IMPORTANT DATES

June 9: Neptune turns retrograde in Pisces, your solar third house. This movement lasts until November 15 and may prompt you to scrutinize your spiritual beliefs.

June 13: The full moon in fire sign Sagittarius impacts your solar twelfth house. A secret comes to light. You may decide to enter therapy or start a meditation practice. You are able to glean information and insights from your dreams. Reach out to trusted friends and family members.

June 27: The new moon in Cancer occurs in your partnership area. Maybe you and your partner decide to tie the knot or otherwise deepen your commitment in some way. In business you could find exactly the right partner.

July—Capricorn

The best news this month is that Mercury turns direct on July 1 in Gemini and moves toward its appointment with Cancer on July 12, where it will remain until July 31. During this transit you and a business or romantic partner or both may be discussing your individual expectations about the relationship. There's a strong intuitive component to these discussions, and it's important to pay attention to your hunches.

On July 31 Mercury enters Leo, your solar eighth house. We'll discuss that in next month's roundup.

Venus remains in Gemini until July 18, when it enters Cancer, your solar seventh house. It will be there until August 12, and during this period you and your romantic partner may deepen your commitment to each other in some way. You could move in together, get engaged, or set a marriage date.

Between July 25 and September 13 Mars finally moves into Scorpio, your solar eleventh house. This transit brings momentum to your social life and the ways in which you pursue your wishes and dreams. There's a bottom-line element to any transit in Scorpio, and since Mars corules that sign, it's happy here and functions well.

Circle July 16. Jupiter enters Leo, your solar eighth house, that day and will be there until August 11, 2015. Resources you share with others—a child, partner, or spouse—will expand. Your partner could land a plump raise or bonus. It should be easier for you to obtain a mortgage or loan. Read more about this transit under the big picture section for your sign.

On July 20 Saturn turns direct in Scorpio, definitely something to celebrate, and a day later Uranus turns retrograde in Aries, your solar fourth house. The Uranus retro lasts until December 21 and urges you to look within about your expectations concerning your domestic life.

IMPORTANT DATES
July 12: The full moon in your sign is a doozy! You receive news of a powerful nature and gain insights into who you are and what motivates you.

July 26: The new moon in Leo ushers in new opportunities in financial matters. With Jupiter closely conjunct, these opportunities are bound to expand your financial base in a significant way.

August—Capricorn

For the first two weeks of August Mercury continues its journey through Leo, your solar eighth house. Then between August 15 and September 2 it moves through fellow earth sign Virgo, your solar ninth house. During this period you're thinking about and discussing a trip abroad that you would like to take. If money is holding you back, take a part-time job or start saving more. Plan for the trip. Visualize it happening.

Venus transits Leo, your solar eighth house, from August 12 to September 5. This period could see your income increasing, so perhaps that will take care of the expense of your trip abroad. You or your partner could get a bonus, raise, or unexpected refund. In terms of romance, it's possible you could meet someone special while you're showing off your considerable talent.

For the month of August Mars continues its journey through compatible water sign Scorpio, your solar eleventh house. Things are intense now with friends or groups to which you belong. You may be doing research on a topic that interests you. Your research is quite thorough, and you find what you're looking for. Now that Saturn is moving direct in Scorpio, you're getting help in terms of structure and grounding for your creative endeavors.

IMPORTANT DATES

August 10: The full moon in Aquarius occurs in your solar second house. It illuminates or brings news about some facet of your finances. Either way, what you learn is sudden and unexpected, thanks to a beneficial angle from Uranus.

August 25: The new moon in fellow earth sign Virgo attracts new opportunities in higher education, publishing, and foreign travel. Pluto forms a wide, beneficial angle to this new moon, so these new opportunities are transformative.

September—Capricorn

Between September 2 and 27 Mercury moves through Libra, your solar tenth house. This transit favors everything connected to your career and professional life. You may be socializing more with bosses and coworkers, pitching ideas, gathering support for a project. This transit is inherently social.

On September 27 Mercury enters Scorpio, then turns retrograde in that sign on October 4, so we'll discuss this more in next month's roundup.

Between September 5 and 29 Venus moves through Virgo, your solar ninth house. This transit favors romance with a foreigner, foreign travel, higher education, publishing. It may be time to dust off that manuscript in your bottom drawer, read it over, and submit it.

On the 29, Venus enters Libra, your career area, where it will be until October 23. We'll discuss this in next month's roundup.

Mars enters Sagittarius on September 13 and remains there, your solar twelfth house, until October 26. During this transit old issues may be stirred up, stuff you have buried over the years. You may be actively involved in a creative endeavor that you're doing by yourself, perhaps with a deadline looming.

On September 22 Pluto turns direct in your sign. Celebrate! Anything that has been delayed should now move forward again.

IMPORTANT DATES

September 8: The full moon in Pisces is a beauty for you. Your imagination and creativity come alive, and there's a beautiful flow to your verbal skills. Your conscious mind is intuitively receptive.

September 24: The new moon in Libra occurs in your solar tenth house. This one ushers in new professional opportunities—a job, new responsibilities, perhaps even a raise.

October—Capricorn

This month is extremely busy—a Mercury retrograde, the last this year, two eclipses, and a change in signs for both Venus and Mars. Let's take a closer look.

Until October 4 Mercury moves in direct motion through Scorpio, your solar eleventh house, bringing your conscious mind's focus to friendships, your social life, research, psychic development. Then on the 4 Mercury turns retro in Scorpio, slides back into Libra on the 10, and turns direct in that sign on the 25. While Mercury is retro in Scorpio there could be miscommunication with friends, and you may have to revise your research plans. If you're doing a lot of writing, revise and review. Don't make submissions during the retro period. Make travel plans on either side of the retrograde.

While Mercury is retro in Libra professional matters may seem to reverse themselves. Don't push for results, tie up old projects and creative endeavors, and wait until after October 25 to start new projects.

Venus remains in your career area until the 23. It helps to mitigate Mercury's retrograde, but the retro also may prevent you from benefiting fully from the Venus transit through your career area.

Finally on October 26 Mars enters your sign, Cappy, and it will be there until December 4. Mars is your booster rocket, particularly when it moves through your sun sign. By nature you're no slouch, but when Mars is in your sign, you're a powerhouse on wheels, zipping around and doing twice the work you normally do. It's a favorable time to get things done.

IMPORTANT DATES

October 8: The lunar eclipse in fire sign Aries occurs in your solar fourth house. Uranus is closely conjunct the eclipse degree, Mars forms a beneficial angle to it, and Pluto forms a challenging angle. These aspects suggest a mixed bag of inner experiences and news about your domestic environment, parents, and family.

October 23: The solar eclipse in Scorpio enjoys an exact conjunction with Venus, so this eclipse should usher in new opportunities in romance, creativity, finances, and friends. Neptune in Pisces forms a beneficial angle to the eclipse degree, suggesting a spiritual and creative component to these new opportunities.

November—Capricorn

Since Mercury turned direct in Libra on October 25, it's certainly safe to pack your bags and hit the road now. Send out your résumés; make your submissions and travel plans. You're in the clear. Mercury remains in your career area until November 8, giving you a second chance to put things right professionally. Between November 8 and 27 it enters Scorpio for the second time, and you have a chance to make amends to friends and others for whatever went wrong during the retro period.

On the 27 Mercury enters Sagittarius, your solar twelfth house. We'll discuss this one in the December roundup.

Venus spends the first fifteen days of the month in Scorpio, a transit that could stir up a flirtation or romance with a friend or someone you meet through friends. You might get involved in a creative endeavor with a group of friends. On November 16 Venus enters Sagittarius, your solar twelfth house, where it will be until December 10. During this transit you can easily tap into dreams and information you receive while meditating. You and your partner may be spending more time alone together, or you could be working on a creative project.

Mars spends the entire month of November in your sign. There's no stopping you. Once you've got your sights set on a goal, nothing prevents you from reaching it. Just be careful that you don't burn yourself out!

Neptune turns direct in Pisces on November 15, so you're able to integrate your spirituality and imagination into your daily life.

IMPORTANT DATES

November 6: The full moon in fellow earth sign Taurus occurs in your solar fifth house. This one illuminates love and romance, creativity, and anything connected to your kids. Pluto and Mars form a close, beneficial angle to this full moon, indicating the completion of a project or endeavor. Any news you hear should be positive.

November 22: The new moon in Sagittarius occurs in your solar twelfth house. Venus is widely conjunct. New opportunities surface in romance, finances, foreign travel, and creative endeavors.

December—Capricorn

As you enter the last month of 2014, take a few minutes to reflect on where you've been this year, what you have achieved, and where you feel you have fallen short. Start your new year's resolution list. It's never too early for that!

Between December 16 and January 5, 2015, Mercury moves through your sign, and for part of this time it will be traveling with Venus (December 10 to January 4, 2015). With Pluto also in your sign, Neptune in compatible water sign Pisces, and Saturn in its final degrees of compatible water sign Scorpio, you've got a lot of astrological energy on your side. Use it well. Remain focused and directed. Tie up loose ends so that you can greet the new year with a smile in your heart.

Mars leaves your sign on December 4 and enters Aquarius, your financial area, where it will be until January 12. This transit and all the other stuff going on in your chart suggest you'll be working hard to bring in more money. You might land a raise or an end-of-the-year bonus.

On December 8 Jupiter turns retrograde in Leo and will remain that way until April 8, 2015. It simply means Jupiter's usual expansiveness goes into a dormant state.

Uranus turns direct on December 21 in Aries, good news for your home life. On December 23 Saturn leaves Scorpio and enters Sagittarius, where it will be for the next two and a half years. Read about this transit in The Big Picture section for your sign.

IMPORTANT DATES

December 6: The full moon in Gemini occurs in your solar sixth house. Your daily work routine is highlighted in some way. News about work arrives suddenly and unexpectedly.

December 21: The new moon in your sign is a gorgeous way to end the year. New opportunities are all around you, and at least one of them involves communication and travel.

HAPPY NEW YEAR!

12

Aquarius

The Big Picture in 2014

Welcome to 2014, Aquarius! It's a 9 year for you. This suggests a year of many beginnings and endings, finishing projects, taking care of loose ends, looking for new ways to expand what exists—as opposed to starting something new.

Now that the tumult of 2012 and the realignment of 2013 are behind you, you're ready to embark on yet another journey. So let's look at how specific areas of your life may be impacted and which dates will be of vital importance to you.

ROMANCE/CREATIVITY
Aren't you lucky! Due to a retrograde of Venus early in the year, 2014 brings you a period in the spring when Venus transits your sign: March 5 to April 5. During this period your muse is at your beck and call 24/7, and your creative drive is powerful, a magnet that draws the people you need when you need them. New ideas come easily, so be sure to have a recorder or pen and paper handy regardless of where you are. You feel more self-confident

during this transit. Others pick up on it and are attracted to you, your ideas, persona, and creative projects. So if you have these ready, start submitting and exhibiting them, doing whatever you need to do in order to advertise them.

You're in a romantic mood during this transit, and that's true whether you're involved or not. If you're already in a relationship, things between you and your partner should be quite pleasurable, fun, and loving. If you're not involved when the transit begins, you probably will be before the transit ends.

If a relationship begins during this period, you could meet this person virtually anywhere—on Facebook, in a grocery store, at some group you belong to, or due to a cause you support.

This stranger catches your eye; something clicks before you even speak to each other. But before that click can go any further, you need to know how this person's mind works. If you mesh intellectually, things can get off the ground.

If you're already involved in a relationship, this transit helps to define it. You and your partner may deepen your commitment to each other.

The Venus retrograde at the beginning of the year—which lasts until January 31—is a continuation of what was going on in December 2013. It occurs in Capricorn, your solar twelfth house, and suggests some bumps in a romantic relationship, perhaps confusion about finances, and snafus with creative projects. But Venus retros can also bring about physical discomforts in the environment—the heat in your office or home stops working, for instance. Or your new shoes don't fit right. Whatever you do during this period, don't purchase art or jewelry.

The other terrific period for romance and creativity occurs between June 23 and July 18, when Venus transits fellow air sign Gemini, your solar fifth house. This transit urges you to enjoy yourself. What a concept, right? Gemini is a mental, communicative sign, so if you get involved during this period, you do so quickly, once things click mentally. In this way Gemini and Aquarius are very much alike.

Romantically you're interested in having fun and probably aren't in the frame of mind for anything serious. If you're involved already, you and your partner enjoy a period of near bliss!

Creatively you're at the top of your game, and anything you tackle works effortlessly.

Other excellent dates:

May 28 features a new moon in Gemini, your solar fifth house. Mars forms a close, beneficial angle to this new moon, Neptune forms an exact and challenging square, and Uranus forms a wide and beneficial angle. Wow. So what's it all mean? New creative opportunities that surface are likely to do so suddenly, activity swirls around you, and there could be some confusion initially about these opportunities. A new romantic interest is also indicated.

Between September 29 and October 23 Venus transits air sign Libra and forms a beneficial angle to your sun. This transit enhances your spirituality and hunger for travel. The travel may involve a spiritual or creative quest of some kind.

CAREER

Jupiter's transits through both Cancer and Leo will help every facet of your life, even your career. The caveat with career matters, though, is that if you're doing something you love, you benefit tremendously. If you're working in a field that doesn't excite you, that has become rather humdrum and routine, then Jupiter, Mars, Venus, Mercury, and your ruler, the moon, could help you to break away and find something that is more aligned with your passions.

Between January 1 and July 16 Jupiter transits Cancer, your solar sixth house. This transit favors an expansion of your daily work routine and forms a beneficial angle to your career area. This transit, a continuation from last year, should expand your professional options and opportunities.

Between July 16, 2014, and August 11, 2015, Jupiter transits fire sign Leo, your solar seventh house. This transit brings in the right partners at the right time.

Let's take a closer look at the beneficial career times:

September 27 to October 4 Mercury is moving direct in Scorpio, your career area. This period favors communication with bosses and peers. Pitch your ideas, and move all professional matters forward. Start a blog, put up a Web site, advertise your products/services or those of your company. Your communication skills are powerful now.

October 23 to November 16: During this period, while Venus transits your career area, you're working steadily and resolutely on a project. Coworkers and bosses are impressed with your ideas and the way you implement them. Others find you so appealing that you're the first to be tapped for team projects. Venus in Scorpio prompts you to research and investigate.

October 23: The new moon in Scorpio should usher in new professional opportunities. You land a new job, get the interview you've hoped for, are promoted, move into a larger office, or sell your book or novel.

Between December 4, 2014, and January 12, 2015, Mars transits your sign, bringing abundant physical energy and drive. It's the perfect time to tackle challenges.

FINANCES

Let's look at Venus transits first for beneficial dates for finances. Your solar second house, which rules money, is Pisces, and there are two periods this year to look for. The first, when Venus is moving direct through Pisces, occurs between April 5 and May 2. The second period occurs between September 5 and 29, when Venus transits Virgo, your eighth house of shared resources.

During these two transits you may earn extra income, get a raise, take a second job. Your income rises, but your expenses may too. Keep track of your finances. During the second transit your partner's income may increase, which benefits you as well, and you could get breaks with loans, mortgages, taxes, or insurance.

Another beneficial date falls on March 1 with a new moon in Pisces, your financial area. Neptune and Mercury are conjunct—Neptune more closely—which suggests a new source of income, perhaps through some type of communication. It's also possible that your involvement in a spiritual organization or one that encompasses your ideals could be a source of new income as well.

MERCURY RETROGRADES

Every year Mercury—the planet of communication and travel—turns retrograde three times. During these periods it's wise not to sign contracts (unless you don't mind renegotiating when Mercury is moving direct), to check and recheck travel plans, and to communicate as succinctly as possible. Refrain from buying any large-ticket items or electronics during this time too. Often computers and appliances go on the fritz, cars act up, data is lost . . . you get the idea. Be sure to back up all files before the dates below:

February 6–28: Mercury retrograde in Pisces, your solar second house of finances. It slips back into Aquarius before it turns direct, so your personal life is also impacted.

June 7–July 1: Mercury retrograde in Cancer, your solar sixth house. This retrograde affects your daily work routine and the ways you maintain your health. Since the retro is in Cancer, it may also impact the people who nurture you and those whom you nurture.

October 4–25: Mercury retrograde in Scorpio. This one impacts your career.

ECLIPSES

Solar eclipses tend to trigger external events that bring about change according to the sign and the house in which they fall. Lunar eclipses trigger inner, emotional events according to the sign and house in which they fall. Any eclipse marks both beginnings and endings. The solar and lunar eclipse in a pair falls in opposite signs. If you're interested in detailed information on eclipses, take a look at Celeste Teal's excellent and definitive book, *Eclipses: Predicting World Events & Personal Transformation.*

If you were born under or around the time of an

eclipse, it's to your advantage to take a look at your birth chart to find out exactly where the eclipses will impact you.

Most years feature four eclipses—two solar, two lunar, with the set separated by about two weeks. Let's take a closer look.

April 15: Lunar eclipse in Libra, in your solar ninth house. Emotions stirred up that pertain to your spiritual beliefs, worldview, or educational and publishing involvement.

April 29: Solar eclipse in Taurus, in your solar fourth house. New opportunities surface in your domestic life.

October 8: Lunar eclipse in Aries, in your solar third house. Uranus is closely conjunct the moon, so you can expect sudden and unexpected emotional issues related to siblings, relatives, neighbors.

October 23: Solar eclipse in Scorpio, in your solar tenth house. New opportunities surface with your career.

LUCKIEST DAYS OF THE YEAR
Every year there are one or two days when Jupiter and the sun meet up, and luck, serendipity, and expansion are the hallmarks. This year those days fall on July 25–26. Circle the dates. Do whatever you enjoy!

January—Aquarius

Mercury begins the year in Capricorn, a holdover from the end of last year, and then on January 11 enters your sign, where it will be until January 31. During this transit you're in your element, right on target with everything you do and think and tackle. Your ideas are cutting edge, so be sure to record them as they come to you. On January 31 Mercury enters Pisces, where it turns retrograde about a week later. We'll discuss this in February's roundup.

Venus begins the year retrograde in Capricorn, another holdover from 2013. This movement occurs in your solar twelfth house and could bring a former lover or spouse back into your life. Creatively you may be revising something you've been working on or tackle something you worked on in the past and didn't finish. On the 31 Venus turns direct in Capricorn and heads for its appointment with your sign on March 5.

Mars begins the year in fellow air sign Libra, your solar ninth house. This fabulous transit may send you overseas in search of . . . well, something. Perhaps it's a spiritual quest. Perhaps you're spending a college year abroad. Or you may be planning to head to grad school or even law school. One way or another, this transit acts as your booster rocket. And until March, it's in direct motion.

Your ruler, Uranus, has been in fire sign Aries for some time and continues that transit this year. It forms a beneficial angle to your sun sign and enables you to really think outside the box. You take risks you might not take otherwise.

IMPORTANT DATES

Three lunations in January keep your head spinning. January 1 features a new moon in earth sign Capricorn, your solar twelfth house. This new moon ushers in new opportunities in writing/communication and your career (because it's in Capricorn) and to work behind the scenes in some capacity. You're in the power seat. Feels good, doesn't it?

January 15 features a full moon in Cancer, your solar sixth house. Something related to your daily work routine is illuminated. If you've been looking for a job, this full moon could bring some positive offers. Expansive Jupiter forms a wide conjunction to it, suggesting the new opportunities expand your venues.

January 30 brings the second new moon of the month, in your sign. This new moon happens just once a year and sets the tone for the next twelve months, so plan for this one. Make a list of what you would like to experience and achieve in the next year.

February—Aquarius

On January 31 Mercury entered Pisces, your financial area. Until February 6, when it turns retro, your intuition, particularly in regard to money, is strong. Follow your hunches on investments. Since Mercury is turning retro in the early signs of Pisces, the planet slips back into Aquarius on February 12, then turns direct in that sign on February 28. While it's retrograde in your sign, be sure to communicate clearly, take nothing for granted, double-check on appointments. It's a good idea to back up computer files on an external disk drive or even on Drop box or iCloud.

On January 31 Venus turned direct in Capricorn, your solar twelfth house. For the month of February it continues its transit of Capricorn. It could bring about a romance that is kept private for some reason. Once Venus enters your sign on March 5, however, the romance won't be a secret anymore! You may be working behind the scenes in some capacity, perhaps on a creative endeavor that is related to your career or something you do on the side.

For the month of February Mars continues its transit of fellow air sign Libra and forms a beautiful angle to your sun sign. You're able to get a lot done this month, Aquarius, so remain focused on your goals and put in the time. It pays off.

IMPORTANT DATE
The only lunation this month falls on Valentine's Day—February 14, in Leo, your opposite sign. Mars forms an exact and beneficial angle to it. Romance, creativity, and an opportunity to put your talents on display: that's part of the bundle with this full moon. Sounds like fun!

March—Aquarius

It's a busy month in the zodiac, with a lot of planets changing signs or direction and three lunations. A wild ride. Let's take a closer look.

On March 1 Mercury turns direct in your sign, and now you're really in your element. Your conscious mind is sharp, discovering new trends, exploring topics that interest you. Your communication skills are exceptional. Then on March 17 Mercury enters Pisces, your financial area, again and you experience some of the same patterns that occurred in early February.

Also on March 1 Mars turns retrograde in Libra and

will be that way until May 19. During this period things slow down. There could be delays in projects, snafus if you're traveling, and a slowdown in your social life. Use this period to delve within.

On March 6 Jupiter turns direct in Cancer, your solar sixth house. Now things in your daily work routine will begin to expand. You might, for instance, have an opportunity to work part-time from your home. Or you could be given additional responsibilities and the pay to match them. Maintain your nutritional and exercise programs. Sometimes Jupiter in this house results in a physical expansion of your waistline!

Saturn turns retrograde on March 2 in Scorpio, your solar tenth house. It turns direct again on July 20. During this period there may be delays of one kind or another in your career. You're able to assess what you need in terms of professional structure.

IMPORTANT DATES

March 1: The new moon in water sign Pisces should bring new financial opportunities. Neptune forms a close conjunction with this new moon, suggesting that one of these opportunities could involve imaginative creative work.

March 16: The full moon in earth sign Virgo occurs in your solar eighth house. This moon illuminates resources you share with others—the fine details, the stuff you may not always be aware of.

March 30: The new moon in fire sign Aries should be beautiful for you. It ushers in new opportunities in communication and travel. With Uranus closely conjunct, these opportunities surface quickly. Be ready to nab them!

April—Aquarius

Compared to March, April is a breeze. There's not too much here to drive you crazy. Between April 7 and 23 Mercury transits Aries, your solar third house, a beneficial period for you. Your conscious mind is active, you take intellectual risks, and you're eager to forge ahead in all your creative endeavors. You may be impatient with others, however, so guard against that.

From April 23 to May 7 Mercury moves through Taurus, your solar fourth house. This transit favors your domestic life and suggests that you may be thinking about beautifying your home in some way. Or perhaps you're talking with contractors about adding on to your home. This transit makes you a bit more stubborn than usual too.

Between April 5 and May 2 Venus transits Aries, so for part of this period it will be traveling with Mercury. The combination favors innovation, romance, and lively discussions at the dinner table! Venus in Aries can be quite ardent and passionate and even somewhat jealous, so be aware of these possibilities when dealing with a partner.

For the month of April Mars remains retrograde in Libra, your solar ninth house. We discussed the effects of this retrograde in last month's roundup, but it's worth noting that Mars is now moving in opposition to Venus, so you and your partner could be at odds over something in your domestic environment.

On April 14 Pluto turns retrograde in Capricorn, your solar twelfth house, and turns direct again on September

22. During this period you may be delving deeply within for answers. Therapy would be ideal, if you're so inclined. But a regular meditation practice could be just as effective.

IMPORTANT DATES
Okay, there are two eclipses this month. The first, on April 15, is a lunar eclipse in fellow air sign Libra. This one could brings news or stir up feelings about your spiritual beliefs. Mars retrograde is widely conjunct, suggesting a lot of activity around the time of the eclipse.

The April 29 eclipse is solar in Taurus. This one ushers in new opportunities in your domestic area. Someone moves in or out, you refurbish your house, rent out a portion of it, sell it, or buy a new one. Regardless of how the particulars pan out for you, one possible opportunity involves writing/communication.

May—Aquarius

From May 7 to 29 Mercury moves through Gemini, your solar fifth house. This transit should be especially nice for you, Aquarius. Gemini is a fellow air sign and your fifth house of romance and creativity. You're going to be thinking and discussing these areas quite a bit during this transit. If you meet someone special in this period, communication will be particularly important in the relationship.

On May 29 Mercury enters Cancer, and this leads to the second Mercury retro of the year. We'll discuss it in June's roundup.

Venus continues its transit through Aries until May 28. You could meet someone special through a neighbor or sibling. Or the special someone *is* a neighbor. Regardless, you'll feel a lot of passion during this transit, and if it's not directed toward a person, it's directed toward a creative endeavor or interest.

From May 19 to July 25 Mars transits Scorpio, your career area. This spectacular period enables you to make great professional strides. You're a powerhouse of physical energy and resolve and are constantly looking for the absolute bottom line in whatever you tackle.

IMPORTANT DATES
May 14: The full moon in Scorpio reveals something about your career that eluded you before. There could be news in this area too, and thanks to a close conjunction from Saturn, any news you hear deserves your serious consideration. Jupiter forms a beneficial angle to this full moon, suggesting that the news is positive and expands your options in some way.

May 28: The new moon in Gemini is a beauty. New opportunities surface in romance, love, creativity, and with your children. Mars forms a close, beneficial angle to this new moon, so things are starting to happen!

June—Aquarius

June is a rather calm month, perhaps because July won't be! But the second Mercury retro of the year begins on June 7 in Cancer. On the 17 Mercury slides back into Gemini, where it turns direct on July 1. In fact, all the

Mercury retros in 2014 impact two signs. While Mercury is retrograde in Cancer, your solar sixth house, you may be revisiting work issues you thought were resolved. Your parents could be involved in whatever you're dealing with, so keep an eye out.

When Mercury slips back into Gemini, your solar fifth house, former lovers could show up. Miscommunication is even more likely than usual during a retrograde period, and you may be revising and reviewing your creative projects. Reread the section under Mercury retro in The Big Picture for your sign.

For the month of June Mars remains in Scorpio, your career area. Take advantage of this. Don't let up on whatever you're doing professionally. Now is the time to make significant strides in your career.

On June 9 Neptune turns retrograde in Pisces, your financial area, and remains that way until November 15. During this period you may be taking a close look at your values, priorities, and beliefs about money.

IMPORTANT DATES
June 13: The full moon in fire sign Sagittarius should be very much up your alley. It lights up your solar eleventh house of friendships, dreams, and aspirations. Uranus forms a wide, beneficial angle to this full moon, suggesting that any news you hear is sudden and unexpected.

June 27: The new moon in water sign Cancer occurs in your solar sixth house. This one should attract new work opportunities and ways to maintain your health and could involve your home/parents in some way.

July—Aquarius

The best news this month is that Mercury turns direct on July 1 in Gemini. So it's now safe to pack your bags and hit the road, Aquarius. Send out résumés, catch up on email, and pitch your new ideas and projects. You get the idea. Life now moves forward again, and with Mercury moving direct in the romance and creativity sector of your chart, you're prepared to talk the night away with your romantic partner.

Between July 12 and 31 Mercury's transit through Cancer, your solar sixth house, brings about discussions and brainstorming sessions with employees and coworkers. If you're self-employed, then you may be scrutinizing new methods of doing business. Once Mercury enters Leo on the 31 the whole tenor of things changes. You and your partner may be discussing strategies and goals for your new business.

Venus continues its transit of Gemini, your romance and creativity area, until July 18. Lucky you! By now, you've probably figured out how delicious this transit is for your love life and that your muse is up close and personal, helping your creative life in unprecedented ways.

From July 18 to August 12 Venus moves through Cancer, your solar sixth house. This transit facilitates things in your daily work routine and the way you maintain your health. You may decide to alter your appearance in some way—new hairstyle, new clothes, a tattoo! You may also decide to try a new nutritional or exercise program. A romance may surface with someone at work.

On July 25 Mars enters Scorpio, your career area. This transit lasts until September 13 and certainly galvanizes your professional life. Research, investigation, and intuitive development are highlighted. Your boss and peers regard you as a powerhouse of energy and ambition.

On July 16 expansive Jupiter enters Leo, your solar seventh house. This transit lasts until August 11, 2015, and expands your partnerships, both business and personal. You and your romantic partner, for instance, could deepen your commitment to each other and move in together, get married, or start a family. This transit enables you to exhibit your many creative talents.

Saturn turns direct in Scorpio on July 20, so it will be traveling with Mars through your career area for a while. Saturn brings structure and focus to your ambitions.

Uranus turns retro on July 21 in Aries, your third house, and remains that way until December 21. During this period you may be scrutinizing your daily activities and trying to integrate more creative elements into your life.

IMPORTANT DATES

July 12: The full moon in Capricorn occurs in your solar twelfth house. Something that has been hidden from you is brought to light. With Pluto closely conjunct to this full moon, whatever you discover empowers you.

July 26: The new moon in Leo is a beauty for you. It attracts new opportunities in business and personal partnerships, new opportunities for creativity, and venues in which you can strut your stuff, Aquarius!

August—Aquarius

Mercury's transit through Leo lasts until August 15, then it enters earth sign Virgo, your solar eighth house, where it remains until September 2. During this period your conscious focus is on resources you share with others—financial and otherwise. But because of the Virgo component, you may be honing in on the details of a financial arrangement. Perhaps it's the details in a pending loan or mortgage? Or, if you're in the midst of a divorce, you may be taking a second look at your partner's finances.

Venus continues its transit of Cancer until August 12, then enters Leo, your solar seventh house, where it will be until September 5. During this period your relationship with partners should unfold smoothly. If you feel you're not getting the attention you deserve, you'll be vocal about it, and things will auto-correct!

Throughout August Mars continues its transit of Scorpio, your career area. It means you've got this entire month plus thirteen days in September to keep your nose to the grindstone and accomplish everything you set out to do. The other possibility with Mars in Scorpio is that you become involved with someone you work with, a purely sexual attraction.

IMPORTANT DATES

August 10: The full moon in your sign illuminates some facet of your personal life. Uranus forms a close and beneficial angle to this full moon, suggesting that any news you hear will come out of the blue, suddenly and unexpectedly.

August 25: The new moon in Virgo, your solar eighth

house, ushers in new opportunities in resources you share with others. You could land the mortgage or loan you've been hoping to obtain. You could get a tax or insurance break.

September—Aquarius

It's a kind of crazy month, a mixed bag of strangeness. But strangeness only makes you more curious. So let's take a probing look.

Between September 2 and 27 Mercury transits fellow air sign Libra, your solar ninth house. This transit may have you in a seminar or workshop that delves into a spiritual topic. Or you could be planning a trip abroad. Be aware that Mercury will be retro between October 4 and 25, so plan your trip for either side of those dates.

On the 27 Mercury enters Scorpio, where it will turn retro early in October. We'll discuss this in October's roundup.

From September 5 to 29 Venus moves through Virgo, your solar eighth house. This transit should facilitate your obtaining a loan or mortgage, but also addresses more esoteric stuff too. You could be delving into your past lives through a regression or perhaps through images that surface during meditation. In romance you may be more discriminating than usual, pickier!

On September 13 Mars enters compatible fire sign Sagittarius, your solar eleventh house. This transit lasts until October 26 and certainly causes your social life to be more active. You may be networking more than usual too, so have your business cards handy!

IMPORTANT DATES

September 8: The full moon in Pisces occurs in your financial area, so something about your income and expenses is highlighted. If there's news about finances, you should be pleased with what you hear. Mars, Saturn, and Pluto form beneficial angles to this full moon and put you behind the wheel.

September 24: The new moon in fellow air sign Libra should be very much to your liking. This one could bring new opportunities in foreign travel, publishing, and higher education.

October—Aquarius

For the first four days of the month Mercury is moving direct in Scorpio, your career area. Then on the 4 it turns retrograde, slides back in Libra on the 10, and turns direct in that sign on the 25. While it's retro in your career area, follow all the usual suggestions for Mercury retros (reread the section on Mercury retrograde in The Big Picture section for your sign). In addition, don't launch any new projects or creative endeavors. Instead tie up professional loose ends and communicate clearly with everyone in your work environment. Recheck all data, make sure emails actually get sent, and do *not* sign any contracts until the retro is over.

While Mercury is retro in Libra your traveling plans may go askew. But if you're in an adventurous mood and can go with the flow, don't worry about the Mercury retro. Your social life may slow down considerably, but former friends and lovers may surface.

Venus entered Libra on September 9 and will be there till October 23. It's unfortunate that Mercury will be retro for much of this transit and will mitigate some of the benefits. That said though, we can't live our lives according to what each planet is doing or not. If you meet someone special, Aquarius, it could be while you're traveling, in a seminar, in a class. Go with your gut.

From October 23 to December 16 Venus moves through Scorpio, your career area. This could be huge. Everything you seeded professionally while Mars was moving through Scorpio could now reach fruition. Make this time count.

For the first twenty-five days of the month Mars continues its transit through Sagittarius, your solar eleventh house. Then on October 26 it enters Capricorn, where it remains until December 4. During this period it's important to clear the decks of your psyche—get rid of beliefs that no longer serve your best interests, end relationships you've outgrown, and actively work with your dreams and intuitive development.

IMPORTANT DATES

Two eclipses this month add to the general craziness. The first is a lunar eclipse in Aries. Uranus is closely conjunct the eclipse degree, so whatever you're feeling is sudden and unexpected and permeates your conscious mind. Mars in Sadge forms a beneficial angle to the eclipse degree too, indicating a lot of activity, movement, perhaps even travel.

The second eclipse is solar on October 23 in Scorpio, your career area. This one ushers in new professional opportunities, and at least one of those opportunities will involve your creativity and romance.

November—Aquarius

As you enter the last two months of the year, you may want to take some time for reflection. Where would you like to be in your life by next year at this time? What would you like to experience and attain in 2015? It's not too early to start thinking about your new year's resolutions. Once Mercury enters Scorpio again on November 8, that will become much easier. Scorpio is always after the absolute bottom line, and that's what you're looking for now. You've got plenty of time to reflect too, since Mercury remains in Scorpio until November 27.

From November 27 to December 16 Mercury transits Capricorn. We'll discuss that transit in December's roundup.

Venus entered Scorpio on October 23, so for a period between then and November 16, it will be traveling with Mercury through your career area. Its transit should facilitate professional matters for you. It could spark a romance too, between you and someone with whom you work. Be careful, Aquarius. Scorpio's passions are profound and transformative!

On November 27 Mercury enters Sagittarius, your solar eleventh house, where it will be until December 16. We'll discuss this in next month's roundup.

Between November 16 and December 10 Venus moves through compatible fire sign Sagittarius, your solar eleventh house. What fun! It looks as if your Thanksgiving holidays will be filled with celebrations, reunions with old friends, and a general sense of optimism. Be sure you have your business cards with you when you network. Connections, Aquarius, are always helpful.

For the entire month of November Mars continues its transit of Capricorn, which started on October 26. This transit enables you to get things done behind the scenes and tie up loose ends so that when Mars enters your sign on December 4 you're ready to seize the energy and run with it. Clean out your psychic closets.

On November 15 Neptune turns direct again in Pisces, your financial area. Now you're primed to integrate your spiritual beliefs and imagination more readily into the way you earn your daily bread.

IMPORTANT DATES

November 6: The full moon in Taurus occurs in your solar fourth house and illuminates something on the home front. Or you hear news about someone in your domestic life. Pluto forms a close, beneficial angle to this moon, indicating that the news you hear empowers you in some way.

November 22: The new moon in Sagittarius should usher in a whole new chapter in the way you think about yourself and the world around you. It's as if you finally grasp the larger picture of your place in the universe. With Venus widely conjunct, a new romance or creative endeavor looks probable!

December—Aquarius

For part of the month Mercury and Venus are traveling together through Sagittarius, your solar eleventh house.

The dates: November 27 to December 10, when Venus changes signs. So during this period your heart and mind are on the same page. Romance is possible with someone you meet through friends, or perhaps you become involved in a joint creative endeavor with a friend or lover. There's a lot of discussion about the bigger picture of the relationship or the creative project.

On December 16 Mercury enters your sign, and yes, you're ready for it. In fact, Mars enters your sign on December 4 and remains there until January 12, 2015, so you've got two planets in your sign for part of this time. Mars is your booster rocket, and Mercury is how you communicate and think about what you're doing. What better combination for taking you into the new year? Even though most people are focused on the holidays during December, you can accomplish quite a bit if you set your mind to it.

Let's return to Venus for a moment. This planet transits earth sign Capricorn from December 10 to January 4, 2015, so it's quite possible that a relationship in which you're involved is private, with the two of you spending a lot of time alone together. Or you're working hard in solitude, perhaps to meet a looming deadline. With Mars and Mercury in your sign for part of this transit, you've got the drive, ambition, and workaholic ethics to complete what you're doing.

On December 8 Jupiter turns retro in Leo and stays this way until April 8, 2015. This movement affects your house of partnerships. You and your partners (business or romantic) may be taking a closer look at your expectations and goals.

Uranus turns direct in Aries on December 21, so now

the ideas really start pouring into your head, Aquarius. Jot them down. They'll prove useful up the line.

Saturn enters Sagittarius, your solar eleventh house, on December 23 and will be there for the next two and a half years. This transit helps to stabilize friendships and the structures you have in place for attaining your wishes and dreams.

IMPORTANT DATES

December 6: The full moon in fellow air sign Gemini sheds light on a romantic relationship or creative endeavor. Or there's news in these areas. With Uranus forming a beneficial angle to this full moon, news is sudden and unexpected.

December 21: The new moon in Capricorn brings new opportunities to delve into your own psyche and could spark a new ambition or goal. With Mercury widely conjunct this new moon, the opportunities may involve writing/communication and travel.

HAPPY NEW YEAR!

13

Pisces

The Big Picture in 2014

Welcome to 2014, Pisces! It's a 1 year for you. This suggests a year of many beginnings. Think of 2014 as an opening chapter in your life that features many new opportunities, contacts, relationships, desires. So now that the tumult of 2012 and the realignment of 2013 are behind you, you're ready to embark on yet another journey.

Let's look at how specific areas of your life may be impacted and which dates will be of vital importance to you.

ROMANCE/CREATIVITY

Aren't you lucky! Due to a retrograde of Venus early in the year, 2014 brings you a period in the spring when Venus transits your sign: April 5 to May 2. During this period your muse is at your beck and call around the clock, and your creative drive is powerful, a magnet that draws the people you need when you need them. New ideas come easily, so be sure to have a recorder or pen and paper handy regardless of where you are. You feel more self-confident during this transit. Others pick up on it and are attracted to you, your ideas, persona, and creative projects. So if you have these ready, start submitting and exhibiting them, doing whatever you need to do in order to advertise them.

You're in a romantic mood during this transit, and that's true whether you're involved or not. If you're already in a relationship, things between you and your partner should be quite pleasurable, fun, and loving. If you're not involved when the transit begins, you probably will be before the transit ends.

If a relationship begins during this period, you could meet this person virtually anywhere—on Facebook, in a grocery store, at some group you belong to, or due to a cause you support.

This stranger catches your eye; something clicks before you even speak to each other. But before that click can go any further, you need to feel your way into the person's psyche using that amazing intuition of yours.

If you're already involved in a relationship, this transit helps to define it. You and your partner may deepen your commitment to each other.

The Venus retrograde at the beginning of the year—which lasts until January 31—is a continuation of what was going on in December 2013. It occurs in Capricorn, your solar eleventh house, and suggests some bumps in a romantic relationship, particularly if you meet the person through friends. Venus retros can also bring about physical discomforts in the environment—the heat in your office or home stops working, for instance. Or your new shoes don't fit right. Whatever you do during this period, don't purchase art or jewelry.

The other terrific period for romance and creativity occurs between July 18 and August 12, when Venus transits fellow water sign Cancer, your solar fifth house. This transit urges you to enjoy yourself. What a concept, right? Cancer is as intuitive as you are, so that quality is certainly enhanced.

Romantically you're interested in having fun and probably aren't in the frame of mind for anything serious. If you're involved already, you and your partner enjoy a period of near bliss!

Creatively you're at the top of your game, and anything you tackle works effortlessly.

Other excellent dates:

June 27 features a new moon in Cancer, your solar fifth house, with great support from Jupiter. New creative opportunities that surface are likely to be expansive and lucky for you. A new romantic interest is also indicated.

Between October 23 and November 16 Venus transits water sign Scorpio and forms a beneficial angle to your sun. This transit enhances your spirituality and sexuality.

CAREER

Jupiter's transits through both Cancer and Leo will help every facet of your life, even your career. The caveat with career matters, though, is that if you're doing something you love, you benefit tremendously. If you're working in a field that doesn't excite you, that has become rather humdrum and routine, then Jupiter, Mars, Venus, Mercury, and your ruler, the moon, could help you to break away and find something that is more aligned with your passions.

Between January 1 and July 16 Jupiter transits Cancer, your solar fifth house. This transit favors all your creative endeavors and enables you to earn a living doing what you love. You still have to make the effort, of course, but once you do the universe brings the right people and opportunities at the right time.

Between July 16, 2014, and August 11, 2015, Jupiter transits fire sign Leo, your solar seventh house. This transit brings in the right partners at the right time.

Let's take a closer look at the beneficial career times:

November 27 to December 16: Mercury is moving direct in Sagittarius, your career area. This period favors communication with bosses and peers. Pitch your ideas, and move all professional matters forward. Start a blog, put up a Web site, advertise your products/services or those of your company. Your communication skills are powerful now.

November 16 to December 10: During this period, while Venus transits your career area, you're working steadily and resolutely on a project. Coworkers and bosses are impressed with your ideas and the way you implement them. Others find you so appealing that you're the first to be tapped for team projects. Venus in Sagittarius prompts you to network, socialize, make contacts, and reach out to foreigners.

November 22: The new moon in Sagittarius should usher in new professional opportunities. You land a new job, get the interview you've hoped for, are promoted, move into a larger office, or sell your book or novel.

FINANCES

Let's look at Venus transits first for beneficial dates for finances. Your solar second house, which rules money, is

Aries, and there are two periods this year to look for. The first, when Venus is moving direct through Aries, occurs between May 2 and 28. The second occurs between September 29 and October 23, when Venus transits Libra, your eighth house of shared resources.

During these two transits you may earn extra income, get a raise, or take a second job. Your income rises, but your expenses may too. Keep track of your finances. During the second transit your partner's income may increase, which benefits you as well, and you could get breaks with loans, mortgages, taxes, or insurance.

Another beneficial date falls on March 30, with a new moon in Aries, your financial area. Uranus is closely conjunct the degree of this new moon, suggesting that financial opportunities come out of nowhere. You are taken completely by surprise.

MERCURY RETROGRADES

Every year Mercury—the planet of communication and travel—turns retrograde three times. During these periods it's wise not to sign contracts (unless you don't mind renegotiating when Mercury is moving direct), to check and recheck travel plans, and to communicate as succinctly as possible. Refrain from buying any large-ticket items or electronics during this time too. Often computers and appliances go on the fritz, cars act up, data is lost . . . you get the idea. Be sure to back up all files before the dates below:

February 6–28: Mercury retrograde in your sign. Your personal life is impacted.

June 7–July 1: Mercury retrograde in Cancer, your solar fifth house. This one affects your love life and creative endeavors, as well as your relationship with your kids. Since the retro is in Cancer, it may also impact the people who nurture you and those whom you nurture.

October 4–25: Mercury retrograde in Scorpio, your solar ninth house. This one impacts education, publishing endeavors, your worldview, and foreign travel.

ECLIPSES

Solar eclipses tend to trigger external events that bring about change according to the sign and house in which they fall. Lunar eclipses trigger inner, emotional events according to the sign and house in which they fall. Any eclipse marks both beginnings and endings. The solar and lunar eclipse in a pair falls in opposite signs. If you're interested in detailed information on eclipses, take a look at Celeste Teal's excellent and definitive book, *Eclipses: Predicting World Events & Personal Transformation.*

If you were born under or around the time of an eclipse, it's to your advantage to take a look at your birth chart to find out exactly where the eclipses will impact you.

Most years feature four eclipses—two solar, two lunar—with the set separated by about two weeks. Let's take a closer look.

April 15: Lunar eclipse in Libra, your solar eighth house. Emotions stirred up that pertain to your partner's income and any resources you share with others.

April 29: Solar eclipse in Taurus, your solar third house. New opportunities surface in travel, communication, and with siblings.

October 8: Lunar eclipse in Aries, your solar second

house. Uranus is closely conjunct the moon, so you can expect sudden and unexpected emotional issues related to money.

October 23: Solar eclipse in Scorpio, your solar ninth house. New opportunities surface with foreign travel, education, publishing.

LUCKIEST DAYS OF THE YEAR

Every year there are one or two days when Jupiter and the sun meet up, and luck, serendipity, and expansion are the hallmarks. This year those days fall on July 25–26. Circle the dates. Do whatever you enjoy!

January—Pisces

It may take you a while to get back into the groove of things after the holidays. For the first eleven days of January, in fact, Mercury (communication, conscious mind) completes its transit through Capricorn, the social area of your chart. So you're still in a celebratory frame of mind.

Between January 11 and 31 Mercury moves through Aquarius, the most private part of your chart, the twelfth house. You may be working behind the scenes in some capacity or in private discussions about an important matter. Or you may be working out of your home and keeping in touch with employees and coworkers through email.

On the 31 Mercury enters your sign, where it will turn retro on February 6, the first Mercury retrograde of the year. We'll discuss that in February's roundup.

Venus, like Mercury, begins the year in Capricorn, your social area. However, it's retrograde until January 31. Even so, you'll still be out and about, hanging with friends and doing whatever is social for you. But with the retro there could be some inconveniences—maybe your AC or heat (depending on where you live) goes out. Perhaps the wiper blades on your car need to be replaced. Stuff like that. There could also be some misunderstandings in a close relationship. But on the 31 all that becomes history as Venus turns direct and heads for its appointment with Aquarius on March 5.

Mars begins the year in Libra, your solar eighth house. This transit, a holdover from last year, triggers activity in resources you share with others—mortgage and bank lenders, for instance, or insurance companies. You may be refinancing your home or renegotiating a loan, or you and your partner or spouse may be launching a joint business.

Your coruler, Jupiter, begins the year retrograde in Cancer, that area of your chart that governs love, romance, and creativity. Until March 6, when it turns direct, there could be delays in those areas, and Jupiter's expansive energy is turned inward. You may be scrutinizing what you really want in romance or what sorts of creative endeavors really intrigue you.

Your other coruler, Neptune, continues its long journey through your sign.

IMPORTANT DATES
January 1: The new moon in Capricorn is a great way to start the year, Pisces. You can expect new friendships to surface, new networking venues, and perhaps even

new career opportunities (that's the Capricorn part of this equation). Pluto is closely conjunct this new moon, suggesting the opportunities are somehow transformative. Mercury is also closely conjunct, so perhaps one opportunity will involve writing/communication.

January 15: The full moon in Cancer illuminates a creative endeavor or romantic relationship. Jupiter is widely conjunct, suggesting that any news you hear should be positive and will expand your creative venues in some way.

January 30: The new moon in air sign Aquarius occurs in your solar twelfth house. This one could usher in new opportunities to delve into your own unconscious or to work behind the scenes in a creative capacity of some kind. If you've considered therapy, this new moon could bring the opportunity to indulge yourself.

February—Pisces

Mercury entered your sign on January 31, always a welcome transit. Until February 6 your heart and mind are in complete agreement, your imagination soars, and your muse is attentive and helpful. Then on February 6 Mercury turns retrograde, slips back into Aquarius on the 12, and turns direct in that sign on February 28.

It's important to follow the rule of the three Rs during a Mercury retro: revise, rethink, review. Make travel plans on either side of the retro, don't sign contracts, and rather than launch new endeavors finish up the ones you've started already. Generally we advise not traveling under a Mercury retro because your itinerary may suddenly go out of the window. But if you're flexible and have a sense of adventure, then by all means hit the road. Sometimes the destination to which you travel during a retrograde is revisited when Mercury is direct. Reread the Mercury retrograde section under The Big Picture for your sign.

Once Mercury slips back into Aquarius, you should have greater access to information and premonitions that your dreams provide. Issues you thought were resolved may crop up again, and friends and ex-partners you haven't seen in years could resurface.

On January 31 Venus turned direct in Capricorn, and for the entire month of February it's in that sign, behaving itself, and your social life should be enormously pleasant. If you're not involved with anyone, you could meet a special someone through friends or through a group to which you belong. This transit should also facilitate avenues for achieving your wishes and dreams.

During February Mars continues its transit of air sign Libra, your solar eighth house. While you're likely to have more contact than usual with banks, insurance companies, and the like, it's also possible that you have experiences with things that go bump in the night—ghosts, communication with the dead. You might even treat yourself to a past-life regression.

February is a relatively slow month in the zodiac, perhaps because March won't be. Since there were three lunations last month, February features just one moon.

IMPORTANT DATE
February 14: The full moon in fire sign Leo occurs in your solar sixth house. This one sheds light on something

in your daily work routine or the way you manage your health. Mars forms an exact, beneficial angle to it, suggesting a lot of activity and general rushing around. There could be news about a creative endeavor in which you're involved.

March—Pisces

Okay, this month is super busy. Not only are there three lunations, but several planets are changing signs, and others are either turning retrograde or direct. Your head is going to spin, Pisces.

March 1: Mars turns retrograde in Libra and turns direct again on May 19. During this period there are apt to be delays in obtaining mortgages and loans. In fact, financial resources you share with others may be somewhat confusing. If, for instance, you're paying certain bills for one of your kids, there could be charges you weren't aware of. Your partner's income comes under scrutiny.

March 2: Saturn turns retrograde in fellow water sign Scorpio, your solar ninth house. When planets turn retro, they essentially go dormant. Things unfold much more slowly. With Saturn, retro until July 20, issues connected to higher education, publishing, foreign travel, and spirituality will slow down.

March 6: Jupiter turns direct in Cancer, a major plus for your love life and creative endeavors. Now you can expect to enjoy expansion in both areas.

Until March 17 Mercury continues its journey through Aquarius. Then between March 17 and April 7 Mercury moves through your sign, a transit that will undoubtedly please you. Your imagination slams into high gear, your intuition is sharper, and your conscious mind absorbs other people's moods like a sponge. It's important to hang out with positive, upbeat people.

Venus moves into Aquarius on March 5 and remains there until April 5. During this month-long transit a romantic relationship may be kept under wraps for some reason. You're doing a lot of creative work in private. You may be paid in cash for a service you do for another.

IMPORTANT DATES

March 1: On the same day that Mars turns retro, there's a new moon in your sign, definitely something to celebrate. This new moon occurs just once a year and sets the tone for the next twelve months. So think closely about what you would like to achieve and experience in the next year, and trust that the universe will bring it your way. With Neptune closely conjunct this new moon, your spiritual beliefs, imagination, and intuition may be part of the new opportunities.

March 16: The full moon in Virgo, your opposite sign, sheds light on a relationship or brings news about a partnership or health matter. Saturn forms a close, beneficial angle to it, so any news you hear strengthens the various structures in your life.

March 30: The new moon in Aries occurs in your financial area. Yay! New income heads your way. Uranus is closely conjunct this new moon, so the opportunities comes quickly and unexpectedly. You simply have to be ready to seize them.

April—Pisces

If March was a hurricane of energy, April certainly promises to be much calmer except for two eclipses.

Until April 7 Mercury continues its transit through your sign, Pisces. Then between April 7 and 23 it moves through Aries, your financial area. This transit has you thinking and talking about finances. Maybe you're even obsessed with the topic. You're discussing your budget, income, and expenses and are perhaps looking for a second job to supplement what you earn already. If you're obsessing, stop it! Help comes from—Venus!

Between April 5 and May 2 Venus moves through your sign. What a glorious period this will be, with other people seeking out your company and being more receptive to your ideas. Your muse is in full attendance too, whispering in your ear, urging you to get moving with your creative endeavors. Your love life should be enormously pleasing now, with your partner attentive and loving. If you're not involved when the transit begins, you may be by the time it ends. This transit and that of Venus through Cancer, which happens in July, are two of the most romantic and creative times for you all year.

Mars, now retrograde in Libra, continues its present movement throughout April. The slowness of things generally may drive you batty, but just go with the flow, Pisces. If you don't have a meditation practice yet, get started. It will prove helpful and grounding for you.

Pluto turns retrograde on April 14 in Capricorn. It lasts until September 22, and during this period you'll have a chance to reflect on what you seek from your friendships. New venues for achieving your wishes and dreams may come to you.

IMPORTANT DATES
This month's eclipses occur in Libra (lunar eclipse) and in Taurus (solar eclipse). Let's take a look:

April 15: The lunar eclipse in Libra reveals something about your joint finances and resources you share with others—partner, spouse, kids, parents. Mars is widely conjunct, so there can be some tension on or around the time of the eclipse.

April 29: The solar eclipse in Taurus should be quite lovely for you. It ushers in new opportunities in your daily life, and given the proximity of Mercury to the eclipse degree, the opportunities could include writing and travel. Also Jupiter forms a beneficial angle to this eclipse degree, so these new opportunities certainly expand your life in a significant way.

May—Pisces

Between May 7 and 29 Mercury moves through Gemini, your solar fourth house. This transit certainly makes for lively discussions around the dinner table! Your home, especially if you have kids, becomes a hub of activity. Music rocks the walls; people are coming and going at all hours of the day. It can be as exhausting or liberating as you make it. Attitude is everything, right? You may be doing writing and research out of your home.

On May 29 Mercury enters Cancer. Since that transit

leads into the second Mercury retro of the year, we'll discuss it in June's roundup.

Venus is active this month. Between May 2 and 28 it transits Aries, your financial area. Wow! Your income should pick up—you might land a raise, get a tax break or refund, or perhaps someone repays a loan. You come up with innovative ways to increase your income too. By the time Venus enters Taurus on May 28, you may be ready to implement your plan.

The Taurus transit lasts until June 23, and during this period your conscious mind is clear, focused, and stubborn. Venus functions well in Taurus, a sign that it rules, so you may be feeling sensuous and sexy.

Circle this date: May 19. Mars finally turns direct in Libra and heads toward its appointment with fellow water sign Scorpio on July 25. Now your life will start moving forward again, and mortgages and loans you've applied for will come through.

IMPORTANT DATES

May 14: The full moon in Taurus illuminates something in your daily life that you probably will have to resolve. Saturn forms a close conjunction, and Pluto forms a beneficial angle to the moon, so you've got plenty of help and support.

May 28: The new moon in air sign Gemini should usher in new opportunities on the domestic front. Perhaps someone moves in or out. If your home is for sale, chances are good that the new moon brings you a buyer.

June—Pisces

It's another nutty month, with the second Mercury retro this year. On May 29 Mercury entered Cancer, the romance and creativity area of your chart. So until June 7 you get to enjoy a momentous time with your muse and romantic partner. Then on the 7 Mercury turns retrograde, slips back into Gemini on the 17, and turns direct in that sign on July 1.

While Mercury is retro in Cancer, you may be revising a creative endeavor, rehashing old issues with a partner, or dealing with some issue with your parents. While Mercury is retro in Gemini, your domestic environment seems to go haywire. Miscommunications may be common. Appliances are prone to breaking down; your computer could crash. You get the idea here. Anything and anyone in your home life is subject to impact!

For much of June Venus continues its transit of Taurus, your communication area. If Mercury weren't retro for most of this transit, the period would probably be quite enjoyable, with things in your daily life moving along at a pace that suits you. Venus can still mitigate some of the impacts of Mercury's movement, but it requires extra effort on your part.

Between June 23 and July 18 Venus moves through Gemini, your domestic area. For about eight days it will be traveling with Mercury retrograde, so there can be some confusing encounters and interactions. After Mercury turns direct, though, it's fairly smooth sailing for you and your home life.

Mars keeps on traveling through Libra. That will change on July 25.

Neptune turns retro in your sign on June 9 and remains that way until November 15. During this period you may feel that your energy is low, and there can be confusing boundaries between you and someone else. Increase your meditation and exercise time.

IMPORTANT DATES
June 13: The full moon in Sagittarius occurs in your career area. A professional matter or relationship is illuminated. Both Mars and Uranus form beneficial angles to this full moon, promising surprises and activity.

June 27: The new moon in Cancer ushers in new romantic and creative endeavors. Neptune forms a beneficial angle to this new moon, so your spirituality and imagination play important roles.

July—Pisces

On July 1 Mercury turns direct in Gemini. Time to celebrate, buy your plane ticket to some exotic locale, send out résumés, make your submissions, return phone calls and emails. On the 12 Mercury enters Cancer again, where it will be until the 31. With both of these transits, look back to what was going on in your life when Mercury was in these signs earlier in the year. Those dates? May 7 to 29 for Gemini and May 29 to June 7 for Cancer.

Until July 18 you continue to enjoy one of the most romantic and creative periods for you all year. Venus is in Cancer, your solar fifth house, lighting up your love life, your creativity, and everything you do for fun and pleasure. There's a wonderful feeling that goes along with this transit, as if you are the golden child, adored by everyone around you.

Mars finally changes signs on July 25 and moves into fellow water sign Scorpio, where it will be until September 13. During this transit you ardently pursue research, investigation, and psychic development and may have contact or involvement with the publishing industry and/or higher education. Your focus and drive are powerful, and you're able to barrel through any obstacles you may encounter.

On July 16 Jupiter enters Leo, where it will be until August 2015. During this transit your daily work routine expands. You could assume greater responsibility for a job, might land a nice raise or bonus, and will have plenty of opportunities to show off your talents. Pay close attention to your exercise routine and nutritional program. Sometimes with Jupiter in the sixth house you can gain weight.

July 20 is another day to circle: Saturn turns direct in Scorpio and moves forward to keep its appointment with Sagittarius on December 23. While direct in Scorpio it brings greater strength and foundation to your worldview and spiritual beliefs. Your educational goals become much clearer.

Uranus turns retrograde in Aries on July 21, and that movement will continue until December 21. You may be taking a closer look at your values and beliefs about money.

IMPORTANT DATES
July 12: The full moon in Capricorn lights up the social area of your chart. Uranus forms an angry angle to this

full moon, so there could be some tension and news that catch you by surprise. However, Pluto is closely conjunct to the moon, suggesting that you come out on top.

July 26: The new moon in Leo enjoys a close conjunction with expansive Jupiter. New work opportunities somehow expand your creative venues and choices about work.

August—Pisces

This month isn't quite as hectic as July. You'll have a chance to catch your breath and enjoy some downtime.

Mercury enters Virgo on August 15 and brings your conscious attention to partnerships—business or personal or both. You're much more attentive to details and able to make course corrections that suit you and your partner. You may be paying more attention to your health too, particularly in terms of what you eat or don't eat. This transit lasts until September 27, when Mercury enters Scorpio. Since this leads to the year's final retro on October 4, we'll discuss it in next month's roundup.

Between August 12 and September 5 Venus journeys through Leo. During this transit your daily work life should be pleasing for you. You're able to put your prodigious imagination to work in a tangible way, express your creativity, and integrate it more readily into your daily work. You have opportunities to showcase your talents and skills and should do so at every opportunity. A raise is possible. Just the right chemistry with a co-worker could spark a flirtation or even a romance.

For the month of August Mars continues its trip through Scorpio, a sign it corules. It travels with Saturn, now direct in the same sign, so these two enhance your intuition, deepen your research and investigative skills, and bring greater structure and action to your life.

IMPORTANT DATES
August 10: The full moon in Aquarius in the most private part of your chart lights up power you have disowned over the years and urges you to reclaim that power. Therapy can be helpful. But so can journaling, meditation, and yoga. Saturn forms a difficult angle to this full moon, so you may be reminded that you should assume greater responsibility for something or someone.

August 25: The new moon in earth sign Virgo, your opposite sign, ushers in new partnership opportunities. Perhaps you meet exactly the right individual to help you market your business ideas. Or to help you build a Web site. You and your romantic partner may deepen your commitment to each other.

September—Pisces

Between September 2 and 27 Mercury moves through Libra, that part of your chart that relates to joint finances. You may be mulling over ways to reduce your debt, refinance your home, or obtain a loan for the purchase of a car or appliance. Right now your best bet is to pay cash for whatever you need. You may be looking for a part-time job to cover holiday expenses.

On the 27 Mercury enters Scorpio, where it leads into

a retrograde early next month. We'll discuss this in October's roundup.

Venus enters Virgo on September 5 and until the 29 brings greater harmony and ease to your partnership area. With both business and personal partners, you're attentive to details and have certain expectations you should discuss. You and a romantic partner may deepen your commitment to each other. Perhaps you move in together or decide to get married. Or better yet, maybe you and your romantic partner become business partners!

On September 13 Mars enters your career area, where it will be until October 26. This transit certainly galvanizes your professional life. Suddenly you're a powerhouse of energy, able to accomplish whatever you set out to do in half the time it usually takes you. There may be some travel involved in your career during this period. You have an unusually clear grasp of your career's larger picture and understand how to make course corrections when needed.

Pluto turns direct in Capricorn on September 22. With the planet of transformation now functioning as it should, you notice that life in general picks up speed and direction.

IMPORTANT DATES

September 8: The full moon in your sign should bring news of a personal nature that pleases you. Pluto forms a beneficial angle to this full moon, indicating that the news you hear is transformative in some way. Saturn forms a beneficial angle to this full moon too, suggesting the news can bring a greater structure and foundation to your life.

September 24: The new moon in Libra ushers in new financial and social opportunities. It could come in the form of investments, a raise, or a tax or insurance break.

October—Pisces

The last Mercury retrograde of the year happens this month. There are two eclipses, and several planets are changing signs. Busy, in other words.

On September 27 Mercury entered Scorpio, and until October 4 it's moving direct, prompting you to think more than usual about your beliefs and to create strategies involving higher education, publishing, or a trip overseas. On October 4 Mercury turns retro for the last time this year, slides back into Libra on the 10, and turns direct in that sign on the 25.

Before the retro begins make sure your computer files are backed up on an external hard drive or a flash drive. Better yet, be really redundant and use Drop Box or iCloud. Follow the rules of the three Rs: revise, review, rethink. Reread the section on Mercury retrogrades in The Big Picture for your sign.

On September 29 Venus entered Libra, and it remains there until October 23. During this period you may be traveling overseas, and if you aren't, you're virtual traveling, perhaps researching a particular destination. In fact, with Mercury retrograde until the 25, virtual travel is your safest bet. In terms of romance and creativity, Venus in Scorpio is intensely emotional. Your muse is ready to help, but you have to engage her (him) first. Be clear on what you desire in romance, back it with emotion, then release it and let the universe manifest it.

Venus enters Sagittarius, your career area, on October 23, and between then and November 16 professional matters should unfold with utter smoothness. It helps that Mercury will be moving direct for most of this transit, and Mars will also be traveling with Venus in your career area for three days. Mars is your booster rocket, remember? And Venus is the facilitator.

Speaking of Mars, it remains in Sagittarius until the 26, giving you plenty of time to make professional strides. You're able to set goals and achieve them. On the 26 it enters Capricorn. Your social life picks up tremendously, and your ambition ramps up. You work tirelessly to implement any strategies you've created and find new venues for achieving what you desire.

IMPORTANT DATES
October 8: The lunar eclipse in Aries occurs in your financial area. There's news about money, and thanks to Uranus, which is closely conjunct to the eclipse degree, the news comes out of the blue. Mars greets this month with a hearty handshake and adds its passion to whatever is unfolding.

October 23: The solar eclipse in Scorpio brings in new opportunities for overseas travel and research and in publishing and higher education. With Venus exactly conjunct the eclipse degree, it looks as if a new love is on his or her way into your life.

November—Pisces

On November 8 Mercury enters Scorpio again, and it will be there until the 27. Now you may be reexperiencing some of the same things you did between September 27 and October 4, when Mercury was last moving direct in Scorpio. Mercury now forms a beneficial angle to your Pisces sun, and this transit bolsters all the qualities for which you're known: your imagination, intuition, and compassion. Just remember that Mercury in Scorpio is always looking for the absolute bottom line, and that can sometimes be abrasive to the people around you.

On the 27 Mercury enters Sagittarius, your career area, where it will be until December 16. We'll talk about that in December's roundup.

Venus enters your career area, Sagittarius, on November 16 and remains there till December 10. Wow, lucky you. This means Venus will be traveling with Mercury for part of this transit, and you've also got Jupiter and Uranus forming strong angles to both of these planets. Think: sudden and unexpected professional expansion. People with whom you work are receptive to and excited about your ideas, and you find all the support you need for your creative endeavors.

Neptune turns direct in your sign on November 15, a nice plus for the end of the year that carries you into 2015 with your spiritual beliefs in place, your imagination in high gear, and your intuition flowing.

IMPORTANT DATES

November 6: The full moon in compatible earth sign Taurus highlights some facet of your daily life and your communication abilities. Pluto's beams are friendly toward this full moon, so any news you hear should be powerful and possibly even transformative.

November 22: The new moon in Sagittarius ushers in new professional opportunities. It could be anything from a new, better-paying job to a raise, new responsibilities, even a new career path.

December—Pisces

As you enter the last month of the year, it's a good idea to reflect on where you've been and what you've experienced this year and then look forward to 2015. Where would you like to be in life at this time next year? Start thinking about your new year's resolutions!

From December 16 to January 5, 2015, Mercury transits Capricorn. You'll enjoy this one, especially with the holidays approaching. Accept every invitation that comes your way, and network like crazy, Pisces. Have your business cards handy at all times. Don't be shy about presenting your talents and skills.

Venus actually enters Capricorn first, on December 10, and travels with the planet of communication until January 4, 2015. This duo brings lively discussions and a possible romance with someone you meet through friends or who is already a friend. With these two planets in Capricorn, there's an element of professional ambition. So even though there's lots of holiday cheer going around, and people are more focused on having fun and enjoying themselves, you're creating strategies for your career.

Mars enters Aquarius on December 4 and remains there until January 12, 2015. During this period you're moving through your own unconscious with greater ease, clearing away beliefs that no longer serve your best interests. You're essentially preparing the way for Mars entering your sign in January 2015.

Jupiter turns retro in Leo on December 8, which lasts until April 8, 2015. This period is when Jupiter goes into dormancy, so the expansion turns inward. It's as if a bright light is shining within you now, and you have an opportunity to take a closer look at who you are and where you fit in the scheme of things.

On December 21 Uranus turns direct in Aries, and on December 23 Saturn enters Sagittarius, your career area. Read about what this means in The Big Picture section of your sign. It can bring delays—or a greater structure. Or both!

IMPORTANT DATES

December 6: The full moon in Gemini highlights your domestic life. It could be that the family is congregating at your place for the holidays, and you're wondering how you're going to accommodate everyone. Uranus brings the answer, and it won't be what you expect!

December 21: The new moon in Capricorn is the perfect moon for greeting the new year. New opportunities surface in your career and with friends.

HAPPY NEW YEAR!

SYDNEY OMARR

Born on August 5, 1926, in Philadelphia, Pennsylvania, **Sydney Omarr** was the only person ever given full-time duty in the U.S. Army as an astrologer. He is regarded as the most erudite astrologer of the twentieth century and the best known, through his syndicated column and his radio and television programs (he was Merv Griffin's "resident astrologer"). Omarr has been called the most "knowledgeable astrologer since Evangeline Adams." His forecasts of Nixon's downfall, the end of World War II in mid-August of 1945, the assassination of John F. Kennedy, Roosevelt's election to a fourth term and his death in office . . . these and many others are on the record and quoted enough to be considered "legendary."